D1491842

Courage and Hesitation

INSIDE THE NIXON ADMINISTRATION

Also by Allen Drury

Fiction

ADVISE AND CONSENT
A SHADE OF DIFFERENCE
THAT SUMMER
CAPABLE OF HONOR
PRESERVE AND PROTECT
THE THRONE OF SATURN

Non-fiction

A SENATE JOURNAL
THREE KIDS IN A CART
'A VERY STRANGE SOCIETY'

Courage and Hesitation

INSIDE THE ADMINISTRATION

Allen Drury

Michael Joseph Ltd

MICHAEL JOSEPH

First published in Great Britain by
MICHAEL JOSEPH LTD
52 Bedford Square
London, W.C.1
1972

7181 1009 9

Set and printed in Gr   by
Northumberland Press
in Georgian eleven on
and bound by Richard   Press) Ltd
Bungay, Suffolk

Dedicated to

THE PIANO PLAYER

who really is,
whether you like it or not,
doing the best he can.

Contents

Introduction

In the bitter cold of the winter-seized city, now almost never free of the sound of sirens for more than twenty minutes at any hour of day or night, sleep is shattered in the hotel room high above the street by the voice of a woman in obvious mortal terror screaming, 'Help me! Oh, help me! Oh God, he's after me! Help me, somebody!' Faster than reaction, faster, almost, than fear, the cry is followed by male voices shouting, followed instantly by silence—secret, ugly, insinuating, containing all possibilities, burdened with who knows what frightful things....

It is 3.22 a.m. in the capital of the world's most powerful democracy, four blocks directly up the street from the heavily guarded, beautifully floodlit Mansion where the favoured family sleeps.

I came back to Washington in a November made disgruntled or delighted, depending upon the political slant of whomever I happened to be talking to, by the results of the mid-term elections of 1970: elections which sounded, from an electorate obviously in as many minds as there are states and territories, more of a damp splutter than a clear, commanding bugle call.

It had been several years since I had been back to spend any length of time. During the course of my visit, which lasted three months, I talked to many old friends and many new; interviewing most of the key people in the White House; talked with the man who lives there; talked to his family; received the informed, amusing and usually acrid analyses of old friends in the press; interviewed members of the Senate and House; attended White House staff meetings, press conferences, briefings, worship services, parties; tried to come up with a few answers about the institution, its present denizens and their operations; may, or may not, have succeeded.

9

I know I owe a great deal to all the staff, but most particularly to Herbert Klein, the President's Director of Communications, and to his amiable and most competent assistants Margita White and Jo Ann Wilson, whose patience, tact, persistence and charm were of invaluable help to me. If I do not owe so much to Ronald Ziegler, the President's press secretary, that is because Ron is Ron, and those who deal with the Nixon White House sooner or later learn to accept the fact and go around him.

One thing I did not do was enter the White House with any preconceived hatred for its principal occupant—a hatred which over the years I have found to be excessive, obsessive and in the long run sadly crippling to many of my old colleagues in the media.

Neither did I enter it with the accolade given me by a writer in a local magazine who saw fit, on grounds mysterious to me, to classify me among 'Nixon's thirty-six best friends'. Any man with that many official best friends is quite apt to have very few or none. I, in any case, was not, and have never been, among them. I had interviewed him a few times when he was Senator and Vice-President, talked to him at some length a couple of times during the years out of power, visited with him on a couple of occasions in the relaxed surroundings of the Bohemian Grove, interviewed him and done an article on him for the *Reader's Digest* after his election in 1968.

I was not unfriendly to his general purposes, philosophy or programme, and I was not unfriendly to him personally. Neither was I overwhelmingly impressed with his record to mid-term, though I thought that on the whole he had successfully begun the disengagement from Vietnam which he had promised, and had pulled the teeth of the carefully stage-managed dissent which had wracked his predecessor's final months in office.

If he had not completely 'brought us together'—who can?— at least we were more together than we had been in quite some time. This, managed under the twin handicaps of continuing flare-ups of organized disruption and the unyielding, implacable hostility of many of my friends who reported professionally upon his activities, did not seem so small an achievement.

Nonetheless, it was as one who was there to be shown that I began my round of talks and chats and formal interviewing; and I did so on terms (or conditions—'The President has accepted all your conditions,' Herb Klein's office told me) which I had taken some pains to spell out before I arrived in Washington. This was a reasonably detailed game plan, as they say in the West Wing and the Executive Office Building, and its basic emphasis was on candour and the right to move about free from any but the most necessary restrictions.

Not, of course, that I ever received anything in writing in reply. I was given to understand that the project had been 'staffed-out', approved by all the people who had to approve it: access had been granted, people would talk, I would receive full co-operation. And with the single exception of the press secretary, I did.

I was not, of course, told any deep, dark, buried secrets of the official White House family—candour and co-operation, after all, can only go so far in any first-term administration that wants to be re-elected, as they all do.

But I was given virtual carte blanche to roam the institution, study its people, absorb its atmosphere. Deep, dark, buried secrets could be discovered elsewhere: they usually get around, in Washington.

Even so, I did not find very many, even from my friends in the press who were certainly as avid as anyone to discover and report them. A 'liberal' Democrat fired here, a 'genuinely *involved*' official pressured out of office there, a 'really *sincere* and *compassionate* individual who *really cares*' forced to yield his powers to a pragmatic, more efficient Republican somewhere else. It was quickly apparent that the sterling qualities of these injured souls very often existed principally in the eyes of the beholders; and frequently I got the impression that their misfortunes were to be moaned over and made much of, via print and tube, only if their treatment could in some way be twisted to the detriment of Richard Nixon.

Usually these great scandals of the Administration turned out to be just the perennial Washington scandal of whose ox is gored. When, in the due course of time and politics, the Democrats recapture the White House, it will seem utterly right and justifiable to the media if they pressure, harass and dismiss Republicans right and left. No tears will be shed then. So the tears shed now, I am afraid, do not prove out at any very valid level of genuine principle or regret. They are good things in which to drown the President, but that is about the extent and depth of them.

Aside from politically inspired 'scandals' of this nature, I did not, in truth, find very many, if any, really reprehensible things in the Nixon White House; nor, I suspect, has anyone else. Instead I found, for the most part, a very hard-working, dedicated, efficient group of men and women—not dedicated to some of the things some would like them to be dedicated to, perhaps—not working for the cause, or in the political direction, that some would like—but hard to fault for intelligence, capability, sincerity and concern for the country's welfare as they conceive it to be.

Their shortcomings—of which, it seemed to me, there were some—lay in more subtle, possibly more serious directions which will appear in due course in these pages. But in the main, 'the youngest staff any President has ever had' seems to suffer mainly —and fortunately not too often in a critical way, either—from being just that—'the youngest staff any President has ever had'.

As for the best way to present them, their employer and their milieu, it seemed to me that it should not be a thing of formal sections and chapters, but rather an informal, relaxed, at times chatty, at times subjective, format—interviews mixed with interpretation, impressions mixed with the moods of the White House and the beautiful, uneasy, crime-haunted city that surrounds it—short takes, long takes, serious moments, lighter moments—quick, episodic, vigorous, alive.

This makes for a rather haphazard book—as haphazard, if it succeeds, as life at the White House, for all its present programmed minutiae, really is. Those who want neat chapters and textbook dissertations can find them elsewhere: these are notes, as I have called them, because notes, it seems to me, bring the life of this particular subject better to the page.

So you will find, as I say, short takes and long takes; regular type and italics, present tense and past; Presidential schedules, thoughts, staff problems and social agendas; interviews and impressions; direct quotations and quotations anonymous because that was the condition under which they were given to me; policies and people. If you roll with it, you may, hopefully, get some sense of the White House and of the shy, lonely, much-wounded, ambitious, courageous and deeply patriotic man who is its principal occupant.

The time is mid-winter 1970-71, halfway in the first—or possibly only—Nixon term. To give the book perspective against the background in which these notes were gathered, I have taken the liberty of including a running mix of headlines from those two banes of Presidents, the Washington *Post* and the New York *Times*. And to get it rolling, perhaps the best thing to do is relate an opening conversation on arriving November 12, 1970, at the northwest gate—

AD to old friend of the press (female): 'I'm here to do a book on the human side of the Nixon White House.' Old friend: 'Human side? There isn't any! We're all dead! It's a massive lobotomy!'

—and go on from there, and try to find out. . . .

I

WINTER SCENE

1. East Wing

THE PROBLEM IS MONEY.
It is lighted at night now, thanks to the decision of the Nixons, and it stands stately and beautiful among its trees against the snows of winter, the leaves of spring, the warm winds of autumn and the sticky summer weather. Begun in 1792, finished in 1800, it contains 132 rooms, a permanent staff numbering in the seventies, a political staff pushing five hundred, and several thousand headaches, many major but some on a more modest scale, such as dusting the china, cleaning the drapes and increasing the collection of antiques among which its principal occupants must live during their tenure. To them, the house is 'fascinating and exciting, but sometimes rather like living in a mausoleum or a museum'. To others, such as the curator of the White House, Clement Conger, and the chief housekeeper, Mrs. Shirley Bailey, it is a practical problem, subject to practical considerations and a practical approach.

'I find it kind of embarrassing and rather heartbreaking, how the public treats this house,' Mrs. Bailey says, her pleasant, efficient face creased with a rather helpless disapproval. 'Of course I know they regard it as theirs, and of course it is, but people will put children on antique chairs, they will sit down and eat food and scatter crumbs on the rugs. They will touch the tapestries and the wallpaper and get them dirty. They will throw cigarette butts in the fireplaces. There seems to be little real respect among the public who visit here. We have police stationed all over the house to warn them, but it doesn't seem to make too much difference. I wish there was some way to

17

convince them that this is an historical house and they should take care of it.'

Clem Conger, bustling about the corridors shrewd and sharp, does his best to take care of it on the historical level, but the task is complicated by that most recurrent of Washington problems: money.

'The President and Mrs. Nixon,' he says, 'were terribly upset at how down-at-the-heel the place looked when they came in. Since Mrs. Kennedy's much publicized "redecoration" of the White House, which consisted principally of the Blue Room and a few things in the other public rooms on the first floor, some nine million visitors have passed through the house, in addition to almost fifty thousand official guests of one kind and another whom the Nixons have entertained.

'The Johnsons seemed almost afraid to change anything left by the Kennedys for fear they would be criticized by the press and the public. But the Nixons are very much interested in seeing the house brought up to its full perfection. They want it to be the most beautiful home in America—not doing it in an extravagant way, but with a steady programme of acquisitions that will constantly improve the place. I am trying to raise a minimum of $250,000 a year to bring back historical furniture, paintings and other furnishings, but it isn't easy. Many pieces are given to us to put in place, but they haven't yet been paid for —if you want to buy a nice antique sofa for us for $10,000, for instance, we have just the thing down the hall. While it is rather unlikely that anybody will take things back once they have been brought to the White House, nonetheless we of course are obligated to pay for them and want to do so as rapidly as possible. There is great competition, however, from collectors and dealers. Even if we are the White House, we find that if we don't grab something as soon as it comes on the market, somebody else is going to get it from under our noses.'

The curator's purpose is to restore the house so that it will look 'approximately as it did in the period from about 1800 to 1850 or 1860. 1825 was probably about the high point of the house and we like to keep that in mind. Basically it is a nineteenth-century house, and we want to keep it that way.'

With this aim Mrs. Nixon concurs.

'We really don't have very many good pieces,' she says somewhat wistfully, 'but with Clem Conger's help we are beginning slowly to build up the collection. You do want the world to see the work of our own citizens, and to see it at the time the house was built and at various stages of its development over the years.

'All over the house, there is something to be done. We have so very many people going through. It is remarkable the house stands it as well as it does.'

For this Mrs. Bailey and her staff are principally responsible. Their day begins at 6 a.m. when the head houseman and several assistants (wearing black suits, white shirts and black ties according to White House tradition) come in to begin the round of cleaning that never really ends. At almost any hour of the working day, members of the housekeeping staff can be found somewhere in the Mansion cleaning something. Mrs. Bailey herself checks in shortly before 8 a.m. At that hour the first tour, that for Congressional constituents and friends of major government officials, gets under way. Before it does, rugs have to be rolled back, certain furniture has to be roped off, other preparations have to be made. Public tours start at 10 a.m. and run to 12.30 p.m. Afterwards, every day, the floors have to be polished, the furniture and china have to be dusted, the gloss of hundreds of brass fixtures has to be restored.

'There are a lot of dust-catchers here because it is an old house with many things in it,' she says. 'The ventilation and air-conditioning systems are overloaded, which brings dust. We are now putting in a fire system which they say will be outdated even before it's finished, but'—with a cheerful smile—'you can't win them all. We do the best we can.

'The time we can really work best is when the family is away. Then we can vacuum the fabrics and the curtains, take the pictures down and dust behind them, go into the family rooms on the second and third floors and really give them a scrubbing. Normally, of course, we can't go to the upper floors, except for minor routine housekeeping, because the family has a right to live as they please and we can't always be running in and out disturbing them.'

The White House has twelve bedrooms, six on the second, main family floor, and six guest bedrooms on the third floor. The housekeeper regards them as 'somewhat overfurnished', and indeed they are, cluttered and crowded with the leftovers of past administrations. Clem Conger, too, tut-tuts about them as he graciously gives his time for a private tour. There, again, the problem is money. 'There are so *many* things to do,' he murmurs unhappily, 'The public got the idea, because of Mrs. Kennedy's much publicized efforts, that the White House is finished. Nothing could be farther from the truth. The White House is never finished.'

Its public rooms and the special rooms on the second floor such as the Lincoln Bedroom and the Queen's Bedroom ('I sometimes wonder,' Mrs. Nixon confides with her characteristic quizzical little smile, 'what royal ladies must really think when they come here from their palaces to stay in our modest Queen's Room. They're very polite, of course, but I can't help wondering what they really think') suffer even more from clutter than the guest bedrooms, because they are the main rooms on display to visitors. Blue, Green and Red, they too seem to have every inch crammed with furniture, paintings, statuary, old maps—a sort of glorified rummage sale of American history, arranged in no particular order or over-all scheme, possibly because there are just so many things that no particular order is possible. Only a handful—the China Room, the Vermeil Room, the newly decorated Map Room off the Diplomatic Entrance which is Mr. Nixon's principal contribution, the State Dining Room and the East Room—possess much unity or central theme. The rest are grab bags, continually being rearranged and redone by succeeding First Families as they and their curators attempt to impose some order on history's hodgepodge.

Redecorations of the ground floor and the first floor, which have been designated national monuments, must have the approval of the Committee for Preservation of the White House. It meets at irregular intervals for lunch, at which time Mr. Conger presents such items as swatches of material for draperies, a suggested acquisition of furniture, a possible painting. Most of the commission members are wealthy, and most have been chosen—though Mrs. Nixon's staff members are very coy about refusing to admit it—because it is hoped they will see fit to contribute. There is no need to be ashamed of it. It is a good cause and there are worse ways they could spend their money.

'In a way,' says Tricia Nixon, head thoughtfully cocked on one side like her mother, speaking in all probability for generations of White House young people, 'living here is like living in some sort of institution. It's not so much its size, or the number of people who come through it, or the thought of those who lived here before and those who will live here after we've gone. It's just the weight of history which lies upon it that makes it not quite comfortable. Prince Charles and Princess Anne exclaimed when they were here and said, "Oh, what a delightful home!" because of course it is much smaller than theirs, and to them it must seem intimate and very warm. I do think my mother has tried very hard to make it warm, and I think she has succeeded very well in the family rooms and in the West Hall of the second floor, where we do most of our living. But there is still that feeling of a museum that you can never quite get away from. To really relax, I go out of the White House, to friends' homes or apartments. You can't really relax here.'

Yet there is one who really seems to—or if not, to give the impression so deftly that he has convinced almost everyone around him.

'He wanted it so much,' says his daughter Julie, 'that he seems to just take it all in stride.'

[142200]

CAMBODIAN AID HIT BY SENATE DOVES ... NIXON'S WEL-
FARE FACES TEST: SENATE PANEL VOTE EXPECTED TO BE
CLOSE ... LINES SET FOR FOREIGN AID BATTLE.

THE BEST IT CAN BE.

Out from the Mansion to east and west stretch the office wings of the White House, operated by the General Services Administration, containing the offices of Mrs. Nixon's staff and of those among the President's who are fortunate enough to have the rank to be there. The game of where-is-your-office is very important to those who play it, in this as in all other administrations, and it is usually a pretty good index of Presidential need and favour if you find yourself in the West Wing or in those sections of the East Wing not occupied by the First Lady's assistants. The enormous old gingerbread cake of a building which is directly west of the White House grounds along Pennsylvania

Avenue is known as the Executive Office Building, and many influential people work there too; but somehow it isn't quite the same as being inside the walls.

Of those who are, none go buzzing along more busily than the First Lady's staff. For them, too, the White House is a practical proposition, geared to the requirements of two people whose every hour and almost every activity is part of somebody's planning, somebody's preparations, somebody's responsibility, somebody's care. Mrs. Constance Stuart, Mrs. Nixon's staff director; Mrs. Lucy Winchester, the social secretary; John Ficklin, chief butler; Sanford Fox, director of the social office; Mrs. Gwen King, director of Mrs. Nixon's correspondence; and Mrs. Helen Smith, director of press relations for Mrs. Nixon, are typical.

Connie Stuart, youthful, pert-faced, red-haired, bright, efficient, brisk and lively, says there is 'no way to imagine what life in the White House is like unless you've lived here or worked here.

'You'll find jobs at the White House are sometimes rather hard to define. People lend their personalities to jobs and just do things. I have two functions. One is to head up the staff here in the second floor of the East Wing, which is really responsible for all the activities of the First Family as a family. And I'm also in over-all charge of Mrs. Nixon's press relations, and head of social activities. If everything goes right, I'm not responsible —but if anything goes wrong—which it does, sometimes, believe me—then I *am* responsible My main formal function is to hold two briefings for the press women who cover Mrs. Nixon, one on Monday morning and the other on Thursday afternoon.

'The pace is very hectic here. You're constantly juggling all kinds of mental walls to make them fit a given situation. You have to shift gears very, very fast sometimes. And it often means late hours. There are no nine-to-fives in the White House.

'It's a pleasure to work for Mrs. Nixon. She is very hard-working, very humble, doesn't want to take stage-centre. But she is always working in a quiet but very firm way to improve the White House, to make social functions here more attractive and more enjoyable, to really present the best that the White House can be. The President wants to do the same, of course.

'The main problem in working for them is that you just don't

22

have the time to do all the things you ought to do in order to accomplish the job you know you should for these people.'

Directly across the tiny reception room from Connie Stuart's office is that of Lucy Winchester: short, trim, grey-eyed, pretty wearing a bow in her hair and looking deceptively like a soft little Southern gal without a care in the world. Behind that sweet exterior hums a mind as well organized as a Swiss watch. It has to be, to handle the social schedules of the White House, those areas in which the President performs his ceremonial function as head of state.

'They told me when I came to work here that anything that happens socially under the roof of the Mansion is my responsibility. It's kept me runnin' ever since.

'My responsibility actually covers any entertaining the family does. For instance, the President is giving a stag dinner tomorrow night. Mrs. Nixon may give a luncheon or reception of some sort. The girls may entertain. For all of these, we are notified of the event. We then recommend where it should be held, what should be served, the type of table decorations that should be used, suitable silver and china. In the case of formal dinners, we are also responsible for making up the guest lists and other details of the dinner, such as the routing of guests: what door they will enter by, what kind of ceremony will be held to greet official guests, where the military aides will be stationed and what they will do. Before we have a state dinner for some visiting president or monarch I attend a planning session with representatives of the National Security Council, the State Department protocol office, the press office here and the military aides' office.

'The President gives two kinds of dinners: if there are to be hard talks on some subject such as nuclear disarmament or economic matters, he plans a small stag dinner to include the working staff people who will be involved in the discussions. If it is to be simply a dinner to reaffirm friendship between our two countries, to say what good friends we are and how wonderful it all is, then we try to have a light, entertaining dinner, usually with a number of guests of various kinds from around the country, followed by some suitable entertainment in the East Room.

'Guests for this latter type of formal state dinner are recom-

mended by the First Family, by the State Department or other Cabinet department, by the military aides' office, by the Congressional liaison staff and sometimes by private individuals who are close to the Nixons or active in certain areas of importance to this country, or to the visitor's country. The President and Mrs. Nixon go over the suggested list and make the final choices. Invitations normally go out about two weeks in advance.

'When a foreign visitor first arrives in Washington, he and his wife usually are brought by helicopter to the south lawn for a formal welcoming ceremony, complete with red carpet and a special platform set up beside the south portico. There is an honour guard which the President and his visitor review, and sometimes a fife-and-drum corps dressed in the costume of the Revolution, with tricornered hats, will play, which is very colourful. Mrs. Nixon usually accompanies the President on these occasions and greets the visiting First Lady. The two heads of state exchange formal pleasantries and then the party goes into the Mansion for a brief reception. After that the guests will be taken to Blair House, across Pennsylvania Avenue from the northwest gate of the White House, where they will stay during their visit.

'Before a state dinner official guests are entertained at a brief private reception in the Blue Room, where the President and Mrs. Nixon serve them coffee before they go into the Great Hall of the White House, which bisects the house from east to west. From there they proceed in a formal procession with the visiting First Lady on the President's arm and Mrs. Nixon on the arm of the visiting head of state. The Marine Band strikes up ruffles and flourishes and then goes into "Hail to the Chief" as the party proceeds along the hall to the entrance to the East Room where the guests are assembled. They then form a receiving line, the guests pass through and go on through the Green, Blue and Red Rooms to the State Dining Room at the west end of the Great Hall, where they are joined by the official party and the dinner begins.'

(Here John Ficklin, chief butler and a White House veteran since 1946 when the Trumans were there, contributes further details: 'I'm in charge of table linens, all beverages, setting up tables, and the staff that serves the dinners. I have a permanent staff of six butlers and one pantry girl. There are also three helpers in the staff kitchen downstairs on the ground floor, and six helpers in the big kitchen who are under me and can be called in to help. We also employ an outside staff of about seventy-five people who come in to help on state dinners. These include butlers, pantry staff, extra kitchen help, extra clean-up people and so on.

('It takes about six hours to set up a state dinner and approximately one and a half hours to tear it down again, remove the tables, china, silverware and decorations and return them to their storage places, which are in butler's pantries all over the house.

('Sometimes the Nixons tell us what they want but usually they leave it up to us. Sometimes Mrs. Winchester or I will suggest what we think will be the right thing and Mrs. Nixon will go along with it. Then if she doesn't like it, she won't criticize but she will simply say that we might do it better next time and will tell us what she would like to have. This has been characteristic of most of the First Ladies that I have known. Usually they just let us do it the way it has always been done in the White House and then if they want some changes, they will tell us later and next time we will do it their way. The Nixons, like all the other First Families, are always very good about expressing their thanks to the staff after a dinner.

('All dinners here are special to me. We don't try to add anything extra to any particular party. We just try to do our best for everybody. It's my feeling that this is the White House and we should make it just as nice as we can for everyone who comes here, so we treat them all alike and try to do our best.')

'Sometimes,' says Lucy Winchester, looking a little rueful, 'we have several months' notice before official dinners. And sometimes we have a week or even less. But usually there is enough lead-time so we can do comfortably all that has to be done.

'We furnish briefing papers for the President and Mrs. Nixon on their official guests, although we usually find that they know more about them than we do and frequently are personal friends whom they have met during the President's eight years as Vice-President, or the travelling he did when he was out of office.

'We also furnish transportation, hotels, cars and even hairdressing appointments for the entertainers, who are sometimes suggested by us, sometimes selected by the Nixons. One of our duties is to check with people who know the entertainers, to find out how they will behave. We don't want another Eartha Kitt. [A Negro singer whose boorish attack on President Johnson at a White House tea gave Mrs. Johnson's innate gentility a priceless opportunity to show itself.]

'For state dinners the President favours the E-type of dining table. For small business dinners he prefers to have a hollow rectangular table. Round tables such as were used in the Johnson administration are now used for small private dinners in the Family Dining Room.

'The President selects all the wines himself. He likes to serve a German white wine at the start of a meal, a domestic red wine with the main course and French champagne at the end of the meal. We usually figure about two bottles of wine for every ten people. Liquor is purchased with the visitors' preference in mind. When we are entertaining the Indians, some of the Asians and some of the Africans, we know they don't drink at all, so we provide fruit juice or a fruit punch of some kind for them. Mrs. Nixon always serves domestic wines for the ladies' luncheons which she gives.

'The President is the first to hold major official dinners outside Washington—the dinner in Los Angeles for the Apollo 11 crew, the dinner in San Diego for the President of Mexico, for example. When he decides to entertain outside Washington, we go to the place and conduct an actual run-through of the dinner in advance. I go out and invite the manager of the hotel, the caterer and the chef to sit with me, and we have the menu exactly as planned. We have the entire meal served by the people who will serve the head table. We decide if the food is correctly seasoned. We talk with the local florist about the decorations. We decide what should be on the table, the size of the platters, the arrangement of goblets, the type of silver and chinaware. We do this because sometimes these hotels out in the country think they are going to plan a big surprise for a Presidential dinner and it turns out to be something quite impossible, such as floral decorations too large for people to see around, or the Great Seal of the United States in ice, so big that it obscures the President from the guests. All of these things have to be taken into account. The Signal Corps, which handles all electronic communications for the White House, also sends out a representative to check on microphones, special lighting effects and the general handling of the programme in a communications sense.

'The Nixons have introduced other social innovations. The Sunday worship service was begun immediately after his inauguration in January 1969, and is held about twice a month in the East Room for approximately 350 guests. Visiting ministers from different denominations conduct services, a choir is brought in and after the half-hour service ends the President and Mrs. Nixon greet their guests in the State Dining Room, where orange juice, pastries and coffee are served.

'The President has also inaugurated what he calls "evenings of entertainment", which have included such things as a Bob Hope evening, a Broadway production, famous singers, Duke Ellington's seventieth birthday and so on. Other special events have included the twenty-fifth United Nations anniversary dinner, a UN reception in New York, Tricia's Hallowe'en party for children of the diplomatic corps, a summer garden party Mrs. Nixon gave on the south lawn for the inner-city children.

'The Nixons have changed the variety of music played by the Marine Band to get away from a certain tendency towards rock 'n' roll and back to musical comedy and light classics. The band is usually told how long the evening is to last, and then they work out their own programme from there. The "strolling strings" who play among the tables during dessert are told how many minutes they will have, and they are also given some indication of the type of music which would be suitable for the particular state visitor.

'This is all part of the Nixons' particular interest in the quality and dignity of the functions at the White House. They are very concerned that the house and its social activities present the best possible view of the United States to those who visit here.'

So, too, says Sanford Fox, a short, stocky, cheerful gentleman with white hair, white moustache and white goatee, who says that he is frequently called upon to play Santa Claus in White House Christmas entertainments. He is an ideal choice for the job, as he seems to be for his more formal duties, which consist principally of making sure that White House gifts, invitations, stationery, programmes, menus and other printed social forms are 'consistent and traditional with the highest calibre suitable for the White House'.

He confesses that he is one who 'likes to have things neat, nice, secure and exact', and in the Nixons he finds kindred spirits.

'Things should be done the way they *should* be done for the President of the United States. The Nixons are anxious to have them done that way. They are always very, very kind in expressing their appreciation for what is done for them by this office—and very kind about not springing surprises. Some people'—refusing to name names from his twenty years of White House experience—'come in at you like a herd of buffalo about scheduling social events. The Nixons aren't like that.'

In addition to formal invitations, programmes, menus and other formal papers, which are engraved by the Bureau of Printing and Engraving, his office also handles stationery. ('I always assist in that, give help and suggestions.') Of the First Ladies he has known, Mrs. Eisenhower preferred a cream-white finish, Mrs. Kennedy a white kid finish, Mrs. Johnson a white kid finish. Mrs. Nixon is partial to a white kid finish in a 'real nice blue' with the words 'The White House' and the Presidential seal embossed upon it.

Cards used by the President to answer requests for his autograph are the same size as those used for White House formal dinner invitations. They are very simple, with the words 'The White House, Washington' in the upper left-hand corner.

Mr. Fox takes great pride in the fact that he assists in suggesting 'the gift' each year—the gift given by the First Family to members of the White House staff. President Eisenhower gave reproductions of his own water colours, the Kennedys and Johnsons preferred reproductions of various White House scenes.

'I suggested to President Nixon that he give pictures of the early Presidents suitable for framing, and he accepted this. Last year they gave George Washington and this year it will be Thomas Jefferson. I suggested to Mrs. Nixon that in the eighth year they should give a picture of President Nixon. She just laughed and said, "We'll think about that."

'It is,' he says with obvious pride, 'a great satisfaction to me to know that I am part of the process of making sure that everything in the social area is done with the right attention to detail suitable to the President and the White House. It makes me very happy that I am able to contribute to this process, and it makes me very happy that the Nixons are so interested and so concerned about it and so anxious to do things the way they ought to be done here.'

Gwen King, director of Mrs. Nixon's correspondence, pleasant, efficient, good-humoured, has been on the White House staff since the start of the Eisenhower administration. Her office sends out all of the First Lady's official greetings (most of which are requested) on wedding anniversaries from the twenty-fifth up, births, birthdays, graduations, bar mitzvahs, get-well cards, messages to organizations and the like. It also handles all letters coming to Mrs. Nixon: those concerning the Mansion, state dinners, entertainments, requests for help, letters from Congressional constituents. They average fifteen hundred a week, some thirty-five of them usually coming from abroad.

'The only ones we don't answer are very nasty ones, which we send on to the Secret Service or FBI for investigation. But we get very few of those.

'In normal cases the answers we send are based on "skeleton letters" that adhere to language that is policy-geared and does not change from correspondent to correspondent.

'I was told at first that Mrs. Nixon was not to receive unpleasant letters on subjects such as drugs and other social problems. I didn't think a mature woman should be sheltered from the things that she reads about in the newspapers, and I was pleased to find she agreed. I asked her about it, she said she wanted to see everything and there was no problem at all.

'She is really terrific about her mail. She doesn't back away from anything. She is intensely interested in it and has never yet turned down a request for an official greeting or message. She gets a weekly report on how much comes in, whether it is favourable or unfavourable. She responds at once and sends us frequent "PN" notes ["From the desk of Patricia Nixon"] about the correspondence and how it should be handled.

'I would describe her as a perfectionist but a very reasonable perfectionist. At first she didn't want to use such phrases as "the President and I", preferring to use "both of us", or "our family feels". Now she realizes people like to have the President mentioned, and she is more used to it. She likes to have letters answered within two or three days, and has a rule that Congressional mail should be answered the same day it comes in, if possible. But she understands that if we have to call a depart-

29

ment or agency to get the facts with which to answer, it may take a little longer.

'She will always follow through on requests for help, as she did recently when we got a letter from a girl who was hooked on drugs and threatening suicide. Mrs. Nixon arranged for the girl to get psychiatric help and now things are much better. 'Mrs. Nixon really cares.'

The First Lady, says Mrs. Helen Smith, director of press relations for Mrs. Nixon, 'does not really like television. She feels that person-to-person contact is her strongest asset. People respond so warmly to her and she is so spontaneous about it. For instance, she will be in a crowd and suddenly she will put her arm around someone or smile and make some personal comment. She is so gracious and so warm and is absolutely unflagging. She wants to shake the hands of all who are waiting to see her, and will continue to do so even though she becomes very tired sometimes doing it.

'She is a wonderful person. If she feels she can help with some cause she will go anywhere to do it. She is extraordinarily well organized, and so accessible. When you send a query to her, you get an answer back sometimes in half an hour. She is full of ideas for improving and showing off the White House to the American people, whom she regards as its owners. Recently she inaugurated the idea of printing pamphlets in different languages describing the White House with a diagram so visitors will know what rooms they are going through. These are being cleared by the State Department and so far have been printed in Russian, Italian, Spanish and French, principally for the benefit of the diplomatic corps and their countrymen who may come to Washington and wish to see the White House.

'I may be prejudiced, but I think she is a very extraordinary woman.'

The press (female): 'Pat Nixon just has no depth of understanding. I think that's the main trouble. She just has no depth of understanding. She just doesn't care.'

The press (female, more charitable): 'She is really a very nice woman but she seems to lack a purpose. She seems to be searching for something. Her attention span is very brief for the projects she gets involved in. She is into them and out again in a hurry. Nothing seems to last. I feel that she is still looking for something to do that will give her a purpose in the White House.'

The press (female, still more charitable): 'The Nixons are a little stiffer than previous First Families. The Kennedys managed to get by on a sort of cool informality that their worshippers were able to translate into great "style". The Johnsons were much easier and more informal. We see now a return to a certain stiffness, in both Nixons. It seems to me that in the beginning, particularly when he gave a party for the press, the President was most easy and charming and was making a real effort to be relaxed in the White House. However, in recent months that has changed again and now they are both rather stiff and determined and awkward.

'I don't think the Nixons want it that way, but they somehow don't seem quite able to relax in office. Pat Nixon is a very pleasant and intelligent woman but she simply does not seem to know how to relax in the White House.'

The press (male, most charitable—mildly): 'I think she does an excellent job of making people feel warm and welcome at the White House. After all, that doesn't seem to me such a bad thing for a First Lady to do. That's really her first responsibility, in my mind, and I think she does it very well.'

And from further down the East Wing staff:

'She is very lovely, very pleasant and very refined. . . .'

'If all other employers were as nice to deal with as Mrs. Nixon, the world would be a wonderful place. She is a very gracious woman to work for and establishes a very pleasant employer-employee relationship. . . .'

'She has the gift of insight into other people that can never be taught or learned. It is a natural gift. . . .'

PRESS BRIEFING.

Constance Stuart and ladies, 3 p.m., Nov. 19, 1970.

Held in the White House theatre, a small grey-green room that can seat perhaps fifty people comfortably, it is used for family movies when so desired, doubles as reception room and conference room. This afternoon several steamer-rugs, mysterious in origin, unknown in purpose, have been left on the front row of seats. There is a lectern and microphone, front: Connie at the

31

ready. Twenty or so press women enter, rear: chattering, gossiping, laughing. Four promptly drape themselves in the blankets.

'Welcome to the *Queen Elizabeth*,' says one of Connie's aides.

'Where's the bouillon?' demands one of the ladies.

Everybody laughs, a trifle warily.

Connie announces there will be no coverage of the Nixon's dinner for the Ash Council tonight. Prolonged and rather testy discussion of why it is called the Ash Council. It appears it is named for its chairman, Mr. Ash. Its job is to acquire Americana for the house.

Several questions about seeing samples of the swatches of drapery material Clem Conger will present tomorrow at Mrs. Nixon's luncheon for the Committee for the Preservation of the White House: When can we see swatches? Why can't we see swatches? What about those swatches?

'If there is something we move *ahead* on,' Connie finally says with a rising exasperation, 'then you will be told tomorrow afternoon at the briefing by Mr. Conger.'

QUESTION: 'Is this Mrs. Nixon's first meeting with the committee?'

CONNIE: 'With the new committee it is. Her last meeting was May 28, as it says in the release.'

QUESTIONS: about Mrs. Onassis, who is a member of the committee. 'Why was Mr. Onassis invited to the luncheon? Is he a member of the committee?'

'No, he is not,' says Connie. 'Spouses are invited.'

'But neither Mr. or Mrs. Onassis will be here?'

'No.'

QUESTION: 'How are people chosen for this committee?'

CONNIE: 'Mrs. Nixon hopes they will have expertise in Americana which she wants for the house. These are people who are interested in this.'

QUESTION: 'The fact they have a lot of money doesn't matter?' (*Much laughter.*)

CONNIE (*doggedly*): 'They are experts in this field.'

QUESTION: 'They are experts in the American dollar and can help buy these things.'

CONNIE (*doggedly*): 'People who are experts usually have the means to enjoy these things. The two seem to go hand in hand.'

QUESTION: about the worship service this coming Sunday. 'Is

it true that only new Republican members of the House and Senate have been invited?'

CONNIE (*doggedly*): 'It will be the people President and Mrs. Nixon have invited.'

'Are any Democrats invited?'

CONNIE (*sharply*): 'I have no idea.'

QUESTION: 'Are there any travel plans after the Thanksgiving dinner?'

CONNIE: 'I have no information on travel. You will have to ask Mr. Ziegler.'

QUESTION: 'It's been printed they will go to Key Biscayne.'

CONNIE (*doggedly*): 'I have no information on travel. You will have to ask Ron.'

QUESTION: as to why Tricia was not at the special performance at Ford's Theatre last night.

CONNIE: 'Tricia was otherwise engaged last night.'

QUESTIONS, UNANIMOUS: '*Engaged?*'

(*Much laughter.*)

CONNIE (*tight smile*): 'Tricia was busy last night.'

QUESTION: reference to Martha Mitchell's front-paged indignation because Connie failed to describe her, in a press release, as hostess of a luncheon today at Blair House for Mrs. Nixon, Mrs. Agnew and the Cabinet wives. 'Did you know that Mrs. Mitchell would be the hostess when you told us Mrs. Nixon was going, or did you forget?'

CONNIE: 'I announced that Mrs. Nixon was going and what she was doing. I didn't know who the hostess was. I was simply doing my job. I said the Cabinet wives and Mrs. Nixon and Mrs. Agnew would receive petit point kits to make state seals to hang on the walls.'

QUESTION: 'Mrs. Agnew will be doing the hula. She is in Hawaii.'

CONNIE (*tartly*): 'I'm sorry. I just said Mrs. Nixon and Mrs. Agnew would receive the kits. I did not say Mrs. Agnew would be there.'

QUESTION: 'Did you know Mrs. Mitchell was the hostess?'

CONNIE: 'No, no. Not as of Monday morning when I told you.'

QUESTION (*softly*): 'Are you sorry you made a mistake?'

CONNIE (*sharply*): 'I don't think I made a mistake. I did my job. I told you where Mrs. Nixon would be.'

QUESTION: about Thanksgiving dinner plans.

CONNIE (perhaps understandably, clicking tongue and rapping on lectern with increasing frequency): 'Details will be given on Monday.'

QUESTION RENEWED: 'What about travel plans after Thanksgiving?'

CONNIE (sharply, rapidly and on a rising note): 'Mr. Ziegler will announce where and when the President is to travel. Is that all, ladies? Well, O.K. then, if that's all—'

And chattering, gossiping and laughing anew, the flock arises and departs, leaving its flushed and harried target. The blankets are abandoned. The *Queen Elizabeth* lies silent and deserted once more until 10 a.m. Monday, when the same type of bouillon will be served, on both sides.

UN MOVES NEARER TO SEATING PEKING. VOTE SEEN AS SET-BACK FOR U.S. ... THE CUBAN SUB BASE AFFAIR: ADMINIS-TRATION DEEPLY DISTURBED ... U.S. RAIDS NORTH, RADIO HANOI SAYS.

Three other White House employees who come generally under Mrs. Nixon's supervision offer interesting sidelights on the house and on its occupants. Two are long-time staff members and the third, Henri Haller, the chef, is not only excellent in his profession but also lively, intelligent and humorous in his approach. This may or may not guarantee job longevity at 1600 Pennsylvania Avenue, but it does make him a perceptive and interesting observer.

Rex Scouton, head usher, is in charge of almost all of the staff operations on the domestic side of the Mansion. Trim, pleasant, dark-eyed, quick-smiling, he came to the White House as a member of the Secret Service more than twenty years ago, was assigned to the Nixons during the President's Vice-Presidential years, is regarded by other staff members as 'almost a member of the family' and as such is friendly, helpful, closemouthed and discreet.

He has somewhere between seventy-five and a hundred employees, a basic staff which has not increased since the days of Harry Truman. Under him come the maids, butlers, housekeepers, doormen, plumbers, carpenters, engineers, electricians, florists and general maintenance crew. He is in over-all charge of setting up for special events and entertainments, and his is the prime responsibility for making sure that the White House runs smoothly as a home. He operates under an Executive Mansion appropriation granted by Congress each year in the U.S. Park Service budget. The Park Service does the paper work for his staff and all employees except the five in his personal office who are paid out of the Executive Mansion budget. He and his four assistants are paid out of the special White House budget granted each year to the President. He says little, very pleasantly.

Rusty Young, tall, round-faced, sandy-haired, a White House staff member since 1953, is the florist squirrelled away in a couple of tiny basement rooms behind what used to be the Roosevelt swimming pool and is now the new and elaborate press quarters. Three helpers assist him.

'We usually make up two or three dozen flower arrangements a day which are placed throughout the Mansion. We place about two dozen of these in the family rooms on the second floor, and we always have at least two arrangements in the President's Oval Office, two in the lobby, two in the Diplomatic Reception Room, several in each of the Green, Blue, and Red rooms and one in the library.

'When we have a state dinner we make approximately six dozen arrangements. Sometimes this can get up to as many as 150 arrangements, as it did when we gave the dinner dance for Prince Charles and Princess Anne.

'Most of our flowers come from the Kenilworth Gardens run by the Park Service, but we also get some from the White House gardens and we receive a weekly supply of carnations from the Colorado Carnation Growers Association, and a regular supply of orchids from a private company. Also, friends of the First Family will sometimes send flowers which we incorporate in our arrangements.

'Arrangements are more or less left up to our discretion, though of course we try to have certain colours for certain rooms, such as the Blue and Red Rooms, and we try to match the decorations to the season.

'I would say we use on the average about forty-eight dozen flowers a day, every day, in the White House.'

Henry Haller, a pleasant, greying native of Switzerland in his forties, wears his white apron and tall white chef's hat in the cavernous kitchens on the ground floor and describes his job with a humorous snap in his steel-blue eyes.

'I'm in charge of all the food needs of the White House, the State Dining Room, the private Family Dining Room, the small kitchen on the second floor where the family's meals are prepared, and the staff kitchen and dining room downstairs in the basement.

'There is nothing fancy here at the White House. Everything is very methodical in the preparation of food, based on my experience and on what the First Family desires.

'Here in the kitchens we work together as a team with nobody trying to outdo the other guy. We have one aim—to make the stay of the First Family in the White House as pleasant as possible. We want to help the President. We don't want to serve food that would distract him, because he has enough problems as it is. We make sure that the food is not cold when it is served to him, and we make sure it is served on time. President Nixon is always on time himself and he expects us to be on time.

'This is a great job because it's not a business. In a hotel, where I used to be, the chef was really a figurehead who had to be responsible for cutting down expenses and making a profit. Here we are not interested in that, because sufficient funds are provided to do the job right. I am in charge of the purchasing, or at least of the ordering, and I am under no restrictions. I am able to buy the best for the best possible price. If there is something I don't like, if the quality doesn't measure up, I send it back.

'I have a food budget of about $1000 a month for the staff. The staff eats good.

'For state dinners, we bill the State Department entertainment fund and they pay the bill. This does not come out of White House funds.

'You can make a character study of how people eat. We have lots of people come here who are very rich and fine people, and we find that proved in the way they are easier to serve meals for than others who are not used to good service.

'On the whole, it's a relatively easy pace here, although we work until we finish and sometimes quite long hours. However, there are other times when there is nothing much scheduled and we can rest for a bit.

'We try to serve reasonable portions so that people will not feel too stuffed when they leave the White House table. I don't believe in this crash diet of taking it off and then going at it again and putting it back on. I want to keep trim myself. I don't ever want to be a fat, sloppy chef, and go on that principle in serving dinners. The best thing is for people to leave the table saying, "I could have eaten a little more but I won't do it." It is a matter of will power.

'Here I can enjoy the art of cooking. I really love cooking, and at the White House I have a chance to do it the way it should be done. At the White House I am impressed with the authority of the President. Whatever he says to the domestic staff is carried out and there is no nonsense about it. In a hotel, you have a question, you take it to the general manager, or he gives orders to you, but here it is the President who gives orders. I am not going to argue with the President. You just don't have a grievance here. You just make the best of it when he gives the orders.

'We deal with the same dealers the White House has been dealing with for many years. They are all checked out by the FBI. Therefore we know the food is reliable to be served here, and the only question then becomes the quality, which is up to me to decide. We want the best here. We pay good prices, and we want to get it.

'The Nixons are very simple people. They don't want a lot of service and they don't want a lot of fancy meals. They seem to get enough fancy food at the state dinners and they prefer simple, ordinary American-type meals when they are dining alone in the private quarters.

'I am very impressed by the President's eating habits. If everybody in the U.S. had the same habits he does and had the will power he has in controlling his diet, the country would be in better shape. He likes to eat but he has the will power to control it.

'The general emphasis in the family is on beef, although the President loves fish. Generally every week for the family menus we have, at some time or other, fish, beef, chicken and sometimes a casserole like lasagna. They are very fond of desserts and like to have sweet souffles or cheese souffles quite frequently.

'We all work well together. Nobody can be a prima donna here. The President'—gesturing upstairs with his thumb—'is the only prima donna here.'

PUNITIVE RAIDS HIT NORTH VIETNAM BASES. U.S. ATTACK IS DEEPEST SINCE '68. HANOI SAYS U.S. BOMBING WILL 'GRAVELY AFFECT' TALKS. RAIDS STIR QUERY 'WHY NOW?' ... OUSTED O.E.O. LEGAL CHIEFS CALL THEIR FIRING POLITICAL ... HEALTH CARE CRISIS SEEN BY MUSKIE.

2. West Wing

Sometimes, if you approach the White House at dusk, you hear a strange screeching sound that seems to be coming from all around you. Startled, you think for a moment that it may be the starlings, which have for so long been the curse of Washington, come to roost in the giant treees. Then you realize the sound is coming from loudspeakers set high in the branches, repeating over and over the high, agonized distress cry of the ubiquitous birds, its purpose to drive away any that might be tempted to tarry here. The strange sound goes on, shrieking over and over again into the cold, misty, luminous evening. Let the imagination run and you are back to the crows cawing ominously over the Capitol in Rome, the Harpies, the Witch of Endor and other dark, foreboding things. The sound goes on and on, frantic, beseeching, agonized, protesting, over and over and over, above the haunted, harried house and all who live and work within it.

Elsewhere in the East Wing there function a few members of the power structure that finds its principal home across the Mansion in the West Wing and the Executive Office Building. Generically, if not physically, all can be lumped under the designation 'West Wing'. This, in Washington, is the easy short-hand for 'power' in the White House. Power in a President's house has many faces, many voices. Some candidly for quotation, some candidly for quotation but not for attribution, they tell the story of an Administration seeking answers to questions never ending.

Harry Dent is in his forties, round-faced, fast-talking, intelligent, able, a former administrative assistant to Senator Strom Thurmond (Republican, South Carolina) who received his appointment as one of the President's political advisers in return for the Senator's help in the 1968 campaign:

'People tend to blame "the President", or "the Administration", for what does or does not happen in Washington. They forget that the President is surrounded by people who are not necessarily with him. Actually we have more than one Administration in Washington. We have the courts, the Congress, the regulatory agencies, the bureaucracy, the press and the White House. People don't realize how difficult it is to get orders implemented through the bureaucracy. It is approximately three million strong and we can name only about twenty-three hundred people in key positions. The rest are all under civil service. Even if the bureaucracy is with you, you have an enormous amount of red tape. When it is largely composed of Democratic-appointed holdovers, it is even more difficult. The Presidency is often referred to as "the most powerful office in the world"—Mr. Nixon said so himself in the '68 campaign—but I don't agree. Compared to the Soviet Union, where the chief gives an order and everybody immediately obeys, the Presidency is very weak and diffused. It requires very strong leadership. The office is not necessarily the most powerful in the world. It probably is the toughest.

'The problem is further complicated by the fact that registered Democrats in the country are five to three over the Republicans. This means a Republican administration always has to paddle upstream.

'Given this situation, I think this President is extremely well organized—he does so much of his own thinking, his own writing and his own work. Most of the actual orders in the White House come from the President himself—right off that yellow pad late at night in the Lincoln Study. This Administration is probably more centrally directed by the big man himself than most others have been.

'The President probably has a better understanding of Southern people and of people in general than almost any other politician in the country. He has travelled in most of the states and many nations overseas and I find that when I take someone from Minnesota in to see him, he knows as much as they do about Minnesota, and the same thing applies to Mississippi or most other states.

'I think that the South in general likes the President very much despite the desegregation that has occurred under his administration. I believe a Democratic President would have had much more trouble. A good part of the credit can go to his vision in establishing racial advisory counsels in the South. The Southerners realize that he is not vindictive in administering the laws, and that he has acted in a spirit of co-operation rather than coercion. He has removed the deliberate provocations of the South and accomplished the job. He has made it easier for the Southern people to do what they had to do.

'I think the President is going to carry the South comfortably in 1972. If George Wallace runs, the President will carry most Southern states by a comfortable margin in a three-way race with Wallace and a liberal Democrat. If Wallace does not run, and I don't think he will, then the President will carry the South with a big majority over the liberal Democrat. The South is so basically conservative that a liberal on a Democratic ticket will almost certainly lose.'

Bryce Harlow, former Congressional affairs assistant to President Eisenhower, former Congressional affairs assistant to President Nixon, is back in the Washington office of Procter & Gamble now, in his old profession of advertising, but his person and his advice are never far from the Nixon White House at any time. 'Bryce knows the score,' everybody in Washington says. 'Bryce is really smart. Nobody's shrewder than old Bryce.' Small, dapper, round-faced, discreet, his tendency to be oracular broken by a sudden sly twinkle that belies his blank, impassive stare and swiftly flowing phrases, he obviously relishes being the pocket pundit of politics.

'For the remainder of the President's term, we have a divided government, which is something too sophisticated for the average guy to understand. The President says one thing, somebody in the Democratic Congress says no, he's wrong, it should be something else. Congress says something should be done, the President says no, that isn't right. It blurs the Presidential image and makes it difficult to establish clear-cut responsibility for either successes or failures. What the President has to do in this situation, it seems to me, is to go up to Capitol Hill with his programme and fight like hell all the way to try to make the country understand his position.

'In areas such as foreign aid, for instance, the President is the only powerful constituent the programme has. He may have to make some big fights at intervals to get things through. This could be either going on TV or flying somewhere in the country to deliver a major speech in order to get Joe Zilch excited about it.

'I think in judging an administration the degree of *unsmoothness* is the question. I would say that the *unsmoothity* in this case is not much beyond par for this particular course. Considering the situation when Richard Nixon took office and considering how he has fared, he has not done badly at all—though the degree of public acceptance of that fact is quite open to question. He inherited a war largely without hope and a domestic scene filled with violence and destruction. These things are in a happier stance today. The President has achieved solidity in pressing towards the redemption of campaign promises he made in 1968.

'He moved into the Presidency with an astonishing calmness and sureness. He was quite ready to be President of the United States. This approach has held true. I think he enjoys the Presidency. It is as though he had picked up the world out there, put it on his shoulders and started walking down the street, visiting with the folks along the way as he did so. I haven't seen him fussed or brittled by it. He is a very, very disciplined person.'

Bob Finch is a former lieutenant governor of California, tall, big-boned, ruggedly handsome in a shoot-'em-up-movie sort of way. When the pressures of being Secretary of Health, Education and Welfare became too hectic, he resigned to move to the quieter realms of the West Wing. A Nixon intimate ever since he was secretary to a Congressman whose office was next door to fledgling Representative Nixon's two decades ago, he concentrates now on the long-range political view and the job of being around when the boss wants to relax with somebody who sees the political realities as he does.

'A President's popularity in foreign policy is closely tied to success or failure of a given issue. In domestic affairs there is not so much that can give him obvious credit. There are more things which can do him discredit.

'In the first two years of this Administration we perhaps spread our shots too much in domestic matters by proposing some fifty different items. We are going to narrow down our proposals for the new Congress and for the campaign.

'The "New Federalism" is really based on revenue sharing with the states. Obviously the key issue in the '70 election was the economy. The governors who bit the dust, both Republican and Democratic, were those who had to raise taxes. Unless we can work out a revenue-sharing programme to ease the burden on the states, there are going to be a lot of one-term governors and other local officials who have to raise money for public services. They have just about exhausted all the taxes they can impose. There have got to be non-conditional grants from the federal government back to the states and local jurisdictions and I believe the Congress will come around to this.

'Of course'—wryly—'if the tax burden is lightened on the states and the federal government shares revenues, the money has to come from somewhere and we may have to look to some sort of increased national taxation, such as a value tax or sales tax.

'All the Democrats do with their authorizing legislation for big spending programmes is to create anticipations they can't fulfil. We think our way is better because their way tends to freeze inequities in the present system. We want to reform the system and it is very obvious that in such areas as welfare, Medicare, the training of doctors and dentists and other medical personnel there is a desperate need for reform.

'There is an awful lot of the old folklore still left about the Republicans getting us out of wars but into depressions. The President is acutely conscious of the damage an economic setback could do politically and he is going to do everything to get employment up as we near 1972.

'He is concentrating on doing the things at hand. He is not trying to ram through all his domestic programme. Rather he is trying to rifle-shot his programme. His mood is more realistic than optimistic.'

U.S. RAID TO RESCUE POWS FAILS. SENATORS APPALLED AT FORAYS.

Like Bryce Harlow, Daniel Patrick Moynihan has gone back

to his former love, in his case teaching at Harvard. Like Mr. Harlow he too maintains his quiet ties with the President. In the White House he was the principal agitator for the Nixon welfare plan, the idea of guaranteed income, the idea of reducing public hysteria in the approach to social problems. Flamboyant, voluble, well-spoken, decent, he believes he sees in the President a man as goodhearted as himself and says so with a forceful and unabashed vigour which brings much criticism from those who were friends of his when he worked for the Kennedy and Johnson administrations. He doesn't care, maintaining his position with a zest that would do credit to a Harry Truman in his younger days. He can stand the heat and, in one way or another, it seems safe to predict that he will always be in the kitchen.

'Perhaps the principal thing that has struck me during my time here has been the way in which the Presidency has been devalued, degraded and even insulted. There has been a steady decline in respect for it and this shows itself in many ways. For instance, there was that girl today who got an award from the President and then told him she didn't believe he was sincere in trying to get out of Vietnam. To me, it's vital to the way our democracy operates that you respect the office and the institutions of the country.

'I had another example coming back from a speech last night. A young man on the plane recognized me and asked if he could make a "citizen's complaint". I said, "Are you a citizen?" He said he was and then proceeded with the usual comments about the war, the minorities and so on. Among other things, he said that he had read somewhere that some friend of the President had called him "Dick" before he took office but since he became President has called him "Mr. President".

'This young fellow said this indicated to him that the President was an egomaniac surrounded by some sort of oriental court. I tried to point out that George Washington made the decision that he was not to be addressed as "Your Majesty" but simply as "Mr. President" and that this has been one of the fundamental features of our democracy ever since. But I could see that he was not really convinced, and that's typical of the attitude a lot of these kids have towards our institutions. They're just plain ignorant of history, of respect, of fundamental knowledge and common sense.

'Perhaps the fundamental issue of our time is the erosion of the authority of our American institutions. Authority relations are consensual, power relations are based on force. If we had a power society and somebody challenged the President, he could say, "Off with your head!" But in a society resting on the authority of institutions by consent, this can't be done. The danger is, however, that if the authority of institutions is eroded enough, it may be succeeded by a power society in which democratic rights and freedoms will ultimately disappear.

'Another aspect of the erosion of the Presidency, it seems to me, can be found in the way in which it is subjected to political attack and the President's purposes thwarted for partisan reasons. For instance, this welfare bill that I have been working on. He will deserve eternal credit for really pushing the idea of a guaranteed personal income, but the bill is going to be defeated on the Hill with the active aid of liberals who have always advocated things like this but are determined that Richard Nixon is just not going to be the one who gets the credit for doing it. [The Nixon bill as such was defeated, but the Nixon principle survived in quite recognizable form.]

'The President's political task is made extra difficult because he represents a group which is not fashionable or popular with the major elements of the media. The silent majority is silent because it has nothing to say. It has no popular intellectuals speaking for it, it represents no major cultural breakthroughs, and so everything it says is ridiculed and put down.

'I do think the President has calmed the country substantially. When we came into the White House after a bitter campaign, we were handed forms whereby the President could call out the National Guard to handle riots. He could just fill in the date and the name of the city. That's how bad things were at that point. His inaugural was the first in which Federal troops were brought into Washington in fear of disturbances. It was really something, it gave you an eerie feeling to see troop carriers and tanks roll in here alongside the Executive Office Building, where a command post was set up. Every major Presidential aide had a phone connected directly to riot control headquarters of the District of Columbia police. Two years later no National Guard is mobilized anywhere, no troops are in Washington, we no longer have our riot phones and as a matter of fact we have a lot more law and order in the country now than when we walked in two years ago.

'The President is very calm about personal attacks and urges us to be too. This can be a weakness, however, because he and the people around him just assume automatically that the press is going to attack things they propose, so they don't defend them—they don't seek even the modest support which I believe they could get if they weren't so sure they were going to be attacked. Admittedly the major elements have been and usually are very unfair. But I still think the Administration could get more support than it does if it had a different approach and a different feeling towards the press than it does have.

'One area, of course, in which there has been great unfairness is the area of his commitment to helping the Negroes. This Administration has been more serious on the Negro than any in history. It has carried through on a rising projection of laws and directives aiding the Negro. I think there is a very genuine compassion on his part—"I was poor, I know what it's like, it's lousy"—yet they have managed to label him anti-Negro.

'He has had the least generous press of anyone I have ever known in the White House. It has been one long presumption of malfeasance, sinister intent, trickery and double-dealing.

'The Vietnam War is killing the American Presidency. Kissinger is extraordinarily brilliant but he is stuck, and the President is stuck, with the end result of other people's mistakes. Personally, I think we should get out of Vietnam even faster than we are, because the stakes involved in world affairs now are so high. I'm a pessimist—I think we really may blow ourselves up. The man you're writing about can literally push the button and destroy the world. And so of course can the others on the other side.'

LAIRD TO PRESS NEW MOVES TO FREE POWS IN NORTH VIETNAM. FIRST FORAYS JUSTIFIED, HILL TOLD ... INFLATION HITS RATE OF 7.2 PER CENT. PRICE RISE IS BIGGEST IN SIX MONTHS.

Former Eisenhower administration official, Washington veteran, long-time Nixon friend: 'How is Nixon doing? I think he is doing very poorly. He's afraid to be tough and ruthless on issues where a President has got to be tough and ruthless, and where the country would applaud him if he were. He is afraid he will live up to the press attacks about his ruthlessness, but that is exactly what is needed. They have him buffaloed so he doesn't do what he should do to provide strong leadership. I find this very disturbing.'

John Ehrlichman is short, stocky, round-faced, dark-haired, dark-eyed, neatly dressed, hair slicked down tightly, trim, compact, pleasant, self-possessed, intelligent, articulate and obviously in full charges of his duties as head of the Domestic Council staff and adviser to the President on domestic affairs. Prior to the appointment of George Shultz, former Secretary of Labour, to the post of Director of the Office of Management and Budget in late 1970, Ehrlichman was *the* principal adviser to the President on domestic affairs. Now he shares his influence with Shultz in an arrangement so far officially amicable. He has a small, intimate, dark-panelled, Williamsburg-style office with a muted-yellow carpet and very comfortable sofas and chairs.

'We divide domestic responsibilities with George Shultz. Our end is the development of, and maintenance of, policies in the domestic area, and development of programmes to further those policies. The Domestic Council is composed of a group of Cabinet officers, experts on domestic problems and such people as Don Rumsfeld, special counsel to the President. The President is chairman of the Domestic Council and I am head of the staff of about twenty professional people.

'The policies we deal with are essentially Presidential—in other words they are things that are nationwide in application. Usually we do this in written form which we send to the President. We call it an "option paper" in which we define the problem, present the agreed facts about it, define the pros and cons concerning it and outline his choices of action. Once the President has decided what we should do we then decide how to do it. Shultz's office handles the budgeting of the programme.

'We develop legislation to present to Congress on the policies that have been decided. We also are consulted by the budget people, and we draw very heavily on the departments for help. My people are basically catalytic. The Domestic Council works through committees of four or five, backed up by staff work groups which may number as many as fifteen, drawn from government agencies, private enterprise, academic circles or wherever people can be of help.

'Our approach to what the President calls "New Federalism" means that it is really the process of determining at what level of government a given domestic problem should be functionally attacked—federal, state or local. We try to determine how to move talent and money to that area.

'For instance, manpower training is essentially a function that can be well conducted at the state and local levels. Federal revenues can be used, but they can be moved in almost untouched to state levels of government. We disagree with the theory that the federal government must set all standards for the use of federal money. We don't think Washington is necessarily more capable or more honest than local governments. For over twenty-five years there has been an ingrained assumption of venality or stupidity at the local level. As a result, local governments have tended to atrophy, and no wonder. We're really being radical because we are challenging local institutions to sink or swim.

'The President is very impatient with people who say you have to have federal rules for local institutions. Local institutions are either going to respond now or they'll be in bad trouble. Two years ago when we came in, there was a widespread disrespect and questioning of institutions. We are setting out on a very deliberate course to prove that democracy can work at all levels. It is a very deliberate Constitutional challenge on the part of the President.

'However, we are not going to see very much in the way of legislation for at least the next two years, because the Congress is controlled by the opposite party. I think there will be more attempts to go directly to the country and try to get national understanding of what we are trying to do. If we are going to leave a mark on the tree to show we were here, we are going to have to go to the country and try to get active support from the citizens. We did this in the case of the family assistance plan when a team from my office travelled around the country. They visited as many influential people as they could in each city, talking to editorial boards of newspapers, to service clubs and chambers of commerce, appearing on radio and television, trying

48

to saturate a city so that it would have a basic understanding of the programme.

'We have very cordial relations with the Republican liberal group in Congress. [The administrative aide to one major Republican senator says Nixon's principal trouble is that 'his two top advisers, Haldeman and Ehrlichman, don't have any concept of congressional relations'.] We play an almost European coalition game on the Hill. Some people are with us on certain issues but leave us on others. So we try to find the broadest possible support on both sides of the aisle. Since the President is as centrist as he is on most domestic issues, we have had some success with this. But it's really an issue-by-issue proposition.

'My office runs essentially like this: Ken Cole, my deputy assistant on the Domestic Council, has breakfast with me every morning. We then move to a joint meeting of my staff, George Shultz's staff, people from the Congressional liaison office, the press office, the science adviser, Rumsfeld, Finch and Peter Flanigan, with Ron Ziegler (press secretary), Herb Klein (director of communications) and Bill Timmons, head of the Congressional staff, coming in for the last part of the meeting. At that point I have had a chance to read the news summary, to get the picture in my own area as George Shultz has in his. In the joint meeting we are in the process of looking at the day's events from the President's standpoint. We are talking about trends and perceptible problems. Shultz and I meet with the President every afternoon at three o'clock. In the staff meetings we get posted on what the issues are and on the legislative problems for the day: whether we can get the departments together to solve something or whether we should buck it up to the President. After the joint staff meeting, the senior staff meets in Bob Haldeman's office. This meeting includes Haldeman, Shultz, myself, Kissinger, Finch, Rumsfeld and from time to time other top people. Haldeman goes directly to the President after this meeting to outline for him what has been discussed at the meeting.

'Part of our job is never to confront the President with a situation in which he has to disappoint someone or take a harsh action. For that reason, we usually send memos to him for decision. He can then be perfectly free to turn ideas down without making his decisions personal. Of course some subjects have to be presented in depth, but rather than burden his time with a lengthy discussion we usually stick to the memo form because they can go into the reservoir, so to speak, and he can read them at the best time from his standpoint.

'In general, he is very prompt in making decisions, although sometimes he will send something back with questions indicating a line of thought that can be quite unexpected. Sometimes he will say, "Please run this through again, get together these additional facts and hold it for me." Then when he is ready to tackle it he will say, "Send it up to me and I'll get busy on it." '

SENATE VOTES DOWN SST FUNDS ... NIXON: NO CUTS FOR NATO. BARS REDUCTION OF TROOPS UNTIL REDS DO SAME ... NIXON SETS GUIDELINES ON DEFECTORS ... DEMO-CRATIC HILL LEADERS URGE WAGE-PRICE FREEZE ... MEIR NOTE REPORTEDLY ASKS NIXON TO PROMISE ARMS, VETO, HELP.

General Alexander Haig, deputy to Henry Kissinger, is forty-six, handsome, greying, possessed of a frank, candid face that assists a clever mind; very intelligent, smoothspoken, capable.

'Nixon established the National Security Council system in its present form because when he came into office he found he had two choices: he could use the rigid staff system of the Eisenhower years or he could use the disorganized, informal, ad hoc system used by Kennedy and Johnson. The latter began because Jack Kennedy had a strong anti-organizational bias and depended upon a system of "Tuesday luncheons" and a series of special committees set up to meet special problems. In many ways the bureaucracy of Defence, State and the CIA were not tapped for their advice or their knowledge. Nixon wanted to go back to a system that would tap this fund of knowledge. He felt that the Johnson-Kennedy system basically gave a President pretty much what he wanted to hear.

'Nixon wanted decisions in the security area to be formally promulgated and the reasons also formally explained on the record. In the Eisenhower system, in which Ike, because of his military background, wanted to be presented with decisions instead of choices, the bureaucracy would hammer out compromise after compromise. The final decision presented to the President would be a mishmash of compromises. Ike held regular NSC meetings every week but all the members came in accompanied by their experts. In a sense these fellows, whom Nixon refers to as "the wallsitters", would keep book on their superiors and report back to the bureaucracy. This sometimes resulted in the top men trying to make points with their own departments instead of contributing to the President's decision.

'Nixon decided he wanted meetings held to a bare minimum. He wanted to avoid what he called "waffle solutions" so he required that no recommendations should come to the President. Rather there should be a series of options giving the President a spectrum of possible courses. By forcing the system to come up with alternative answers, he has stripped away old shibboleths. Now people on the council don't seek to compromise but seek to present dissenting views. For instance, with a subject such as SALT (the U.S.-Soviet strategic arms limitation talks) we prepared a range of proposals we could use, in a fairly limited package. At the same time we considered various steps that could be taken in the event that the Soviets refused to co-operate on one or all of the proposals. The system has been strengthened by the President's past reputation of being tough on the Soviets. This has permitted him to come up with more forthcoming proposals than a more liberal President might have been able to get through the bureaucracy. There are more real limits to the powers of the Presidency than people imagine.

'Nixon is not a consensus President. He doesn't want to determine policy on the basis of consensus. He never takes the temperature in the room to find out what people are thinking. He will never make a decision in these meetings. He will discuss the options. He will then take his own private counsel on it and sometimes it will be two or three weeks after the meeting before he sends back word of his final decision. He makes his own decisions, keeping his own flexibility. Then he promulgates his decisions in writing.

'Kissinger wears two hats. He is a catalyst, a transmission belt for the National Security Council. He has an academician's religious conviction that he should maintain his own neutrality. He wants to make sure that all views get to the President in manageable form, that options are reasonably presented. Even so, there is a tendency for the boys at the working level, still, to try to get together and work out compromise solutions. Many times he will bounce papers back and force them to be redone. This does not make him popular, but his own aim is not to package things in such a way that his views are the only ones emphasized to the President.

'At the same time, he is also the President's adviser on national security affairs. When the President asks his views he gives them. His influence is probably strong because basically he and the President have a real empathy. They view the world in much the same way. Henry is more theoretical, the President is more pragmatic. They very seldom clash on essentials. Where the Democrats tended to make the Secretary of State a very dominant figure in national security policy, President Nixon felt he personally had to take responsibility. In a sense he has been his own sole counsel on policy issues. He also decided that although the chairman of the Joint Chiefs of Staff was not a statutory members of the NSC, he would like to have the advice of the professional military, and so put him on the council.

'At the start of each meeting the President requests a basic, almost fundamental, briefing. He wants everyone on the same basis, starting with the same facts. Many times this is done by Richard Helms, director of the CIA.

'Sometimes in periods of crisis there will be two meetings a week; sometimes in quieter periods it may be every two or three weeks. It averages out at roughly one a week. Of course, in between meetings there are many relatively minor foreign policy issues which have to go up to the President for a decision. For these we usually resort to memos which we send to him and he then makes his decision and sends a memo back.

'On the NSC we have a staff of thirty-five to forty substantive people and probably another thirty secretaries and administrative people. The thirty-five or forty substantive policy people break down into three general categories. We think of them as the "operators", who are experts in a given geographic area; the "planners", who either handle system programming in their special areas of knowledge or work on estimating long-range trends; and the "programmers" who measure the allocation of U.S. resources in a given country, measure what we are getting from it in terms of foreign policy. On balance this works very well because it shreds the emotionalism from a lot of problem areas and permits us to take a good hard look at them.

'The President's style is very thoughtful, that of a policymaker who doesn't shoot from the hip. He wouldn't be human if he didn't have a temper sometimes, or sometimes react in rather starchy ways when he is dissatisfied with a presentation. But almost consistently his style is to weigh things very, very carefully and to move cautiously. Once he does move, he's exceptionally good about pouring in assets to back up his decision. He doesn't sit and worry. In Cambodia, for instance, he knew he was swimming against the tide of the bureaucracy but he was confident he had made the right decision in spite of protest from a lot of the public and even his own Cabinet. He didn't lose his cool, though many around him did. It was not a snap judgment he had made on his own. He felt he had got a tremendous in-put from all pertinent sources before he acted. Once he had acted, his entire emphasis was on how we would follow through. Looking back now, it is clear that he was almost 100 per cent correct.

'Another example of the way he acts when the heat is on came in the crisis in Jordan. The public does not know it yet, but we came very, very close to a major catastrophe in the Middle East. He stepped into it, kept control, made his decisions precise, positive and unequivocal. That really turned events away from a major confrontation.'

EUROPE RAISES OUTCRY AGAINST TRADE BILL ... INDO-CHINA RAIDS SAID TO BE AIMED AT FOE'S BUILD-UP. NIXON IS BELIEVED TO SEEK TO PREVENT ANY OFFENSIVE IN THE COMING MONTHS ... GI'S IN GERMANY: BLACK IS BITTER.

Former high Nixon staffer, amicably resigned, still friendly and concerned: 'There seems to be a reluctance in the White House to come to grips with certain problems, both of personnel and of policy. Consequently a lot of people are still hanging on who are diametrically opposed to the Nixon programme and they simply can't seem to get up the guts to get rid of them. Bob Haldeman and John Ehrlichman have got too far too fast. They have not really been tested in getting where they are. They don't have the experience. They don't really have the backbone about various things. Also, there seems to be a reluctance on Nixon's part to really go after some of these people who are obstructing him. It is a curious thing, which extends also, it seems to me, to foreign policy and what seems to be a reluctance, sometimes, to come to firm grips with the challenges that face him as President from the Russians and elsewhere around the world.'

James Keogh, former *Time* magazine executive and head of the President's speech-writing staff for the first two years of the term, has left the White House as per agreement to return to private life. White-haired, helpful, he has a quick smile that lights up his face and a very pleasant manner. His duties have been taken over by Ray Price, a Nixon campaign speech writer who is supposed to be the official 'liberal' on the speech-writing staff; but the essential nature of the office and the man it serves remain as Jim Keogh describes them.

'Everything that comes out over the President's name originates in this office through this staff. You might say it is the research and writing shop of the White House.

'The President insists so much on being his own writer of the things which he says directly in public that we basically provide him with material and "suggested remarks". These will number from two to six major points. In an off-the-cuff speech, what he does is look at our suggestions, absorb them, possibly delete or add some of his own, underline them, think about them and then spin out his own thoughts. Much of it is in his own words, based partially on our suggestions and on his own ideas.

'In a major speech the process is different. He tells us what he has in mind. We provide him with a draft or drafts. He comments, dictates memos, makes suggestions. We will then redo it and send it back to him. He usually then goes over it very thoroughly, works it over in varying degrees, depending on how well we have met his original suggestions. He is very insistent that any major statement that he makes in person will bear the stamp of his own words and personality.

'In the area of statements, routine messages to Congress and other kinds of routine official statements over his signature, he does not bother too much but often takes our suggestions. He is

54

much more willing to take what we offer in this less important area.

'The same thing applies to official proclamations, executive orders and some major correspondence. The head of the staff is closer to being a managing editor than any other particular title. We have a three-girl research office to assist us.

'There are an amazing number of minor messages the President sends out: messages of greeting to various organizations and banquets, special greetings to a local hero who is being honoured by some civic function, and so on.

'Major correspondence may consist of form letters to some thousand people, for instance, soliciting contributions to the White House historical fund, VIP letters, diplomatic statements to heads of state and the like. Some of these are checked over carefully by the President and some are rewritten, but in the main these go out as we prepare them, in a routine way.

'Pat Buchanan is responsible for preparing a "news summary" with the help of the staff. This summary, sometimes consisting of as many as fifty typewritten pages, goes to the President every morning. It consists of a digest of the views and opinions and statements of all three major TV networks, the top stories on government by the AP and UPI and at least forty newspapers and all of the major magazines. This summary contains some editorial comment by the staff as to the overall impact of a given broadcast or article.

'It excludes the New York *Times* and the Washington *Post*.

'The President wants to read those himself.'

The White House switchboard, in-put and out-put for half the world these days, presently has seventeen trunk lines, nineteen girls and two men who work the late-night shift. The board is open twenty-four hours a day. It handles all White House calls except top secret military and the 'hot line' to Moscow, which are handled by the Signal Corps.

Traffic runs between five thousand and ten thousand calls a day, depending upon calm or crises. Perhaps two hundred are crank calls—they increase when the moon is full, says Mrs. Mary Burns, assistant operator, staff member for twenty-two years. 'We get the lunar lunatics.' Occasionally someone will call and ask for Jesus Christ. A favourite caller is 'Marjorie', who lives in the Washington area, has been institutionalized and usually begins her calls with a hum. Whoever receives her call will say calmly, 'Now, Marjorie, stop bothering the White House operators, we're all busy.' She is, however, 'really quite intelligent and rather nice', and presumably a break in the busy day.

Perhaps one call a day is genuinely threatening to the President. It is referred immediately to the Secret Service's Protective Intelligence Division, which handles all suspicious matters involving the White House or its occupants. Sometimes it takes as much as an hour and a half to trace the call, during which Mrs. Burns and her colleagues try to keep the caller talking.

When the President goes to San Clemente, seven or eight switchboard girls go with him, but operators are not sent to Key Biscayne. All Presidents have been very appreciative of the switchboard's service, which sometimes involves tracing people down on planes, ships, island retreats, or in the backwoods.

Nowadays the operators get quite upset because many people in government outside the White House make use of the switchboard for their calls. Members of Congress and Cabinet officers will call in and ask the board to get people for them, instead of using their own facilities on the Hill or in the departments. This, as the girls admit rather ruefully, is a tribute to their skill they don't always appreciate. 'Those White House operators,' one Cabinet member remarked. 'If you're dead, they'll dig you up.' They had really rather not—'but what can you do about it?'

Dwight Chapin, the President's appointments secretary, is thirty, dark-eyed, dark-haired, rosy-cheeked, good-looking, earnest, intent; he gives the impression that he has so many things on his mind that he simply can't relax for a moment. This is probably true. Like Finch and a good many others in the official family, he makes notes on a big pad of legal yellow note paper just as the President does.

'We're responsible for the general scheduling of the President's time and also the daily schedule. I also act as advance man, or send out members of my staff as advance men, when the President is travelling. In addition I participate with Herb Klein and various public affairs officers at a regular Saturday meeting in which we take up things that might help the President in dealing with the public and decide whether they are worth his taking the time to do them. We are already considering what we want to do on television and radio next year; we are also considering how we want to involve the First Family in the holiday season next year. This year's schedule was already locked up a long time ago. Most of the things we decide upon are locked up at least two weeks ahead of time. We may want to refine a schedule but basically we know well in advance what he is going to do. We also handle special mailings to important groups, such as the pocketbook we did on the voluntary army. It didn't do very well, actually. This group is involved, in other words, in the whole merchandising part of the operation.

'The President averages about twelve appointments a day. He also does a lot of telephoning. It's all on the same sheet, a log which is kept by our office and his secretary's office.

'The President says he really works two days in one. He comes to work between eight and eight-fifteen and usually works steadily until 2 p.m. Then after a lunch break he resumes at three-thirty and works until seven. Then frequently he will return to the office after dinner and work until 10 or 11 p.m. He figures the energy he puts in and the hours he keeps qualifies his claim that he works two days in one.

'Of course, he can do this because, unlike the ordinary businessman, everything is scheduled for him. He doesn't have to stop and decide whom he's going to telephone or see because his secretary knows already who it will be, or maybe someone has been told to call in at a given time. Bob Haldeman is my boss and we try to see that whatever the President puts his time on will be worth doing. When he does something we make sure that it is something that he can do something about.

'When we get a request for an appointment we staff it out by sending a memo to the President and to others concerned describing what is to be covered in the appointment, who favours the appointment and who opposes it. That way we make sure his time is not wasted. He has recently established what we call an "open hour" once a week, during which eight or ten people may see him for as much as five or ten minutes apiece. In addition, we have the "congressional half hour" once or twice a month in which Congressmen who want to talk to him personally can make an appointment for five or ten minutes.

'The President has a real warmth about him. He's very considerate of others. To my knowledge he has never once yelled or got boisterous. He is also very quick to think of things to make people happy. For instance, the other day I went in and saw two Rose Bowl tickets [for the Stanford-Ohio game] lying on his desk. I said, "Isn't there somebody we could give those to who would appreciate them? Someone, for instance, who was born in Ohio but grew up in California?" He thought for just a minute and then he said, "You go find some wife of a prisoner of war who was born in Ohio and grew up in California and I bet she'd like to have them." So we did find one and the letter has gone out. I don't know whether she'll like them or not, but at least we're starting it through the mill.'

('One thing that annoys me a little with the staff,' says the President's longtime campaign associate Murray Chotiner, 'is that all they release of the President's schedule each day are the formal things, greeting visiting firemen or the medal-giving ceremony in the Rose Garden. There are about three of these, maybe less, each day. This goes right in the paper alongside Congress with maybe twenty-five committees at work in the House and another twenty in the Senate. It makes him look almost frivolous compared to Congress. I wonder what the tourists must think who come here and know only his cere-monial schedule that they read in the papers.')

From the daily log kept by Dwight Chapin's office come the records of two typical days, showing that the President actually does considerably more than hand out medals in the Rose Garden:

PRESIDENT RICHARD NIXON'S DAILY DIARY

THE WHITE HOUSE, Thursday, November 5, 1970:

9.15 a.m.—The President had breakfast.

9.25—The President went to the Oval Office.

9.45-10.05—The President met with his assistant, R. H. Haldeman.

10.08-11.48—The President attended a Cabinet meeting in the Cabinet Room.

11.48—The President returned to the Oval Office.

11.50-12.24 p.m.—The President met with Lee Kuan Yew, Prime Minister of Singapore, Ernest Steven Montero, Ambassador of Singapore, Henry A. Kissinger, Assistant, Emil Mosbacher, Chief of Protocol.

11.50-11.51—White House photographer photographed group.

12.24 p.m.—The President went to the Blue Room.

12.26-1.00—The President received the diplomatic credentials of three ambassadors. The President met with each ambassador and his escorts in the Blue Room and then in the Red Room, as follows:

Emilio O. Rabasa, Ambassador from Mexico, Emil Mosbacher, Chief of Protocol, Robert A. Hurwitch, Deputy Chief of Protocol.

Pierre Ileka, Ambassador from the Democratic Republic of the Congo, Emil Mosbacher, Chief of Protocol, Robert S. Smith, Acting Assistant Secretary of State for African Affairs, Alec G. Roumayan, interpreter.

Julio Asensio, Ambassador from Guatemala, Emil Mosbacher, Chief of Protocol, Robert A. Hurwitch, Deputy Chief of Protocol.

Following the presentation of credentials, the President held a brief private discussion with each ambassador in the Red Room. Press and photographers were also present.

1.00—The President returned to the Oval Office.

1.15—The President went to his office in the Executive Office Building.

1.17-2.10—The President met with H. R. Haldeman, Assistant.

1.44-1.45—Lawrence M. Higby, Staff Assistant.

3.11-3.13—The President left his office in the EOB and went to his Oval Office.

3.15-3.34—The President met with his assistant, John D. Ehrlichman.

3.35-3.45—The President met with: George P. Shultz, Director, Office of Management and Budget, and Caspar Weinberger, Deputy Director, OMB.

3.45-4.00—The President went to the Roosevelt Room, where he met with undersecretaries and budget officials for a budget meeting.

4.00—The President returned to the Oval Office.

4.01-4.06—The President met with his assistant, H. R. Haldeman.

4.11-4.35—The President met with H. R. Haldeman, Assistant. and Henry A. Kissinger, Assistant.

4.39—The President went to the Mansion, where he joined the First Lady.

4.42-5.08—The President and the First Lady went to the Blue Room where they hosted a reception for Adams family descendants.

5.08-6.25—The President went to the Map Room, where he met with newspaper columnists.

6.25—The President went to the Oval Office.

6.28—The President met with: H. R. Haldeman, Assistant, and Robert H. Finch, Counsellor.

7.15—The President went to the Mansion.

7.23—The President telephoned his assistant, H. R. Haldeman. The call was not completed.

7.49-8.02—The President telephoned his special counsel, Harry S. Dent.

8.10-11.13—The President hosted a black tie stag dinner in honour of the Earl of Mountbatten of Burma, K.G.

THE WHITE HOUSE, Tuesday, November 17, 1970:

7.44 a.m.—The President had breakfast.

7.55—The President went to his Oval Office.

8.14-9.22—The President attended a Republican leadership meeting in the Cabinet Room.

9.25-9.45—The President met with Ronald L. Ziegler, press secretary, Sen. Hugh Scott, and Rep. Gerald Ford.

9.49-10.00—The President talked long distance with chairman of Procter & Gamble, Neil McElroy, in Cincinnati, Ohio.

10.15-10.47—The President met with his assistant, H. R. Haldeman.

10.49-11.32—The President met with Ellsworth Bunker, Ambassador to South Vietnam, and Henry A. Kissinger, Assistant.

11.32-12.25 p.m.—The President met with John D. Ehrlichman, Assistant, Elliot L. Richardson, Secretary of HEW, and Sidney P. Marland, Commissioner of Education Designate.

12.14-12.25—The President met with Securities and Exchange chairman Hamer Budge.

12.26-1.45—The President met with Senator Robert J. Dole and H. R. Haldeman.

3.07-3.40—The President met with: George P. Shultz, Director, OMB, Caspar Weinberger, Deputy Director, OMB, John D. Ehrlichman, Assistant.

3.41-4.41—The President met with his assistant, Henry A. Kissinger.

3.43-4.23—The President met with: Rolf Pauls, Ambassador of Germany, and Klaus Schultz, Mayor of West Berlin.

4.43-5.15—The President met with his counsellor, Daniel Patrick Moynihan.

5.17-5.38—The President met with his assistant, H. R. Haldeman.

5.38—The President went to the Mansion.

6.04—The President went to the south grounds.

6.05-7.05—The President and the First Lady flew by helicopter from the south grounds of the White House to Philadelphia, Pennsylvania.

7.08-7.15—The President and the First Lady motored from the helipad to the Pennsylvania Academy of Fine Arts.

7.15-8.22—The President and the First Lady attended a reception at the Pennsylvania Academy of Fine Arts. Their hosts were: President of the Board of Directors and Mrs. John Gribbell, Director of the Academy and Mrs. William Stevens.

8.22-8.28—The President and the First Lady motored from the Pennsylvania Academy of Fine Arts to the helipad.

8.27—The President was telephoned long distance by National Committee woman Meredith Clark in St. Croix, Virgin Islands. The call was not completed.

8.31-9.31—The President flew by helicopter from the helipad to the south grounds of the White House.

9.34—The President went to the Mansion.

9.38-9.39—The President received a telephone call from his special counsel, Harry S. Dent.

10.00-10.04—The President telephoned Attorney General John N. Mitchell.

George Shultz, short, stocky, blond with a rather roundish, know-ing face, is obviously intelligent and shrewd; smokes a pipe, has a good sense of humour, speaks very softly, frequently breaks into a quietly humorous little smile. Formerly Secretary of Labour, in late 1970 he was appointed Director of the Office of Management and Budget. As such he is the President's top adviser on domestic affairs, John Ehrlichman notwithstanding. He is tough and he is competent, and in his gentle, self-possessed, dryly humorous way he deprecates his power and influence and that of the OMB. This fools nobody in Washing-ton.

'We have four jobs here. The first is organizing the budget process. The second is trying to figure how a greater awareness and skill in the managerial area can help the government work better. The third is providing participation in the process of developing economic policy. And the fourth is coping. Most of the day we spend coping. Sometimes we cope with what we did but more often we cope with what others did. I figure that if people have a sense of policy and direction the events they cope with get the policy attained bit by bit and in better style. I sometimes tell my staff, "As you cope, so shall you reap."

'This job has the potential of putting one in touch with almost everybody of any stature in the government. The budget goes across the whole spectrum of the government. For instance, just yesterday the Chief Justice called me to try to get some more funds to provide more guards for the courts so that his judges won't get shot at.

'The impression has gotten around that because we touch so many things we must have a vast power. The Budget Office is undoubtedly powerful, but our job is not to decide. Rather it is to insist on a process of policy making in the economic field that will make everybody responsible to the President.

'The budget-making process has many time-honoured aspects but we have tried to add a few new things. Our aim is to give the principal officers of the government a continuing picture so that their in-puts of information to the budget process will be as informed as possible. We have been trying to make sure that the in-puts will be timely so that they will really mean something. We have also changed the structure to try to eliminate a "budget director's mark" and substitute a "President's mark" on the budget. We withdraw ourselves in a decision making sense and provide information so that the Cabinet officers and the President can be the decision-makers. Our principal aim is to try to keep everybody posted on the whole budget. We try to make a series of approximations of what can be done in a budgetary way rather than a single definite command.

'In the budget meetings we have tried to outline the economic philosophy of the budget as we saw it. We showed them what everything they all want adds up to, and when it was over it was pretty obvious that what they want isn't there. We make a very tough review of the fiscal picture without reference to political factors, then we say, "That's the rock bottom, Mr. President. If you want to dig in deeper you can do so, but it probably would be a waste of time."

'We go over what the agencies have requested and lop off some of the obvious junk. In between the agencies' requests and rock bottom, the items that have to be paid under existing legislation, there are a range of very tough things.

'Some are politically sensitive. Some are things that everybody wants to do, but how do we do them? Here they are. We try to present the President with the total picture. Then we go through them item by item and see what can be cut. We winnow away at the list and make it smaller. Then we go back to the President and see if we can cut again below that. We see how we can fit it all together. We give the agencies and departments the opportunity to appeal the decisions in writing and we see that their appeals get to the President.

"We work with Ehrlichman on the domestic budget. On Defence, State, CIA and other security matters, we try to work with Henry Kissinger. We conduct our review in tandem with the secretaries. For instance, our people go to the Pentagon for a joint examination and data-collecting session with the secretary. This allows both of us to operate off the same facts. Then we can both independently make our decisions. Then the President makes what we call a "President's mark" on the items he wants to cut further. It's an exhausting process, looking at things you don't know much about, but it's a good way to get it worked out.

'The President's guideline is that expenditures should not exceed revenues engendered by the tax system when the economy is at full employment. It is a severe discipline, because the thrust of uncontrollable items (such things as highway funds obligated in past legislation) is always upward. The President says that we aren't always seeking to avoid a deficit, we want to do what is worth doing. But in general we try to keep expenditure related to revenues as closely as possible. He is not a doctrinaire President—it isn't the good old rip-roaring concept of "balance the budget at any cost". The problem of how to find full employment in a rising economy and still keep inflation under control is a very difficult one that no country has solved yet. We are doing our best.

'One of the interesting things about the budget is that by the time the President sends the '72 Budget to Congress three fourths of it will be already locked in under authorized expenditures and programmes.

'The federal bureaucracy is actually getting smaller, which is an aim of this Administration. As for such things as government waste, particularly in the defence area, we try to get down to it, but the fundamental responsibility lies with Cabinet and sub-Cabinet officers. On the other hand, it probably makes them do it better if a knowledgeable group can raise penetrating questions.

'We have 550 professional people in the OMB, the same as the old Budget Bureau, which we absorbed. We will probably add about 125 more. When I was Secretary of Labour, I told my people that we wanted to be a swinging outfit, out in front working on problems. I think the OMB should be "the good grey OMB" with a strong analytical capability, giving objective analyses in an effort to see that the options are properly staffed out and understood by the people who make the decisions.'

Nixon intimate No. 1: 'As of now'—that favourite politician's phrase—'there is no strong dump-Agnew movement. But a lot will depend on how the Vice-President conducts himself as we come into the homestretch before the convention. He has a lot going for him, but there is a razor-thin line between a voice which points out things that a lot of people agree with and a voice that becomes strident by talking too much. Of course, the Vice-President also has going for him the President's vivid memories of the sort of treatment he received when he was Vice-President. There was a dump-Nixon movement in those days, remember.'

Nixon intimate No. 2: 'There are four reasons against a dump-Agnew movement. The first is that the possibility is raised in columns and news stories out of an obvious, and to the President offensive, hope that it will occur. The second is that even the hope is premature, because Presidents make that kind of decision in the spring of an election year, or maybe in the summer just before, or even during, the convention. Thirdly, I know of no disposition on the part of the President's staff or advisers to do such a thing. And fourth, Mr. Agnew has a rather devoted following among some elements of the Republican Party and an attempt to get rid of him could have quite interesting results. Having talked to him many times, I know that he is very philosophical and is not worried about it. I really think he would be happy either way—and after all, what else can a Vice-President do?'

None of which means, of course, that these two suave gentlemen would not gladly and eagerly assist in the political execution of Spiro T. Agnew if their boss asked them to; or that their boss, bound by the imperatives of Presidents, which are sometimes less subject to conscience and friendship than those of ordinary men, might not perfectly calmly and logically decide to order such a thing at the coming national convention. An Agnew aide sums up the perils of being No. 2, an office in which you do not necessarily, if you wish to retain it, try harder:

'We have received excellent co-operation from the White House staff, partly, I think, because the President is so wholeheartedly for Agnew. However, I think that if they got the word, or if they felt he was a detriment to the President, they would axe him in a minute.

'One interesting episode occurred when the Vice-President was speaking to the Associated Press Managing Editors' Con-

vention in Hololulu recently. He had about a page and a half in which he specifically named people like the New York Times, Newsweek, Time, Look *and* Life, *NBC, ABC and CBS as those he meant when he talked about the Eastern press establishment. This caused great excitement in the White House staff. They were horrified that he would name these people.*

'*His point of view was that he wanted to say specifically whom he was criticizing, and not make it just the press in general. However, there was great upset about this in the staff and they took it to Nixon. He overruled Agnew and asked him to take it out of the speech, which he did. –*

'*I don't really understand this attitude of the President or of some of the White House staff in this, because the way I look at it, these people are your enemies for life. They are not going to change, there is nothing to be gained by appeasing them, and you might just as well sail into them with everything you have. However, the President is apparently still trying to make some points with people who are bitterly critical of him and are never going to change. That could be a factor in what he does about the Vice-President next time.... It could be a factor.*'

Sitting quietly in their Sheraton-Park apartment with Mrs. Agnew after a relaxed and intimate family dinner, the storm centre of all these battles, pressures and controversies speaks quietly and shrewdly about himself and the perils of his country as he sees them.

QUESTION: What do you think of the Vice-Presidency as an office now that you have been in it for a while?

'I think it's the most flexible office in the government'—sudden laugh. 'Certainly it has given me, I think, more opportunity than any other Vice-President—thanks to the kindness of the President—to do things in the government. I didn't really want to get so far away from the Senate, where constitutionally I'm president of the Senate and presiding officer, but it's worked out that way.

'I went up to the Senate my first day here, all full of idealism and sentiment. I had spent five or six sessions with the parliamentarian trying to learn the rules of the Senate; I knew the Senators by name and I knew their faces; I was prepared to go in there and do a job as the President's representative in the Senate. I even prepared a little four-minute talk to express my pleasure at being there on the first day. When the session opened, the Majority Leader spoke in a perfunctory way for about a minute to welcome me to the Senate and this was followed by the Minority Leader doing the same thing.

'After that the Majority Leader said, "Mr. President, I move that the Vice-President be given two minutes to reply." I was then faced with cutting down a prepared four-minute speech to two minutes, which was awkward in itself. It was like a slap in the face.

'However, I tried hard to get to know the Senators and to work with them in those first months. Then, unfortunately, the President was called away to Europe at the time of the ABM fight. I was given the job of helping to get that legislation through. When it got to a vote, I went up to Len Jordan [Republican, Utah] during the vote and just said casually, "Len, how are you going to vote?" He drew himself up, stared at me accusingly and said, "You can't tell me how to vote! You can't twist my arm!" Within a minute he was off the floor calling in the press for a press conference, saying I was going around the Senate twisting arms.

'It seemed to go on from there after that. And so, after trying for a while to get along with the Senate, I decided I would go down to the other end of Pennsylvania Avenue and try playing the Executive game.

'Down here the President has found many things for me to do, and on the whole I have been much happier working here with him in the Executive Branch. I still go up to the Senate and preside. And when I preside, I make very sure I impose the rules, and if somebody is talking too long I gavel him down and force him to obey the rules. I've decided that if that's the way they want me to be, that's the way I will be.

'However I find up there, as I do in the Executive Branch, that I have no real power. It is a damned peculiar situation to be in, to have authority and a title and responsibility with no real power to do anything. I think this is the hardest adjustment for a man to make, both coming to the Vice-Presidency and coming to the Senate. He has been, as many of us were, a governor, say, in an administrative position, and suddenly he finds he can't do anything effectively. It's a strange sort of limbo, particularly for the Vice-President. In the early days I used to say to myself, "Now, tomorrow I'm going to do so and so" ... and then I would stop and think, "You aren't going to do anything, you don't have the power."

'I find the Senate very exclusive and withdrawn into itself ... almost an arrogance in the club feeling up there. It makes it difficult to deal with them, even in the rather remote fashion that I now do. And yet, you know'—dreamily—'the Senate might not be such a bad place to be, someday....

'I am very much disturbed by the trend of American policy under which, prodded on by the press and the liberals, we are steadily withdrawing from commitments around the world. It is not so much that this reduces our power militarily to a dangerous level as it is that it erodes the faith other nations have that we are strong enough to do something should a crisis arise. When I went to Asia I found that they said, "You can't do anything, really, if a pinch comes, because you are withdrawing."

'In the same way when we sometimes appear to be retreating before the Soviets in some other area, this erodes the world's confidence that the United States will really do what it says it will do. Frankly, it scares me."

QUESTION: Then how do you explain why the President appears to be withdrawing our power around the world?

'He's in a hell of a position. He has the press and the media and the liberals and the academic community and all the rest after him all the time. He is forced to take that into account. No one who doesn't sit in the cat-bird seat can really understand his problem. It is all very well for people to criticize, but until you are there, you don't know the pressures he must operate under.

'I find these fellows on the Hill very disturbing, particularly the attitude of the Senate Foreign Relations Committee. Of course, Fulbright is going to get away free. Events will never catch up with him. He'll be dead by the time the results of what he advocates afflict this country. We're talking now about our grandchildren, or at least about the next generation. Then is when the blow will come from the Soviets. By that time we will be so weak that we will not be able to respond unless we were willing to launch a massive retaliation that could blow up the world. They have been extremely clever in never forcing a crisis. Their method is to work around us and weaken us on every side without forcing a confrontation. Again I say it scares me, because these fellows in the Senate and in the House who oppose our foreign policy are doing things to this country which cannot possibly be reversed unless we start soon to do them. They will soon be irreversible.

'There is an almost masochistic desire on the part of the liberal community to surrender and to back away from any confrontation with Russia—for us to be twice as fair in dealing with them as with anybody else, twice as long-suffering, twice as permissive as we are with anyone else. I find this almost impossible to understand, but I know it exists among many in the liberal community.

'I wish there were some way to create a conservative paper in New York and also a conservative television and radio network. It is very hard to get people who have the money to co-operate with one another. It is an example of the difficulty of getting people on the conservative side to organize to combat this intensive liberal drive all the time on the other side.

'I really love foreign policy. I have thoroughly enjoyed my trips abroad and I am looking forward to making more. It is getting now so that they stop by to see me when they come through here. I spent an hour today with King Hussein, whom I had met before. The first time is a formal visit, the second time they get more relaxed and about the third time they really begin to talk to you. You begin to understand the signals in their diplomatic language. You know their situation and you know what they are saying to you. I find it very interesting and I'm glad the President has seen fit to give me this kind of responsibility.

'I'm standing the gaff pretty well. I keep in good shape and they aren't getting to me. When I first began the '68 campaign there was a terrific drive to destroy me as a candidate and at first I took it very seriously. For a little while I thought, "Well, I've got all those marbles out there. Am I going to be able to keep control of them?" But the President was a tower of strength to me in that situation: "Ignore them, they're going to be after you all the time anyway. It's a political campaign and there isn't much we can do to stop it, so just say to hell with them and just keep right on doing what you're doing." And presently I realized when I read the attacks that they were so extreme and exaggerated that they simply were ridiculous. They simply did not make sense. Once I understood that, I got to the point where I could shrug them off and then they didn't bother me any more. Now I'm just going to go ahead and do what I want to do.

'But I do find that one has to be very specific in one's comments, because if not, the press immediately shreds away all the qualifications that you put in. For instance, I said originally that those who *encouraged* the student riots were "effete snobs". Within two or three days it had become, in the press, not the people who had *encouraged* the students, but the students themselves. Then presently it became *all* students. Then presently it became *all youth*. And that is the way it goes.

'People asked me why I attacked Kingman Brewster of Yale and I said "Well, if I don't make it specific, within a week I will be accused of having attacked *all* college presidents instead of just one college president." This is a very dangerous thing that the press does, and they do it all the time.'

Mrs. Agnew, when asked how she thinks her husband is standing it: 'I think he's doing all right. He manages to keep himself in good shape and seems to be in reasonably good spirits. We've learned to roll with the punches and we don't let it bother us any more.'

He seems genuinely unconcerned about his political future. He seems to be really, completely philosophical about whether he stays on the ticket in '72 or leaves it. At one point when we were discussing the Vice-Presidency I said humorously, 'Anyway, you're stuck with it.'

He raised a finger with a sudden smile.

'Not forever,' he said quickly. 'Not forever.'

SST KEPT ALIVE BY HOUSE ... RAIL HALT LINKED TO PAY RISE. UNIONS SEEK THIRTEEN ONE-HALF PER CENT BOOST IF TALKS GO ON ... STATE DEPARTMENT REPORT: TWO DECADES OF 'ATROPHY' ... 1971 SOVIET BUDGET RISES SLIGHTLY, BUT DEFENCE FIGURE IS UNCHANGED.

Bob Brown, special assistant to the President for domestic affairs, is thirty-six, a pleasant, articulate, well-spoken Negro, obviously convinced and idealistic about his job. Like all the Administration's blacks, he is under a lot of pressure from his own people. He seems to be able to take it, aided by an overriding conviction that what is being done is in the right direction.

'As special assistant to the President for domestic affairs, I might be getting endorsements for a programme, I might be helping to form policy as it relates to a domestic problem, I might be looking with others at some problem down the road, trying to get an idea of a proper programme that we can form to meet it.

'I deal also with minority business and civil rights and I try to help initiate and create opportunities for the disadvantaged, not only blacks but many other minority groups and the poor. I also deal with the black colleges and universities, of which there are 112 in the country. Very little federal money heretofore has gone into these schools. But at the end of fiscal year 1969, the figure had risen to more than $122,000,000, compared with somewhere around $10,000,000 to $20,000,000 a year in past administrations.

'We have set out unequivocally to see to it that higher education funds get to these schools. The President has said he wants it done and we have proceeded on that basis. These are not basically new appropriations but they are designed really to help smaller colleges, whereas in actuality they have in the past largely helped bigger ones. The reason for this is that many smaller colleges had to turn back the money—which would have helped students to study by working their way through—because it was required that the universities and colleges deliver matching funds. The poorer schools naturally could not do this. Under the President's prodding, Secretary Richardson of HEW has redrawn the regulations to provide that all schools whose student bodies are more than 50 per cent composed of students coming from families making $7500 a year or less should be given government funds outright without any requirement that they match the funds. Things like these have to come from the President himself to get them done, and he has been very vigorous in pushing them.

'As far as minority enterprises, particularly black enterprises, the government is putting up a great deal of money and it is increasing. In 1969 it was $7,657,000 in government contracts going to minority group contractors. In fiscal year 1970 this rose to $37,456,000. For fiscal year 1971 it will be up to $142 million, so you can see we are making rapid advances in this area. Heretofore blacks and other minority groups in this category received little or nothing from past administrations.

'This was done by a memo put out by the President in 1969 and since then contracts to minority contractors have risen 1300 per cent over what they were before his directive.

'Are blacks taking advantage of this?' He shrugged. 'Our objective is to make the money available to whoever wants to go into business. Then they fail or succeed if they're able to. It is up to them. We aren't interested in just proposing programmes but in doing something. It's up to them to take advantage of it. We can get into the rhetoric bag if we want to but we don't want to. We want to make it real.

'Those who say the President is not minority-oriented or young-oriented are crazy. As far as the young are concerned, we have the youngest staff any President has ever had around him. As far as minority-oriented, I think that many of us come from poor families. Certainly my own family was on the other side of the people on the other side of the tracks. We were p—triple o— poor. I know what it means to have no shoes and not enough to eat, and while the President probably never went without shoes or without something to eat when he was growing up, still his family was very poor at one time and they did not have any luxuries. So he knows what it is like.

'I think the same thing applies to a lot of us on the staff who come from modest backgrounds. A lot of the opposition to the family assistance plan comes in large measure from people who are eating three squares a day. Either they've forgotten how it is to live on a thousand dollars a year or they are totally insensitive to the kind of problem we will have if we don't have welfare reform. Unless we have reform it's going to overwhelm everything in a little while.

'One of the things I like about my job is being able to help so many people with just something as simple as one phone call. In a job like this you can change people's lives, and this can't help but touch one down deep. For the first time, this Administration has set up a liaison group on poverty and we make sure that things are taken care of in that area. I am chairman of the group and we monitor the whole effort. We don't just let an Executive order be issued and then forget about it. We keep tabs and we keep pushing.

'I get a response all the time from people about it. Recently I got a letter from a young fellow who works for the Tennessee Valley Authority. He had a job but he said he had tried to better himself and become an electrician having been an electrician's mate in the Navy. But he said, "They won't let me through. Every time I try to break into a better job, the whites stop me." So I wrote the TVA chairman, and asked the Civil Service Commission to look into it and see what could be done, and now that young man is the first journeyman electrician TVA ever had, and there are others in training. They tell me my name is pretty big down there in the Tennessee Valley area because I have helped to give blacks and poor whites a chance to make it. I don't think this is enough. I don't think the President feels this is enough—that what we are doing is enough. I know we both want to make it better, and I spend all my waking hours trying to make things better.

'There is no doubt of the President's commitment. He knows what it is to be poor just as I do. In my family, as I said, we were p—triple o—poor. My grandmother, who raised us, never let us accept any kind of government aid. She scrubbed the floors in white houses and told us to mow lawns and so on to make some money when we got big enough to do so. And she drilled into us that we should always be self-reliant and make our own way in the world if we possibly could. . . .

'You ask if the Administration has established credibility with the minorities, with the blacks and the poor. No, I don't feel we have established the kind of credibility that we need. It would be dishonest to say that. More needs to be done to highlight what is being accomplished by the Administration. Many blacks are very hostile towards the Nixon Administration and towards the President. We have to emphasize more what we are doing. However, the President feels that until we make great strides we don't need to blow about it. He wants us to have real accomplishments to talk about and we are still working. We have hired more blacks and minority group representatives in top jobs than any other Administration. No Administration before this has given out free food stamps. A massive food stamp programme and a massive school lunch programme are being conducted by this Administration. The President proposed them and now it's happening. We've met the toughest problems head on. But the more you do, the more you have to do.

'You ask if I receive criticism and suspicion from my own people. I certainly do, but my response is, I couldn't care less. I'm trying to do a job. I worked for the President in the campaign and during the last two years, and I shall continue to work for him. I'm going to stand by him in or out, whether I'm still on the staff or if I go back to private life. If I leave, I'm going to be working for him still, because I believe in what he is trying to do and I think he is sincere in it. I don't give a damn what people say about it if I believe I'm doing right. I want to be helping people—that's what a man's life is all about.

'To go back to my grandmother who raised me, I used to ask her, "Mom, why are we so poor?" She'd say, "We really aren't poor. Look at those people in our community, they're worse off than we are, many of them. They're poorer than we are." So I looked and I could see others were worse off than we were. She'd say, "If there's any one thing I want to teach you, it's to share with other people." And she did. There was always something in our house. She kept a big pot of beans and a big pot of potatoes and whenever somebody would go by and they wanted something, they'd say, "Miss Nellie, can I come in and eat something?" And she'd say, "Sure you can," and then she'd say to us, "If I don't teach you anything else, life is all about sharing. That's what it's really all about." Now, she was a woman who never got beyond the second grade, who taught herself how to read and write, whose father was a slave and so on. She drilled into us that sharing and helping other people was the best thing in life. If I believe in Richard Nixon, I'm going to go to whatever length I can to help him, even to the extent of giving my life if necessary. If a man doesn't want to give his life for what he believes in, then he can't really believe in it.

'I was almost broke in 1960 but I packed up my wife and I

went back to North Carolina from New York, where I was working as a Treasury agent, and I set myself up in business as a public relations firm, with a borrowed desk and a chair in an abandoned office over an abandoned theatre. I put in a telephone. They were just about to take it out. I owed money to everybody and suddenly a call came from a friend in New York who wanted to give me an assignment. That assignment led to other assignments and they parlayed into a pretty good business, and then I had contracts all over the nation. And it goes to prove what my grandmother told me: It seems like when you do something to help people things work out for you, if you just hold on things will work out and soon you'll have more business than you can shake a stick at. Well, I held on, and after a while I had more business than I could shake a stick at, and all because I followed what she told me, which is that to help people and share with them is the best thing a man can do in life.'

Of all the serene and happy men in the White House who tell you how wonderfully everything is going, none is happier or more serene than Peter Flanigan, special assistant to the President in the area of economic affairs. In his forties, sleek, trim, well-clothed, smooth-spoken, he is the Administration's most conspicuous resident millionaire. He occupies a light, pleasant, bamboo-papered office in the West Wing looking towards the Mansion. The flag over the White House is clearly visible and he comments on how often he looks at it and thinks how nice it is to see it, and how wonderful it is to be here helping a President in whom he believes.

'My area is principally commercial, financial and economic. I attend the Troika meetings on the economic direction of the government. The Troika includes the Secretary of the Treasury, the chairman of the Council of Economic Advisers and George Shultz, Director of the Office of Management and Budget. I also attend the meetings of the Quadriad, which is those three plus the chairman of the Federal Reserve Board. [These names are almost too cute to believe, but they are current at the White House.] When a particularly serious problem comes up, I am called in to consult and advise on it, such as the Penn Central bankruptcy, the broker-dealer relationship and things of that

75

nature. I have been consulted and active on oil questions, on trade policy, on NASA, on the Atomic Energy Commission, on the regulatory agencies of the government—these latter perhaps give me the most concern—airlines policy, the gas shortage and so on. We make a great point in this office of having no connection with any individual company, route, or rate case because we must not give even an appearance of interest, otherwise our decisions and activities would be called into criticism and question.

'I also am involved in the field of insurance, which includes flood insurance, crime insurance, insolvency insurance, wavewash insurance and so on.

'I also work on consumer problems with Virginia Knauer. I also was involved with draft policy and draft legislation, with negotiations to re-establish relations with the Vatican, with the hijacking deterrence programme, with the textile negotiations and with the trade bill.

'I also help do staffing at the upper levels of the agencies and I am not too worried that we have some holdovers. I don't think that many people out there in the bureaucracy are saying, "Let's axe this guy". Furthermore, if we win in '72 the proportion of holdovers in the super grades of Civil Service will be enormous—but virtually all the super grades are at retirement age or will be very shortly. Therefore we can slot the government with lots of Republicans who will be young enough to be around awhile.

'While the President is a consummate politician and a pragmatic man, there are a few fundamentals he won't be moved on. In Southeast Asia he is going to do what he thinks is right, and he is going to do what he thinks is right to stimulate the economy. The problem is to bring unemployment down without starting a rapid inflation, and I believe this is going to be done. It may mean a deficit but we can stand a deficit if it is not inflationary and does not go beyond the full employment level. We can have a deficit as long as it is not putting a demand on the economy that the economy can't handle.

'One of the things you finally learn here is not to agonize over what has been done, say in Vietnam or in the Civil Service. You are here to go forward, not back. There's no point in worrying about it.

'Here we're sort of a little band of brothers, at the top, most of us having come into the campaign to work with the President, some of us going back as far as his campaign of 1960. It gives you a nice feeling to be here working together with old friends for someone you believe in.

'The staff here is very non-competitive with one another, dedicated, happy, working together to support him and make his success the greatest possible success. There is no self-aggrandizement. People are not thrusting themselves forward at the expense of the President's programme.

'We have a sort of community belief in his positions here. All of us share that thrust of thinking. Sure, we consider the political aspects, but there is a strong philosophical basis which we have in common with the President.

'Henry Kissinger once said that it's futile to try think you can work individually on the staff, because if the Administration is a success, no single individual will have the credit but we all will. And if it is a failure, then we all will have to share the blame.'

Top White House aide (not P. Flanigan) with a bemused smile: 'Clark MacGregor, our new staff member [for Congressional relations] *had a social gathering the other evening for eight or ten of the top members of the White House staff and their wives. And you know, that was the first time the staff had ever got together socially. And it took a newcomer to do it!'*

Bill Timmons, top member of the White House Congressional liaison staff (bumped down a notch when the President appointed former Republican Rep. MacGregor [of Minnesota] to be director of the staff after he lost in 1970 to Hubert Humphrey in the latter's successful bid to return to the Senate), is forty, tall, sleepy-eyed, slow-spoken, intelligent. He worked for many years on Congressional staffs on both sides of the Hill. He has the manner of one who has spent most of his life in politics, yet with something a little fresher and more candid about him than that might imply. He of course denied the constant complaint from the Hill that the Administration's relations with Congress are in serious need of repair.

'It's largely a matter of the President's time—there's just so much of it every day. Most Congressmen are convinced that if they could just talk to the President personally they could make him see things their way. I'm not convinced that liaison is all that bad, although it's been true, maybe, that some of the staff here may not have been quite as obliging about running up there all the time, or about answering Congressional complaints all the time, as some people would like.

'We are going to make some changes and try to meet them halfway a little more. Bob Haldeman and John Ehrlichman and some of the others are going to go to the Hill more often, attend such things as the House Republican Conference meetings, the Senate Republican Policy Committee luncheon and the fraternal groups in Congress such as the "Chowder and Marching Society" in the House and the "Wednesday Luncheon Group" of Republican liberals in the Senate.

'We're going to try to have a regular series of briefings for all these groups on major Administration programmes from now on. They do have a valid point that perhaps there has not been as much contact as would have been advisable, both from their standpoint and ours. We're going to try to make that better from now on.

'I look for a hardening of political activity on the part of Democratic Presidential hopefuls. They will feel they have to impress their colleagues and the country. They will try to embarrass the President. It is going to be a tough two years but I think the end result will be that the progress of the Administration will be substantial when it is all over.

'I'm optimistic about the prospects of ultimately getting through a good part of the President's social legislation. In foreign policy he will face a continued isolationist approach by the Democrats, and that attitude is going to be harmful. It will affect military assistance, foreign aid and economic development. There will be those who are going to try to cut foreign commitments and redirect the funds into domestic matters.

'In this office we try to handle the day-to-day problems of the Congress as quickly and as well as we can. We handle approximately eight thousand incoming telephone calls per week and place perhaps sixteen thousand outgoing. We process some five thousand pieces of paper a month, principally letters to constituents and to agencies on behalf of Congressmen, requests for greetings from the President, signed pictures, etc.

'The staff consists of two guys working the House, two working the Senate and a fifth who does case work on projects concerning Congressmen. In addition, we provide some help in researching and writing speech material for members of Congress, and another fellow has just been added to act as liaison with the OMB. In addition there are some twelve secretaries—about twenty people all told in the office.

'We work twelve to thirteen hours a day and sometimes eight on Saturday. We're just constantly running to put out fires. We are always running. We figure there are perhaps twenty-five votes of a legislative nature, either on the floor or in committees, every day on the Hill. All of these we are concerned with. Also, a lot of our work is stopping pernicious legislation, such as the Cooper-Church amendment against the war.

'It's tough work but it's exciting and I would rather be here than anywhere else. In fact, I turned down a chance to run for the seat of Congressman Brock of Tennessee, who just beat Albert Gore for the Senate. If I had won I would have been a very minor new Congressman, whereas here I am right in the thick of things all the time. Occasionally I get invited to a dinner upstairs where I can take Mama, and it just is generally a lot of fun, even though it's very hard work.'

Chuck Colson is a thirty-nine-year-old, round-faced, tough, pleasant, shrewd-eyed, hard-headed and hard-nosed political operator, one of the most incisive and effective performers in the White House. He used to be administrative assistant to former Senator Leverett Saltonstall (Republican, Massachusetts). He occupies a suite of offices in the Executive Office Building overlooking the West Wing of the White House and is plagued by a telephone that rings practically all the time. He announced as he whirled into the office that the President had just decided to appoint John Connally Secretary of the Treasury, and that he and his staff would have to begin notifying the business community and others who might be interested, as they always do when a major appointment comes up.

'My principal function is to keep liaison with the outside world. This covers a multitude of activities both public and private, including the business community, contacts with labour leaders, contacts with dairymen who want special protection for dairy products in the trade bill, contacts with hard-hats, contacts with other special groups, contacts with—you name it.

'I am the focal point for contact between the outside world and the President. My job is to see that the President isn't isolated. It makes me laugh when I hear that he is isolated because I spend all my time making sure that he isn't isolated.

'I'm general handyman, advising him on various things: for instance, I was sort of a legal adviser on the Carswell nomination, on the relationship between the Senate and the President. I gave the legal opinion which was the foundation for the President's letter to Senator Saxbe, at the height of the nomination fight, concerning the Senate's role in the nomination.

'I give the President major advice on federal communications problems, under what circumstances he should use television and can use it legally under the law. As far as his press conferences are concerned, for a period there we were running into complaints that he was dominating television, and of course if he holds his conference in prime time then it does give him an advantage which perhaps can be legally and fairly challenged. However, I think it likely that he will address the people more often from now on.

'I think the President has done extremely well with his contacts with major labour unions, and in terms of the attitude of labour towards a Republican President. We have worked very hard on this together, because the President believes in the workingman as distinct from the unions. I think that we are doing a great job here in terms of the President having a very even-handed relationship with both business and labour. They are in to see us as much as anybody. His approach to both groups is fair and equitable.

'The unions have an enormous respect for him as an individual. You don't hear the President being accused of being the captive of big business, or other clichés which used to be thrown around about Republican Presidents. Labour is a changing animal, an emerging middle class much more concerned with protecting what it has than it used to be.

'When we contact certain groups after a nomination, or sometimes before a nomination or other major policy decision of the Administration, we do it on the basis of record books, maintained in my office, of leaders in about fifteen different fields of endeavour over the country. We borrow eight or ten guys from the White House staff and we immediately begin making calls or sending out mailings. We think it is important that the movers and doers understand what the President is doing. We try to explain to them, either beforehand if there is time, or, as with today's Connally appointment, as soon as we can get to it after the decision is reached.

'Frequently the President will call me back later in the day and ask how people are reacting to a nomination or to some decision. He really does seek out fresh viewpoints. He wants to know what other people think and what their ideas are. After all, we don't have any monopoly on ideas in the White House—in fact, we talk to ourselves too much, if anything. Sometimes if the President wants to make a preliminary check on something himself, he will use the lists we have to call maybe ten or twelve prominent people and get their advice.

'I have to emphasize again that he is not isolated. I do everything I can to get people in to see him, and he wants to see them.'

White House insider (not C. Colson), musing on a major Cabinet appointment: 'The thought was that it was a good idea because Bill's a great pal of Kay Graham [publisher of the Washington Post] and Senator Fulbright. But—wistfully—'it just hasn't seemed to work out....'

John Whittaker, deputy assistant to the President for domestic affairs, is a tall, pleasant-faced, youthfully grey individual who is another of those White House assistants who work in a number of different areas. He is concerned with pollution, long-term and emergency planning for fuel and power, how to develop a better atomic reactor for domestic power. He is also involved in 'national growth policy'—how to reverse the migration to the big cities and encourage people to go back to smaller centres. In this latter field he is trying to work on policies that will provide the states with funds to give incentives, particularly to industries, to move out into areas that will draw people to them. At the same time the states are to be assisted to provide better schools and other inducements to people to encourage movement to new areas.

'I'll admit there is little evidence that people are starting to get out. The response in general is negative. But I feel there is a good chance that in time the programme will take effect.

'The President takes an active interest in all these areas, particularly in the national growth policy. Legislation on the environment is a little discouraging in Congress at the present time, because many people talk about doing something but they actually do very little.

'I wouldn't say we're involved directly in politics, but of course the Domestic Council looks at bills not just on the basis of economy but in terms of the real political world as well. We have to. We make recommendations to the President as to whether he should sign a bill or not, bearing in mind all the factors including the political. We are not, after all, in the business of political suicide. We are not going to send a bill to Congress which is not politically oriented. That isn't how the democratic system works.

'It's surprising to me how little we think of re-election. I am always amazed by this. It is just a day-to-day operation.

'There are a lot of professionals on the staff below the top level, but they don't know the President intuitively so that they can play President themselves. The top people have to know when to play President and make a decision, rather than buck it on up to the President for decision. Sometimes there is a time element involved here in making these decisions in the President's name. You have to be able to sense when to take the responsibility.

'It is extremely helpful to have all the professional people and experts who work in the Office of Management and Budget under George Shultz. We can go in and get a twenty-year background on some legislative proposal. Frequently we find that we think of something which seems brand-new, but actually there is a long record of Presidents having attempted to do it in the past. This is very helpful in plotting our strategy on how to go about it.

'The main thrust from now on will be to concentrate on revenue sharing. The governors want local control of funds given them by the federal government and I see why they do. You sit here making decisions that are local and you really have no knowledge of local conditions. I think they have a good argument for wanting money put back in the states without strings. Revenue sharing is a way of turning the New Deal around. I don't think you'll get confidence really re-established in government until you get money back to the states and let them dispense it.

'I don't think anybody has really tried, as President Nixon has tried, to run the bureaucracy. I think there is still a definite problem, because you hear so many screams and so much backbiting. But I think that means we are getting at the problem, because usually this means that the people who should not be there, or who are opposing the programme in holdover positions, are being removed. I think, however, that Democratic holdovers are somewhat overrated as a problem. Actually I think there have been times when we were a little ahead of both Kennedy and LBJ in removing holdovers who stood in the way of our policy.'

H. R. 'Bob' Haldeman, chief executive officer of the White House, is in his forties, crew-cut, with deep-set dark eyes; youthful-looking, trim, frank, straight-talking, obviously intelligent and efficient. He received me in his comfortable office, done in Williamsburg style with dark green paint and heavy drapes. A fire burned in the grate. (Outside the window we could hear King Timahoe, the Nixon's Irish setter, barking as I heard him barking on many occasions during these interviews. He does not like being confined and seems to be ever hopeful that someone will come out and let him run. Haldeman says the Nixons quite frequently let him run on the south lawn and he is constantly reminding them of it.)

'You ask what I do. It's a monumental problem to tell you because I don't exactly know. A little bit of everything, I suppose. My function is basically to be a sort of commander in chief of the White House, basically the administrative manager of the office of the President.

'I handle the President's schedule and anything that relates to his personal office and job—the people who see him, the people he wishes to see, the papers that go to him, the papers that he originates and sends out to other people. My role doesn't fit old patterns of the way Presidents operate. I am not a Jerry Persons or Sherman Adams [aides to President Eisenhower], for instance, because the operation varies according to the President.

'The President needs one person he can turn to quickly to cover anything he wants to cover. I of course will turn to someone else down the staff, but it saves him having to take the time to determine who to send things to and who to contact. It is simply a convenience for him, to make his work easier. He doesn't like to leave things hanging fire. He wants to be sure they are quickly taken care of. He makes wads of little notes to himself about things and I am the beneficiary of that. I send his requests and desires out through the staff and make sure that someone reports back to him as soon as possible with the answer or the result.

'Yesterday, with the Connally announcement, was probably a typical if somewhat unusual day, in that it really showed how you get involved in things around here.

'This was one occasion when the President made the decision on his own. He did not want it discussed by anyone in advance because of its effect on the money market. This is always very important with a Secretary of the Treasury, because his fiscal policies have such a bearing on the economy.

'I spent a lot of time on the phone Sunday with the President and I made arrangements to set up the Cabinet meeting Monday morning at which there were present John Tower [Republican Senator from Texas], Cabinet members, Connally and others who were concerned. I also made sure that those who should be notified early among the staff were notified about the appointment, and that the staff began spreading the word immediately to the financial community.

'The Connallys and the Nixons had breakfast Monday morning and after that the President called me to the Map Room, where he and Governor Connally and I set up procedure about announcing the appointment—the points that the President would make in his statement, the points that Connally would make, where the announcement would be made and so on. This took pretty much the whole morning.

'The President then came over here to the West Wing from the Mansion to meet Tower and the Cabinet and then went to his office to notify various members of the Senate and the House. Then Mrs. Connally and Mrs. Nixon came over from the White House, and Secretary Rogers, Secretary Kennedy and the Connallys and Nixons went to the press room to make the announcement. Then they came back to the President's office, where the two men, with their wives, chatted for a bit. Then the Connallys left.

'Then I came back to my office to go over the President's appointments for the afternoon while he had lunch in his office, as he so often does. I went back to his office at two in the afternoon to go over the morning routine and things that were hanging fire from that, and to make final plans for the Congressional reception in the afternoon at which he would entertain the first half of Congress, entertaining the second half tomorrow afternoon.

'Then Governor Connally came back and we discussed the first steps of his taking over at the Treasury. He met with Shultz and Ehrlichman and then left to see Arthur Burns [chairman of the Federal Reserve Board]. I then was back on paper work for a while. Then I had a meeting with Don Rumsfeld, who is shifting from the Office of Economic Opportunity to a full-time role as a White House counsellor. Then Henry Kissinger came in—he comes in and out a lot—and there were some more last-minute things that the President wanted done.

'Later the President met with Senator Goldwater and I sat in on that conference. After that we went over things the President had stored up, the people he had met over the noon hour and what thoughts had come to him during that time and what he wanted done with them. At 5.30 p.m. I went with him over to the Mansion and the reception for the first half of the Congress; stayed about an hour, talked to various Congressmen and Senators, came back here. Bob Finch and I had a meeting. Then Kissinger came back in on a late-day problem and then I left about 7 p.m.

'My office is really the central point short of the President. People can check with me on things that they don't need to bother the President with or, frequently, do not want to bother him with. I am able to get things to him for decision and he in turn uses me as a channel to make his wishes known to the staff. I basically don't have substantive responsibilities. I am more the operative man.

'I keep myself free—I don't run a calendar of my own, which is why it has been hard for us to get together for this interview. I am always available to the President so that any time he wants to turn a problem over to me he can do so and I can arrange for somebody to work on it as quickly as possible.

'He is an amazing guy to work with—has a great sensitivity not to interfere with other people's feelings. He is very considerate of the staff—very demanding of results and expects that things be done right, but he is very thoughtful about the people who work for him. Of course, he has so much stuff under way that he has to keep putting it out just to stay abreast of it. He can't afford to slow down for a minute.

'The staff basically breaks down into the political staff and the professional staff, which has been here for what seems like a couple of centuries. They handle the basic functions of mail, accounting, messenger service, payroll and so on. These are career people and they stay on as we come and go.

'There is a staff secretariat whose head reports to me and follows through on personnel matters. Each individual office under the President also, of course, has its own staff and they talk over with me the hiring and firing of personnel when this becomes necessary.

'We started out trying to keep political coloration as much as possible out of policy and hiring matters. However, we realize that these things make for variety in decision making, and so within reasonable limits we have tried to keep a spread of opinion on the staff, so that no one is to the left of the President at his most liberal or to the right of the President at his most conservative. In a staff such as the speech-writing staff, someone like Ray Price could be categorized as "liberal", someone like Bill Safire could be categorized as being in the middle and Pat Buchanan could be categorized as being on the right.

'This type of spread is not accidental. The President goes on the theory that a person's philosophy can be contributive to the ideas around here, that there has to be a counterbalancing, that you don't want people thought of as "house conservatives" or "house Jews" or "house blacks"—but you do need that type of person in each of those areas in order to contribute ideas to the Administration.

'Ehrlichman, Kissinger and I do our best to make sure that

all points of view are placed before the President. We do act as a screen, because there is a real danger of some advocate of an idea rushing in to the President or some other decision-maker, if the person is allowed to do so, and actually managing to convince them in a burst of emotion or argument. We try to make sure that all arguments are presented calmly and fairly across the board.

'I'm aware that there has been criticism in Congress that relations have been bad but I don't think Congress is supposed to work with the White House—it is a different organization and under the Constitution I don't think we should expect agreement. There is a clear-cut division of power which was intentional, and I think that a certain amount of distance is healthy. I feel that we have developed a situation in which the President is too much responsible for developing initiatives for Congress, and consequently it has become too much a measure of his Presidency whether his initiatives succeed in Congress or not.

'We find that Nixon is measured by a totally different standard in the press, the academic community and elsewhere than either Johnson or Kennedy was measured. We are told that if he gets something through it doesn't mean anything, because it should have gone through anyway. But if he fails in getting something through, then this is a big mark against him. I don't think there is much we can do about this. We recognize it simply as something we have to deal with. We've got a good many things through and more are coming. So I think the President cannot be judged on a day-to-day basis. I often find it fascinating to ponder by what standards Nixon is going to be judged by history when all the partisan battles we face now are over.

'We are trying to get our case over to the country. Our getting it over has a direct relation to our ability to govern. We hope that things will be understood by some intelligent and effective segment of the population because this is necessary to govern. If this is not perceived by them, then it becomes very difficult.

'However, we don't intend to lie down just because the general run of analysts don't like what we do. I think we have had a pretty damned good two years, in terms of where we were when we came in and where we are now. Nixon is now fighting, in the family assistance plan, for the most far-reaching piece of social legislation perhaps any President has ever proposed. He says we don't know how it will work, but we do know that if we don't try it, we may never know if it will work or not. We are almost at the point in welfare where some change is better than no change and where a change has to be made ...

'Has the President changed in office? He may be more no-nonsense than before, but the thing that has impressed me is apparently a great inner feeling of self-confidence in the job. He likes being President. He moved right in and he obviously enjoys it now. There are times, of course, when he gets fed up with petty annoyances, and he works and worries hard over the big decisions. But he likes stepping up to decisions, particularly hard ones. Occasionally, being human, he will get annoyed with the ways things are going. But usually he manages to conceal this and to keep going himself in a calm and effective manner.

'He doesn't particularly like the ceremonial aspects of the White House but he has done a good job of it. He has made very thoughtful innovations in the use of the White House. He has the feeling, as the Spanish say, *está en su casa*—"you are in your home"—when you come to the White House. He has a very real sense of history and never forgts what the White House means to an individual who comes here for the first time.

'He puts a lot of time and thought into the toasts he gives at state dinners. They are always personal, thoughtfully and carefully done. This is a feature of them that is not generally felt, except by the people who are there, because the press usually does not write up the toasts unless they are political in some way.

'His feel for the ceremonial side is interesting to me because that is not the side where his real interests lie. His interest lies in being head of the government and really being in charge of things. But he does a much more careful job of being head of state as well than I would have thought he might do. He does it with a great style and sensitivity, as do Mrs. Nixon and the girls. They are not the kind of people who exploit what they do. But they manage to do a great deal.

'I would say that he works harder than he used to—in fact, too hard, which is one of my worries. He doesn't do very much for exercise, aside from a little running in place every day, and that is about the extent of it. On the other hand, he doesn't seem to need a great deal of exercise, so perhaps it all works out all right after all.'

Don Rumsfeld, then head of the Office of Economic Opportunity, was about to be promoted to the post of counsel to the President when I talked to him. He is in his early forties, handsome and aware of it; soft-spoken; intelligent and capable, and aware of that too. After some sparring on the OEO, which was then in hot water from the customary quarters because of his attempts to control its legal services branch, he decided to be reasonably candid and said that there were many problems involving lawyers who exceeded their authority and violated their trust by representing people who were not poor—who got involved in such things as defending the underground press and pornography, or in representing people who were not poor in criminal cases, even murder. All of these were in direct violation of the law and regulations. He said the agency had pretty much been allowed to run loose in the past but that now the Administration had gone through and pretty well straightened it out. He said that part of the problem in OEO was that 'there are people on the staff around the country who are just dedicated to not doing what the law says.

'My own experience, including twelve years in Congress and two years in the Executive Branch, both with the President and in the OEO, has been most fascinating—really a great, great, great, great experience. Decision making and governing are really the process of rolling up and rolling down a decision so that you touch all bases and get all the in-puts for a decision.

'You have to do this because there is no lever for the President —no handle marked "President" that you move forward and something happens.

'My activities in OEO have been designed to do everything possible to correct shortcomings and still keep the flak at an acceptable political level. In administering a situation, a person has to decide the atmosphere he is in—how much he can move without breaking the china. He has to know how to move the parameters of the playing field, so that six, eight, ten months down the road he will have the tools and the climate in which he can do what he wants to do.

'A President should keep movement on all the time inside the government. Sometimes he has to go to the people to do it. You have got to get the people—get them attitudinally oriented to where you want them to go. The people are not ideologues. They are hopers and strivers who want something done and are willing to follow a man who can make it happen.'

These thoughts on the Presidency, volunteered and sound, left the lingering thought that just possibly young Mr. Rumsfeld might be looking six—eight—ten—years down the road to the day when he himself may be able to extend the parameters of the playing field—and perhaps control the game.

NATIONAL RAILROAD STRIKE BEGINS. LENGTH OF TIE-UP IN DOUBT. UNIONS ACT DESPITE BAN BY CONGRESS ... PRESIDENT IS ASSAILED OVER LAG ON OPEN HOUSING IN THE SUBURBS ... HOUSE INCREASES FUNDS FOR FOREIGN ASSISTANCE ... PANEL UPS OLD-AGE BENEFITS. SENATE GROUP FINISHES WORK ON WELFARE BILL.

Harry Flemming, then special assistant to the President for administrative affairs and now working on the swiftly growing 1972 campaign, is in his thirties, saturnine, with long sideburns and eyes that narrow and grow cold when he talks about people he dislikes. He has been the hatchet-man in getting rid of people in government the Administration disapproved of and replacing them with people it does. It is clear that he has done his job with a certain relish.

'I am engaged in what you might call the non-violent overthrow of the government. We have been successful in the main on what is readily available to us in the way of jobs. But to say that you have control of the government, or have a government friendly to you, by simply putting certain friendly people in certain positions, is foolish. We have turned over close to three thousand jobs and have achieved a reasonably friendly team, but that does not necessarily mean that it is a completely effective team. Some people are very, very loyal but have no grasp of the responsibilities of a position once they get in it. Others, who have a grasp of the position, turn out to be not as loyal as what you might hope and find it difficult to mould themselves into what the President's objectives really are.

'Actually there are about thirty-four hundred top jobs available to the Administration but some, such as judges, depend on death or resignation before we have a chance to fill them. And about ninety-five are ambassadorial posts which traditionally have been filled by career Foreign Service officers. These technically might be available, but as a practical matter they are not, because the tradition has grown up that they come from the career service. In addition there are some minor scientific and technical jobs which are not really involved in policy.

'The available manpower pool for top positions in government is very large and very wide. Few men will turn down positions of real responsibility in the government—but whether they will really be effective in government is more difficult to say. You can have a strong background in industry or academic life or some other part of American society and not necessarily be able to cope here. Contrariwise, I have seen people come in whose experience in business or other areas has been more marginal, and yet they really have known how to handle it well when they got down here.

'Of course, there are some people who come into government and find that the social aspects of it, the prestige—or what they think is prestige—are more important than doing a good job for us. I read the local society pages, as one does to keep up with what's going on in Washington, and many of the dashing figures I read about there aren't worth ten cents over here in the Executive Branch. They like that car with the light in the back window and the telephone, but some of these heroes of the society page are almost total disaster areas for doing the job the President wants them to do. They aren't really "beautiful people". They're just being used by Washington hostesses and they aren't astute enough to know it.

'Others have a certain unchecked ambition and try to operate in this area without knowing where the political strength really is, and this gets them into trouble too. Wally Hickel [fired by the President in late 1970 from his post as Secretary of the Interior] is a case of one infighter. He was apt to take positions and try to undercut the President, and then not have the political savvy to know how to defend himself when the chips were down. His department was administrative chaos most of the time he was in there. He was encouraged by certain people around him to write his famous letter to the President [urging Mr. Nixon to pay more attention to student dissenters] which of course brought things to a head. So when we fired Hickel we took occasion to get rid of several of those people at the same time.

'As for the question of deliberate sabotage by holdovers in the bureaucracy, we always say there are three political parties in Washington: the Republicans, the Democrats and the bureaucrats. The bureaucrats are going to be here longer than the rest of us and they know it. They have their own way of going about things. It may not be clear-cut or deliberate sabotage of certain policies, but they do have ways of obstructing things they don't like. However, I don't think there is very much evidence of deliberate sabotage. I think on the whole they go along with what is decided at the top. If they do sabotage change sometimes, it's usually because it may involve a policy they themselves began years ago and they are wedded to it. When they see the Administration trying to change it, they dig in their heels and balk.

'Part of the problem there, I think, is that our administrative appointees have a tendency to come into government and immediately become absorbed in the larger problems—their relations with Congress, with the White House, with the budget. They start dealing with people on that higher level, worrying about larger policy questions instead of dealing with the people below them who are responsible for carrying out the policies of their agencies or departments. Those who are directly responsible, the implementers, the career people, often do not have a clear set of guidelines from some of the top people. I would say that 75 per cent of the blame when policies are not effectively implemented lies with our policy officials and only about 25 per cent with holdover subordinates.

'The barrier between career and non-career people in government is a great one. It creates considerable problems in this area. I am convinced, however, that most employees are sincere and are doing a good job as they see it.

'Another over-all problem is that the government does not

rotate its top career officials on a regular basis. It tends to reward seniority, it tends to foster stagnation, it tends to leave a guy in for decades, defending old policies and being unable to adapt to new ones. There is a tendency in the career service to reward technical expertise rather than managerial expertise.

'People just get impacted and stagnant at a certain level. Consequently, each person down the line below them tends to get impacted and stagnant. The government has got all kinds of programmes for dealing with this but they are simply not carried out.

'The President is not really satisfied with the work we have done so far in changing the personnel of the government, and I hope he never will be satisfied. The structural changes he's made have been due to a feeling on his part that the structure is simply not suited to push the government in the direction he wants it to go.

'This is very important, this business of the government being able to deliver effectively on its policies, because the people have been promised so damned much in recent years, and delivered so little, that there is a real crisis of faith in the federal government. So many federal programmes have been promised and not done that something has got to be changed in order to restore people's faith in government. In a basic sense, that's what we are trying to do in this office, by getting in people who will go along actively with the President's programme and help to put it over.'

The press (bull-session with old friends): 'He is the most complex man who has ever been in the White House. He doesn't have any intimate friends. Nobody is close to him. He should have at least somebody, but all he seems to have is Bebe Rebozo.

'He definitely tries to get away from the press. The anti-press feeling permeates the whole Administration. He is the first President to duck out of parties early to avoid the press. He deliberately avoids us. He wants to stay away from us.'

When I pointed out that the press, after all, had been extremely harsh with him over the years, this was conceded. 'But the majority of publishers are Republican.'

'And the majority of reporters are Democrats and "liberals".'
Reluctantly this was conceded too. But—'Nixon has no sense of

style. No grace. He is always escaping from us. Why is he always escaping?'

It is Friday, December 11, 1970. For this first Presidential press conference in more than three months, snow threatens. It is cold and sharp, with a sting in the air, as the press enters through the northwest gate, going first past the press office below the main drive and then up stone steps to the drive and so to the main entrance. Secret Service and police check credentials, greet friends, study strangers. There are perhaps three hundred of all ages, shapes, sizes, dress and hairdo in attendance on this night strained with the excitement, the tension and the frustration of the long Presidential news drought. Much bitter comment has filled columns, editorials and news stories in the past few days. A group of major correspondents, fantastically, has actually held a secret meeting, their ostensible purpose to arrange the sequence of questions, their real aim to get Dick Nixon.

Every seat in the East Room is filled and many stand along the walls under the glare of television lights and cameras. Between the enormous portraits of George and Martha Washington on the east wall a lectern and many microphones have been set up.

The press is in position approximately fifteen minutes before the appointed hour. Promptly at 7 p.m. the voice of the press secretary, heavy and portentous, calls out, 'Ladies and gentlemen, the President of the United States!'

'Unfortunately,' murmurs someone, not too *sotto voce.*

The President comes in from the hall, looking tanned and rested, moves to the microphones, turns immediately to the room and says, 'Won't you be seated, please.' Helen Thomas of UPI is first on her feet with a question concerning the 'understanding' on the bombing of North Vietnam.

His face sets and he gives the toughest answer he has given on the subject in many months, saying that if there is any misunderstanding on the part of the North Vietnamese or anyone else, he wants to indicate 'the understanding of this President with regard to the flying of reconnaissance planes over North Vietnam'. He says he must insist that there be continued reconnaissance because, as American forces are being withdrawn, 'I have to see whether or not there is any chance of a strike against those forces that remain. And we have to watch for the build-up.'

He adds that if our planes are fired upon he will not only order that they return the fire, but he will order that the missile site be destroyed and the military complex around that site be destroyed.

'That,' he says firmly, 'is *my* understanding.'

He adds that if he concludes that the North Vietnamese are infiltrating in such a way as to threaten the remaining U.S. forces as they withdraw, 'then I will order the bombing of the military sites in North Vietnam, the passes that lead from North Vietnam into South Vietnam, the military complexes and the military supply lines.

'That shall be the action I shall take. I trust that that is not necessary, but let there be no misunderstanding with regard to this President's understanding about either reconnaissance flights or about a step-up of the activities.'

By now there are many sceptical faces among the reporters, many annoyed and upset expressions, much indignant whispering back and forth among those—and they are much in the majority—who are openly appalled by what seems to be a new and tougher line.

The question then jumps to further Cabinet changes. He says he has none to announce tonight, says Don Rumsfeld will leave the OEO to become a Presidential counsellor, says they will have to wait until the press secretary's briefing at 11 a.m. tomorrow to hear about the rumoured appointment of defeated Republican Senatorial candidate George Bush of Texas to the post of UN Ambassador.

With the sort of snidely polite hostility with which many members of the press address Richard Nixon, he is then asked by a youthful reporter whether he approves of J. Edgar Hoover's statements on a possible conspiracy to kidnap 'a high government official'.

He sidesteps blandly by saying Mr. Hoover has rendered great service to his country, he generally approves of the actions he has taken and he is not going to go into any specific actions.

He is then asked, again with the same hostile pleasantry, whether he will not elaborate on why he lost confidence in

Walter Hickel and removed him from the Interior secretary-ship.

He explains that he did indeed lose confidence in Mr. Hickel and therefore thought a change was right. But, he adds with equal blandness, he has 'a great admiration for him. I think he rendered sincere service. I wish him the very best.'

He is then told by another questioner in a tone of increasing insolence that there is a feeling in 'some quarters, not just among blacks and students but also among some of your natural Republican allies, some voters and certainly, as you may have noticed, some columnists'—his expression grows a little wry but he listens patiently—'that you have yet to convey a suffi-ciently sharp and clear sense of any direction, vision and leader-ship on many matters to end the divisions in this country as you said you hoped to do two years ago, and as your own Scranton Commission on Campus Unrest has urged you to do. Do you recognize this as a problem for yourself and for the country, and, if so, what can you do about it, and what will you do about it?'

He answers calmly that he should emphasize that 'divisions in this country are never going to end—there's always going to be a generation gap and there's always going to be differences between the races and between the religions. The problem is trying to mute those differences, to litigate them to the greatest extent possible and to develop a dialogue.'

He cites the winding down of casualties in the war and says that in other areas 'I trust that we can give that sense of direc-tion that you refer to, and I particularly hope I give it to the columnists. I want them to have a sense of direction too.'

He chuckles, and with an annoyed reluctance but knowing he has them, his audience joins in.

Questions return to Vietnam. He is asked if his comments on the bombing of North Vietnam, plus indications 'we've had from other officials of probably more raids to try to free American prisoners' mean 'that you have abandoned hope for the Paris peace talks to reach a negotiated settlement?'

He answers stoutly, 'Not at all,' not at all fooling anyone. He says that we are continuing the talks in Paris and notes that Ambassador Bruce has offered to return some 8200 North Viet-namese prisoners as against approximately 800 Americans and other allied prisoners. He says North Vietnamese failure to accept that offer 'will pinpoint something that is pretty generally getting known around the world, and that is that this nation [North Vietnam] is an international outlaw, that it does not adhere to the rules of international conduct.' But, he says, the United States is going to continue the negotiations as long as the North Vietnamese are willing to negotiate, and as long as there's some hope of making progress on the prisoner of war issue or on a cease-fire to bring an earlier end to the war than the Vietnamization process will inevitably bring.

The questioning then goes to the supersonic transport. He says he is satisfied that arguments regarding its effects on the environment can be met, and the prototype should be built.

Herb Kaplow of NBC, one of the fairest-minded of the press corps, asks if the President feels that sufficient public interest has been generated so that he might hold another press conference sooner than the nearly four-month lapse preceding this one.

He replies smoothly that as President he has a responsibility to help the press do its job but as President he has a primary responsibility to do his own job. His job is to inform the American people and he ticks off the ways: press conferences like this, formal reports to the nation, television interviews with a small group of correspondents. He says he thinks the American people are entitled to see the President and to hear his views directly, and not to see him only through the press. 'And I think any member of the press would agree on that.'

The expressions of his audience indicate that not too many would agree with that, but he continues, still blandly, inviting suggestions on how to keep the country informed without dominating television too much, because he reminds them he has been accused of trying to dominate television too much. Perhaps there should be 'more conferences in the office'.

His audience, met and answered to a standstill, ruminates for a moment. Then someone thinks of Cambodia and it is off again. Does he foresee any circumstances in which the United States will use ground troops in Cambodia? Firmly and quickly he responds, 'None whatever.'

Once more the snide, insinuating, oily non-politeness enters a questioner's voice as he is asked, 'With unemployment and inflation rising do you think it's fair to say that your economic policies have not worked, and do you plan any quick change?'

He replies calmly that he thinks his policies are working. He says he hopes to bring unemployment lower than 5 per cent without a war situation and he thinks the Administration can achieve that goal.

Asked whether the federal government plans to use its leverage to promote racial integration in suburban housing, he says flatly, 'Only to the extent that the law requires. I believe that forced integration in the suburbs is not in the national interest.'

Once more the oily unction, the phoney politeness bristling with undercurrents of hostility that almost visibly hang in the room: at various times he said My Lai was a massacre, Charles Manson was guilty; and in mentioning Angela Davis, he said that those responsible for such acts of terror should be brought to justice. 'My question,' says the interrogator with the rancorous relish he can never quite keep out of his voice, 'concerns the problem of pre-trial publicity and the fact that it could jeopardize a defendant's rights at a trial. How do you reconcile your comments with your status as a lawyer?'

Looking them straight in the eye he says with a disarming candour that catches them completely off balance that he thinks that's a legitimate question. 'I think sometimes we lawyers, even like doctors who try to prescribe for themselves, may make mistakes. And I think that kind of comment probably is unjustified.'

Taken aback but still game, his questioners move on to the election, to third-partly candidates, to wage-price guidelines, to the Soviet role in the Caribbean. Asked if he considers Soviet activity in that area a threat to this country, he says flatly, 'No, I do not.'

The questioning skims the Middle East, reverts for a moment to Cambodia, touches on the trade bill, returns again to campus unrest, moves on to U.S.-Soviet relations. He says the significant thing is that 'we are negotiating and not confronting. We're very far apart [at the SALT talks] because our vital interests are involved, but we are talking.'

Asked to comment on potential Democratic aspirants for the Presidency, 'and speculation that you might be a one-term President', he smiles and says, 'I think I'll let them speculate about the one-term President.'

Things hop, skip, and jump again: China (relations hopefully will come to be based not on expediency 'but on principle ... in which the government will try to have some communication and eventually relations with Communist China'), the hapless Lithuanian seaman turned back to the Russians ('I can assure you it will never happen again'), withdrawal rate from Vietnam ('... as long as we're negotiating ... I am not going to indicate a withdrawal schedule'), a possible purge of liberal dissenters in the Republican Party in 1972 ('We welcome them. We want them'), the trade bill (he is not satisfied with the progress in the Senate).

He concludes with a graceful little comment that Mrs. Nixon has reminded him that his audience and their families are invited to the annual White House Christmas party for the press on December 23.

Someone says, 'Thank you, Mr. President,' he says, 'Thank you,' and leaves the room. The press gets up and mills away after him out into the main lobby, chatting and gossiping. Many realize with some astonishment that he has not been asked a single question about the railroad strike, which has just begun.

Someone remarks, 'I don't think anyone laid a glove on him.'

'We never do,' someone else agrees wryly, 'which always amazes me, because we certainly come in here prepared to try.'

PRESIDENT WARNED BY HANOI. ALL U.S. FLIGHTS IN THE NORTH FACE FIRE ... NIXON ASKS LEADERSHIP ON CAMPUS ... MILITARY SEES CAMBODIA AS KEY FRONT ... WHO TURNED THE COLD WAR BACK ON? [The United States, of course, Who else, in the Washington *Post*?]

Virginia Knauer, the President's adviser on consumer interests, is a bright, lively, bubbly little grandmother, round-faced, pretty, full of vivacity and so enthusiastic about her job that it is almost impossible to interrupt once you get her talking. She obviously loves her assignment.

'They refer to me around here [Federal Office Building, Number 7, a block up Connecticut Avenue from the White House] as 'the den mother' because I have had political experience that many of the staff have not had. This office exists under an executive order, the idea being that ultimately we will get legislation to establish a permanent agency. I am to advise the President on consumer concerns and I represent the Administration's point of view on various bills before Congress. Our policies are based on the in-put from various leaders represented in the consumer advisory council which the President has set up to assist us.

'I maintain, I think, a very close contact with the people at all levels who are working on legislative programmes dealing with this area. President Nixon gave me responsibility for one of the hottest things in his administration. There are of course hundreds of consumer programmes in various bureaus and agencies. He told me to co-ordinate them.

'We try to find practical solutions to consumer complaints. We are building, through consumer boards around the country, a quite powerful force of public opinion on behalf of the consumer. Our concern is basically with quality and reliability of products and not so much with prices, which do not come under our jurisdiction. We have done such things as the recent flap about hot dogs—how much fat there should be in the meat. We also are involved in the various drives to eliminate certain pesticides that may be dangerous to human living.

'I attend the seven-thirty "team" meeting at the White House every day and I am encouraged to speak out and bring the attention of those attending to the problems facing consumers. A lot of policy is formulated there for the President's consideration. I also work closely with the Office of Management and Budget. The President doubled my own budget last year and I expect there may be a further increase this year.

'Recently I have begun to ask business to contribute to fellowships for people to come back here and study consumer problems in Washington. I don't know whether I legally can accept the funds'—a cheerful little giggle—'but I'm not going to get into that, I'm just going to go ahead and take them. Much of our work is directed towards the "inner city" and I have recently had the Government Printing Office prepare me some brochures on things as fundamental as how to buy a car, what you should check in a contract and things of that nature. I have required that they be printed in interesting colours. I hate dull folders and I can't stand this government brown. They have the colours over there to do the job. You just have to keep after them to get them to do it right, I do.

'It is good for the President to have someone who can speak in an authoritative way on these matters as I do—someone who can say to business, "The President told me to do this, gentlemen, and it's going to be done." Of course, at election time you find a lot of the boys on the Hill putting in bills for consumer interests, but somehow this interest always drops after the election and nothing much is done in the form of legislation. The boys are just running for office and making Brownie points.

'The press always thinks the government is testing brand names but actually less than one tenth of one per cent are comparatively tested by the government and then only when it purchases them through government contracts. One specific of how we help is that the Veterans Administration used to purchase hearing aids for distribution to veterans from only certain firms. Now we have required them to establish better standards and the bidding has now doubled on the part of private concerns seeking government contracts in this area. We intend to put consumer caveats into government purchasing.

'Recently I got excited about the quality of toasters. Some of my experts around here said to stop talking about toasters, that wasn't interesting to anybody. I said nonsense, I'm a housewife and I relate with millions of other housewives. I know that they're as interested as I am in the right kind of toaster to put on the table for breakfast.

'I refer to government, consumers and business as "the happy triangle", although sometimes it isn't so happy if one has to keep after all the branches to make the triangle work.

'We have working arrangements with over two hundred business associations and we are gradually bringing about a greater responsiveness to consumer complaints. Our largest source of complaints comes from automobiles: Congressmen send us whole stacks of complaints about cars. Right now this office is getting about seven times more letters than my predecessor did and also many, many telephone calls from outraged citizens. One fellow around here is very good at handling these screaming voices on the telephone. We average approximately seven thousand complaints a month.

'We do our best to help the people who are concerned. I think we have brought consciousness of consumer unhappiness into the board room. The businesses who have failed to live up to normal expectations of performance on the part of their customers hear from us. Many of them are beginning to agree, and to co-operate in getting things straightened out.

'I try not to be abrasive. I try to be challenging with business and get things done that way. Now when I visit a business or contact someone about a consumer complaint they say, "Don't try to con her—she's done her homework." They also know that if I get really upset I can go on TV and blast them, I can go to court to try to stop what they're doing, and therefore they pay some attention.

'Recently I suggested to the Better Business Bureau that they capitalize on their 140 offices around the country and share their information with me so that we can all work together. A number of chambers of commerce are also beginning to do so. What I have is sort of a combination of the needle and the carrot. I feel there has been responsiveness on the part of business—not 100 per cent, but good. Certainly their major interest is self-interest, and that is to be expected and respected. However, we are more and more encouraging them to pay attention to the consumer. I think we are making real progress.

'We are also working with the bureaucracy—this granite group that doesn't like to be nudged one way or the other. We are making headway.

'I find that overseas in Europe they are very much interested in what we are doing and that they are beginning to establish consumer protection agencies there. We're just a little ahead of everyone else—we speak up more and so we are helping these great industrial nations of Europe to catch up on these things. It forms a good image for our country when we can take our expertise abroad and help them in this area.

'I am establishing consumer voluntary groups around the country and mobilizing American consumers in a constructive way. I don't necessarily think they should burn down the local Safeway, but I do think that a reasonable, dignified protest against unreasonable prices and poor quality can really do a great deal and we are moving in that direction.

'I don't like red tape—I like to see action.'

Jim Rowley, chief of the Secret Service, is sixty-two, a tall,
pleasant-faced, grey-haired veteran of the White House, where
he served for many years as part of the President's bodyguard.
He is understandably cagey about certain aspects of the Secret
Service, but talked in a guarded and friendly way about what
they do.

From other sources it developed that the Rose Garden and
other areas immediately around the White House have been
implanted with electronic devices, television cameras and
various superspy mechanisms that alert the guards should anyone attempt to get into the Mansion without proper authorization. Similar precautions throughout the grounds make of the
White House virtually an armed enclave. Even so, once in a
while someone will manage to slip in: machines cannot always
compensate for human error, and human attention is not always
100 per cent unflagging. Fortunately in each instance the visitors
have been innocent of purpose and as surprised as the upset
gentlemen who have finally descended upon them as they
neared the Mansion.

It is not the grounds, as Jim Rowley points out, that give the
Secret Service its greatest problem. It is the Presidents, who to
this day, although improving, cannot quite restrain themselves
from meeting the people more directly and openly than their
harried guardians would prefer.

'I think the Warren Commission recommendations in their
report on JFK's assassination were the biggest help to us in
getting adequate men and material to protect the President, his
family, and the Vice-President and his family. Prior to that time
the government did not think in terms of professionalism
resources and equipment. Now, however, it does.

'We have advance men, technical men, command men, radio
communications men whenever the President travels. We use
the helicopter as a surveillance instrument and also as an aid to
evacuation in times of trouble. We also have special men on

strategic rooftops in a given area where the President is to appear.

'You might say that the helicopter is the outer perimeter of what we do. In the inner perimeter we have the fellows who ride with the President's car and in cars surrounding his car. Then there are those who parallel the route of travel, and so on. We have a certain strategy we work out and follow which you might say is comparable to football. We find the areas and the problem we have to face and establish something like a zone patrol.

'At the present time we have approximately 880 special agents, not only for immediate protection of the President and others, but in some 65 field offices throughout the nation, all keeping an eye for us on potential trouble spots for the President. Under law our responsibility covers the President and his family, the Vice-President and his family when the family is with him, Presidential and Vice-Presidential candidates at the time of a national election, the former Presidents and their wives, the widows of former Presidents and children of a former President up to age sixteen. When Mrs. Onassis got married we ceased our coverage of her but President Kennedy's children are still under our protection and will be until they reach sixteen.

'We also cover heads and chiefs of state who come to Washington and we also do special details such as assisting in New York with the twenty-fifth anniversary of the United Nations.

'We are also involved in the sky marshal training to stop hijacking of airplanes. At the present time we have twenty-four men who are taking classroom instructions on that and we will have a number of them travelling internationally, in addition to those twenty-four, until the Customs Bureau replaces them with other agents later on. In time that responsibility will be passed to the Department of Transportation.

'We have recently established within the over-all Secret Service complement what we call the Executive Protective Service, which is in reality a group of White House police who guard the White House itself and also those foreign embassies in Washington that request help. This also is extended to the consulates and embassies of the UN delegations in New York. We decided to call it the Executive Protective Service for a simple public relations reason: if we said the White House police were guarding these embassies it would soon appear in the papers as NIXON'S POLICE GUARD RUSSIAN EMBASSY or NIXON'S POLICE GUARD BRITISH EMBASSY or what have you.

'There are perhaps 250 in the Executive Protective Service now—basically, the White House police force—which is up from 170 in recent years. We have been given many additional responsibilities, since more and more sensitive offices have begun to be located in the Executive Office Building. We found that we were having to patrol corridors with three or four men and having to guard a great many entrances to the building, so finally we said why don't we simply establish certain doors where people can come in and out and have television circuits established in the corridors to keep an eye on everyone in there? Now we can handle the whole thing with much fewer men and with a much more sensitive and expert system of protection than we did before.

'We are constantly studying new techniques to protect the President. I remember vividly when I went to Moscow how Stalin travelled. The gates of the Kremlin were flung open and several cars going at ninety miles an hour dashed out. No one knew which car Stalin was in. There were troops lining the entire route of march that he followed. The same thing is used for the President of France. Compared to many other countries, our protections are extremely subject to being attacked.

'However, the President can't be imprisoned. It's a calculated risk whenever you leave the White House. But it has to be done. I've always contended that he has to meet with the people and therefore it is our problem, difficult as it sometimes is, to give him protection if we can. We have to be flexible, we can't be rigid, we have to stay loose. Most Presidents sooner or later want to get out of their cars and go and shake hands with people. This gives us grey hair, but it's our job to protect them even so, and we do the best we can.

'All of the Presidents have been co-operative but the conditions prevailing around the country at the given moment they are visiting somewhere will sometimes prompt them to leave our protection and do things that we would not advise. However, since the Kennedy tragedy everyone has been much more sensitive about things and we have been able to get better co-operation from the Presidents.

'All of our facilities are right here close to the White House, within a couple of blocks [1801 G Street, N.W.], so that if there were any emergencies over there, our manpower would be available immediately to go to the site of the trouble.'

The press (columnist, male, veteran, long-time friend of the President): 'I am very puzzled by Nixon. He does things that an experienced politician wouldn't do. It seems to me that there's almost a feeling that he just isn't interested somehow, almost as though he doesn't want to run again. I can't believe this, but look at some of the things he's done. The Carswell nomination —Carswell's a nice little guy, but he has no more business on the Supreme Court than I do. Firing Wally Hickel from the Interior Department—the only man in the Cabinet who has any kind of reputation for being a conservationist—and then appointing Rogers Morton who has no interest in it, when the Democrats are making hay over the conservation issue. Some of the things he has done in foreign policy also seem very puzzling to me.

'I'm disappointed because I like Nixon, I want him to succeed and I think it is vital to the country that he do so. And yet I feel in a sense that he is letting down his country and his party because there's just this curious lack of political smartness about doing things it seems obviously necessary to do—things that a smart politician would not overlook if he were really on top of the job ... I find many things the President does very puzzling these days. It just doesn't seem to hang together, somehow.'

He was running very late: our interview had originally been set for 4 p.m., then been delayed until 4.15. I was accompanied from the EOB to the West Wing by Herb Klein and Jeb Magruder, Herb's top assistant. The President was closeted with Dr. Arthur Burns, chairman of the Federal Reserve Board. Time passed. His receptionist, Steve Bull, became more and more apologetic, knowing that the President had a reception for members of Congress over at the Mansion at 5 p.m. At approximately 4.45 the buzzer sounded and I was taken into the Oval Office. The huge room is now almost devoid of furniture except for the President's massive desk and a few chairs and sofas along the walls. 'The first thing I'm going to do,' he told me soon after his election in 1968, 'is take those damned television sets out of the Oval Office.' He has done so.

The windows were opened to the cool winter evening and the curtains billowed out from time to time with the wind. Photographs were taken for the first couple of minutes while we chatted about innocuous things. Then the photographer and the others left. He leaned his head in his hands, rubbed his eyes, stayed that way for a moment. But when he looked up he did not look tired, and that was the only time during our talk that he gave any sign of being tired. Mostly he looked, and talked, and appeared to be, entirely relaxed, comfortable and as though he did not have a care in the world. It was perhaps the single most impressive thing about him at that moment. Tiredness and strain are easy to spot: they were not present here this particular late afternoon.

We began with his suggestion that I submit questions in writing and that he take occasion when at Camp David or San Clemente or Key Biscayne to dictate extended answers into his tape recorder. After that, he suggested, I might want to come back and question further on certain points. He said that if he could go to the tape recorder first he would be able to be more relaxed, frame his answers more intelligently and contribute more substantially to what he hoped would be 'a thoughtful and worthwhile book'.

I told him this would be fine with me and then expected him to boot me out, since Congressmen and their ladies were gathering at the Mansion and the clock was moving on. Instead he sat back and chatted for half an hour, ranging from the press, on which he has some definite and occasionally acrid ideas, to the nature of the questions I wanted to ask.

I said that some of them might be critical in nature, but that I didn't intend to offer hookers: I would simply be seeking answers to some of the opinions I was running into around town.

'Don't worry about that for a minute,' he said. 'Give me any hookers you want. Be the devil's advocate, make them just as tough as you like. After all, it's my job to answer these criticisms and if you simply ask me bland questions without any bite to them—"Mr. President, what did you do to save the world today?"—the interview won't add up to very much. I'd prefer to have you make them tough whenever you feel it is justified.'

I asked him if he wished to impose any restriction that his answers be paraphrased rather than quoted directly and he said no, he would be perfectly willing to turn them over to me and let me use them in direct quotes as I pleased—with the exception that on some extrasensitive subjects it might perhaps be wise to paraphrase. In that case he would do it himself, dictating, 'It is known that the President believes—' or, 'The President is understood to feel—' or some such protective, if easily detected, formula.

He was very curious as to whether I was getting sufficient co-operation from the staff and suggested that I be sure and talk to such people as the chef and others on the domestic staff as well as the professional and political staffs. He said both Julie and Tricia would be good sources about White House operations, as both were very thoughtful and perceptive young ladies.

'You should try to talk to a lot of people and not just these grey men around here'—and from his tone it was impossible to determine whether he meant the description as it stood or was dryly mimicking the press attacks upon them.

I said I would.

Aside from a couple of minor items, I did not ask him anything particularly vital, since he had suggested written questions and I intended to ask them in that form; but I was impressed with how fluently and easily he did talk about things. Earlier in the day I had received intimations that various people on the staff were very concerned that I might be going to ask his opinion of other political leaders and they did not want me to do so. 'You won't ask him about Muskie and Kennedy, will you?' asked one earnest staffer with a real anxiety, as though this were an unsuspecting innocent who could be trapped instead of a fifty-eight-year-old political veteran perfectly capable of taking care of himself. Even if I had, I am sure he would have responded directly or sidestepped gracefully. Top men are almost always more relaxed about themselves than their staffs are, and this seems particularly true of the President of the United States.

After a pleasant and comfortable half hour, already fifteen minutes late for the Congressional reception, but not really seeming to mind so very much, he rose and started towards the door: 'Now I have to go and shake hands with four hundred

Congressmen.' Confused a little by the Oval Office's several hidden doors and thinking he was showing me out, I followed him, for he gave no formal farewell but simply moved along still talking. In a moment we found ourselves outside in the arcade along the Rose Garden and I realized he was on his way to the Mansion. I asked directions to Steve Bull's office, he told me, I said, 'Good night, Mr. President' and turned back into the empty office. He waved and walked away, all by himself in the chill winter night: a suddenly lonely and touching moment. Back in the hallway outside Steve Bull's office I found some consternation on the part of Steve and the Secret Service. 'Where is he? Is he gone? Has he left for the Mansion? Is he by himself?'

This was apparently against all the rules. It was hard not to escape the feeling that he had taken one of those small, secret delights known only to Presidents, in going off, thus unescorted and unannounced, to where he wanted to go.

BOMBER DOWNED IN LAOS. SECOND PLANE SHOT DOWN IN CAMBODIA ... DAYAN BARS ANY PULLBACK, KEEPS DOOR OPEN TO TALKS ... KHRUSHCHEV RECALLS CUBA, JFK ... SOVIET VIEWS OF U.S. SHOW A FRIGHTENING 'MIND GAP'.

Intimate comments from one in a position to know:

The President is 'unusually inhibited by strangers', but once he gets used to someone on the staff 'it is very comfortable and he hardly pays any attention to the routine work we do for him around here....

'I find this job a very strange one and this house a very strange place to work. I expect a good many of us do too, because actually, here we are and many of us have a lot of talent, many much more than I do, and yet we are all geared to simply helping one man get through his day. Many of us may sit around doing little chicken things such as I do most of the time, and yet you have to figure that you're helping the President and that is what makes it worthwhile, I guess. There are so many small details that have to be handled and they get split up in so many different hands that a lot of us find ourselves sort of spinning our wheels and not accomplishing a great deal in any sense of personal satisfaction or achievement. I guess in the long run it will all add up, but sometimes you wonder what the purpose is, and what you're doing here....

'Sometimes he is under strain and when he is, he shows it in ways that those of us around him can tell. On the whole, however, he remains very calm. One thing that struck me about him when I first came here is that he is quite profane. This startled me when I first heard him speaking but I've got used to it now.

'Most of the good ideas that originate here come from him. He does take much staff advice, but usually the ideas are his own. When he does something it will be on the basis of his own thoughts and those of many others on the staff. The opinion really flows in from the staff. He solicits the staff's advice on every point. Sometimes he is overruled by the staff—which means that when the weight of evidence or the weight of argument is against him, he will sometimes yield to the advice. Then if the staff is wrong, he will not say anything in particular, but he will let us know by his manner or his way of saying things to us what he thinks of us for having given wrong advice.

'He does not like to bawl people out and he gets upset when he has done something or said something harsh to us. I remember that on a couple of occasions when he has chewed me out, which I deserved, he has never apologized for temper the next day but he has done some little extra, thoughtful thing, which is his way of saying that he is sorry for the argument and hopes that it will not happen again.

'He is terribly hard-working and well-disciplined. He is also very fair to everyone—and amazingly patient. I have been struck here at how easy going some people are in replying to his requests. Of course, many of them have been with him for many years and maybe that's why: *they* know he's not going to fire them, and *he* knows them and knows he will keep on depending on them as he has in the past. However, I have heard him say many times, "I want this or that on my desk by eight o'clock tomorrow morning." Well, it isn't on the desk by eight o'clock the next morning and frequently it isn't there for several days. Except for a couple of very conscientious people around here, there is a rather slow method of replying to the President's requests. However, as I say, they know he is not going to fire them, so he just grits his teeth and goes along with it.'

And from others, less candid about temper and strain but in fundamental agreement on methods of operation, similar sidelights:

'I have never seen this man really upset. I don't see him chew people out. Possibly he does so occasionally in some moment of great strain, but so far, most of us have never seen this in him. He is very nice and generous and takes a very philosophical attitude towards embarrassing things that sometimes appear in news stories or columns critical of the Administration. His attitude seems to be, "You win some and lose some, and if you're human you're going to make mistakes sometimes, so don't worry about it." Maybe he is almost too good about it, but his own long experience as a target for criticism seems to have given him this philosophical approach....'

'A photographer told me he wanted to get some shots of the President striding up and down, gesturing with his arms, and so on. I said, "It just doesn't happen. This is not that kind of President. I have never seen him do those things." He is calm even under great stress. As a matter of fact, he conducts most of his business sitting down. He comes in in the morning and sits down in that chair, and that's where he stays all during his working day except for meals and an occasional nap in the afternoon in his office over in the EOB ...'

'In my experience, the President always manages to keep calm under the provocations of the press and the Hill. I don't know and perhaps no one else knows, maybe not even himself, how much he is torn up inside by the strain of it. I do know that no one shows greater civility to both his supporters and his opponents. The White House is the most exquisitely simple society that you'll find in this country right now. It is a pretty closed society, but it is a civil one. There is less meanness in the top people of the Nixon White House than in any recent administration ...'

'He doesn't have a great deal of camaraderie. He is not a fraternizer but he is very thoughtful of others and very careful not to make people unhappy. He is demanding but civil. This makes his criticisms more biting and much more effective when they do come. But they do not come very often....'

'The President loves the Presidency. I have never really noticed a moment's frustration in him, and I did work for him before he got here and there was lots of frustration then, when he wanted to get here. Now I find a complete serenity. He does not seem to be "burdened" by the office, as the popular cliché would have it. I think it is because he prepared for it for so long and now he's like someone who is given the tiller of a ship that he spent all of his life thinking about, and he is just going about sailing it.

'The first Cabinet meeting was typical. He came in and we held the meeting in a very matter-of-fact fashion. Nothing very dramatic happened. It was all very routine and I was disappointed, because I had come to it with quite a bit of excitement and anticipation of drama. But then I reflected that after all, he had been Vice-President for eight years and had presided at many Cabinet meetings in the past, and therefore it was nothing new for him ...'

'I have never seen staff work more efficiently done than it is here. Of course, we do have some people who try to see the President all the time. It's amazing to me how many people just want to get near the presence of the President. He protects himself from that, and also streamlines his own work with his system of memos. That way he makes sure that he can be informed of what he needs to know from a staff member without a lot of palaver. If you get a memo in by 5 p.m. you can almost be sure that he is going to read it that night. He will then dictate into his tape machine and usually the next morning you will receive an answer. That means that we don't go to see him with just trivia. If we request a personal meeting, he knows it is a serious matter worthy of his time. This way he has provided himself the freedom to do the writing, reading and studying he must do ...'

'As near as I can see, there seems to be a genuinely good feeling and rapport among the top members of the staff. You hear reports of friction and jealousy and occasionally somebody does a big piece on it in the papers, but I haven't seen it. Even between Haldeman and Ehrlichman there seems to be a real friendship and ease in dealing with one another.

'Haldeman is the man who really gets things done. If you

have a problem and go to him—if you can get to him—he can take care of it right away ...'

The press (male, veteran, many years' experience covering Presidents, long-time friend of Nixon): 'Nixon is like all Presidents —he can be brutal about people sometimes. Maybe it's the Merlin complex or something, but he thinks he can use you for something and then go away for three years and when he comes back you're supposed to be standing there waiting and still be just as much of a friend as you were before. He expects you to maintain your loyalty to him regardless of whether he's shown any loyalty or interest in you in the meantime. They all do it, it's a funny thing ... I've talked to him several times and I've generally found him so serene and untroubled that I sometimes wonder a little whether he really knows what's going on, or what could hit him if things go wrong. I think he does, but I really wonder sometimes ... They give you this picture of everybody loving everybody else on the White House staff, and it's probably truer in this Administration than in any other I've known in four decades. But when you get up near the top there's a lot of jockeying for position behind the scenes. I don't think it's erupted into any real feuds like we've had in some administrations—yet—but there are frictions there, though they try to hide them. You can't avoid it when people are human beings— and these, although they seem a little bland and faceless sometimes, are human beings. There's this great desire to get near the President, to be the one who's always seeing the great man —they can't help it. If they can't do it, they pretend it. I remember the other day X started to say to me, "When I saw the President the other day—" I interrupted, "Now, X, don't give me that crap. When did you actually see the President last?" He grinned a bit sheepishly and said, "Well, actually, it was about six months ago." But to hear him tell it, and to read how the press tells it, you'd think he was in there every other day. Among those who really are, there's a lot of competition for the great man's smile. I think it amuses him. He's an intelligent man. I think he rather enjoys it, like all Presidents. They're really all sons of bitches, in some ways. They enjoy being President and they secretly enjoy what the Presidency does to other people.'

The President's press secretary, Ronald Ziegler, is thirty-two, efficient, effective—and nice when it suits him, which it often does not. It did not suit him to be pleasant to me.

I had an appointment with him one dark winter afternoon and waited for fifty-five minutes without even the courtesy of a secretary's hello, after which I picked up my marbles and went home and did not try to see him again. Next morning, after I had mentioned to others on the premises that I now thought I had found out all I needed to know about the character of Ron Ziegler, he called with loud apologies and a long tale beginning, 'Jesus, I just didn't know you were out there, Al.' I told him not to worry, these things will happen.

I was told by his colleagues later that indeed they do, and often to people who come to him in good faith for the help he is theoretically supposed to provide on projects basically friendly to the President.

But—those magic words in this or any other White House—'the President likes him.' So he stays. And, of course, he does have his troubles. And on the whole he handles them well, under often extreme and deliberate provocation. A sampling of excerpts from the press briefings he holds morning and afternoon on almost every working day gives some of the flavour of the White House press corps and his own flavour:

Tuesday, January 5, 1971, morning—
QUESTION: 'Can you give us a rundown on what happened at the Cabinet meeting?'
ZIEGLER: 'The Cabinet meeting lasted for an hour and a half. When the President walked into the Cabinet meeting he received a standing ovation, I think marking the Cabinet's approval of how well the President did last night in the conversation [with three television commentators]. Then before the President could get into any topic of discussion, they generally went around the room to express their views as to how the President covered the many areas he covered last night ...'

QUESTION: 'Did anyone at the Cabinet table say that the President's answers to any questions were lousy?'

ZIEGLER: 'No. They didn't.'

QUESTION: 'Is that the first time the President has received a standing ovation in a Cabinet meeting, Ron?'

ZIEGLER: 'No. He has after other—(laughter)—are you going to ask me about what went on in the Cabinet meeting and then chuckle among yourselves, or do you want to know?

'The President has received standing ovations in Cabinet meetings following addresses that he has given on television. I have recalled the Cambodian speech and also others that he has given on family assistance, when he introduced the family assistance plan and other speeches that he has given on nationwide television explaining United States policy in South Vietnam ...'

Tuesday, February 2, 1971, morning—

QUESTION: 'Can you say whether the President had any contact with Souvanna Phouma [Prince Souvanna Phouma, Prime Minister of Laos] in the past several days?'

ZIEGLER: 'No, I wouldn't take that question ...'

QUESTION: 'Why won't you take Helen's question, Ron?'

ZIEGLER: 'I just am not prepared to do that.'

QUESTION: 'When do you expect the news blackout in Southeast Asia to be lifted, Mr. Ziegler?'

ZIEGLER: 'I have no comment on that.'

QUESTION: 'Ron, when the American and South Vietnamese troops entered Cambodia last April, the Administration said this was not an invasion because it was done with the assent of the government of Cambodia. Would that definition apply also to Laos, since the head of the government says they have not approved any entry of foreign troops?'

ZIEGLER: 'I am not prepared to take hypothetical questions such as you put forth and will have no comment on it ...'

Wednesday, February 3, 1971, morning—

QUESTION: 'Ron, there is an AFP [the French news agency] report which is datelined Quang Tri which says, "Thousands of military trucks moved bumper to bumper along two highways. Along the sides of the roads, troops with full field packs and arms were also moving in uninterrupted columns. Hundreds of helicopters passed overhead, airports throughout the northern provinces were buzzing with activity."

'Is that story true?'

ZIEGLER: 'As you know, Dan, we don't address [that subject] from the White House and it would be inappropriate for us to talk about details of movements of forces. So I can't answer your question.'

QUESTION: 'Could you explain to us why we have to learn from the French and the Japanese what—this question is asked in good spirit—what American soldiers are doing?'

ZIEGLER: 'You have read a portion of a report to me, Dan. It related to movement of forces. I assume you were referring to what forces? You didn't say, the portion that you read.'

QUESTION: 'I don't know whose forces. If they aren't ours, I would be interested in that as well.'

ZIEGLER: 'That goes to the thrust of my point. Anything regarding movement of forces within South Vietnam, United States forces, would, of course, come from MACV [Military Assistance Command Vietnam] or come from Saigon....'

QUESTION: 'Ron, do you mean to say that if there is an entry into Laos, that this would be merely details of movements of forces that the White House would not address?'

ZIEGLER: 'I don't think he raised that point in his question. You raised Laos and I assume—'

QUESTION: 'That is right, but you were asked several times in the last couple of days for information about possible entry into Laos and you have referred us to the Defence Department in essentially the same way.'

ZIEGLER: 'I have no information to give you from here this morning. I think all of you are aware of the fact that correspondents on the scene and in South Vietnam are being regularly briefed under the basis which you are familiar with. I have no information to give you.'

QUESTION: 'Have you had the opportunity to discuss your views on the value of an [information] embargo that applies only to one kind of correspondent in situations like this?'

ZIEGLER: 'No, I haven't.'

QUESTION: 'Do you have any views on that?'

ZIEGLER: 'None to express here at this time.'

QUESTION: 'Do you think that is a fair situation?'

ZIEGLER: 'I have no comment on that.'

QUESTION: 'Ron, this is a question that you were asked yesterday. I would like to ask it again. Has President Nixon been in touch with Prince Souvanna Phouma?'

ZIEGLER: 'Gentlemen, I am just not prepared to get into any discussion regarding Indochina with you at this time.'

QUESTION: 'Do you plan to co-ordinate any announcement on a stepped-up military activity in Laos with a successful landing [by Apollo 14] on the moon? ...'

ZIEGLER: 'Let me just go on Deep Background with you for a moment. In the questions that have come from several of you this morning, you have drawn certain assumptions and so forth. I obviously can't address those. But I would caution you as to some of those assumptions....'

QUESTION: ' "Deep Background" means what, Ron?'

ZIEGLER: 'Administration officials indicated, without direct quotation ...'

QUESTION: 'Ron, going back on Deep Background, you said that "you have drawn certain assumptions" and cautioned us against those assumptions. Are you referring to the assumptions based on foreign press reports that there have been entries of South Vietnamese troops into Laos?'

ZIEGLER: 'You will have to determine, without my assistance, what assumptions I was referring to.'

QUESTION: 'Back on the Deep Background remark, it seems a little silly to me that you won't define the assumptions we are supposed to have made. Why won't you do that? It seems nonsense.'

ZIEGLER: 'I didn't mean it to be, as you say, nonsensical. I was referring to the premises put forth in some of the questions which were remembered from previous stories, Pete. I wasn't relating it to a question that some here asked on their own.'

QUESTION: 'Would you consider this question, Ron: Because of the confusion and the embargo and silence and everything, which is a very distorted ball of wax, is there anything on a positive note that you can tell us with that in mind?'

ZIEGLER: 'I could probably give you some positive answers to some questions, but I can't bring one to mind yet.'

QUESTION: 'I am asking you whether you can tell us. It is a constructive question.'

ZIEGLER: 'I really have no information to provide you.'

QUESTION: 'Without reference to any of the discussion so far, are American troop withdrawals from Vietnam continuing at the present time?'

ZIEGLER: 'Our policy has not changed.'

QUESTION: 'But our withdrawals are under way at the present.'

ZIEGLER: 'The level of U.S. forces, which will be in effect in May, which I think is a level of 284,000 that was previously announced, the process leading up to that level is continuing ... I think it should be quite clear that the President's policy objective from the very outset is not to widen the war. Indeed, it is to reduce U.S. involvement under the Vietnamization in South Vietnam and in Southeast Asia. We are proceeding with that policy and there is no change in that policy ...'

Wednesday, February 3, 1971, afternoon—

QUESTION: 'Does the President feel this operation is going well?' (*Laughter.*)

ZIEGLER: 'I would not comment on that ...'

Thursday, February 4, 1971, afternoon—

QUESTION: 'Ron, is the embargo lifted? Has the full embargo been lifted?'

ZIEGLER: 'MACV has lifted the embargo, yes.'

QUESTION: 'Is there an embargo by the South Vietnamese government?'

ZIEGLER: 'Not to my knowledge. But I think Defence would be able to handle that question for you. You could get that from South Vietnam ...'

QUESTION: Ron, if there were no border crossing or none planned, why was the embargo allowed to run as long as it did?'

ZIEGLER: 'The embargo was an embargo, and again this is being discussed extensively at DOD [Department of Defence], but the nature of this embargo was similar to previous embargoes which have been put into effect in South Vietnam. The embargo was placed by the commander, General Abrams, for the safety of participating troops and because it was the judgment of the military commander in South Vietnam that it was essential to embargo this movement for the safety of the participating troops ...'

QUESTION: 'Ron, can you acknowledge the existence of considerable public apprehension during the past week over this operation? Secondly, in the light of it, if you do acknowledge it, do you think you would do anything differently in regard to embargo or the control of information than you have done in the past week? ...'

ZIEGLER: 'The commander placed the embargo, as is the normal procedure, to protect the security of forces who are making such movements. The fact that there have been no casualties inflicted by the enemy in the operation, I think, points to the wisdom of that judgment.'

QUESTION: 'Ron, you were asked this question before, but now that the embargo is lifted, perhaps you can answer it. Has the President been in touch with Prince Souvanna Phouma within the last few days?'

ZIEGLER: 'No, he has not been ...'

QUESTION: 'Ron, as the commander in chief, what was the President's involvement in this operation? Did he take part in the planning or approval of the plans or was all of this carried out at the theatre level?'

ZIEGLER: 'You can say that the President approved this operation ...'

QUESTION: '... how much time during the past six days did he spend on this operation?'

ZIEGLER: 'I am not prepared to break out an amount of time.'

QUESTION: 'Was it a majority of his time?'

ZIEGLER: 'No, I wouldn't say that.'

QUESTION: 'A great deal of time?'

ZIEGLER: 'No, I wouldn't say a majority of his time.'

QUESTION: 'Have the objectives been achieved? ...'

ZIEGLER: 'I am not prepared to characterize the nature of an operation. It appears to be going well ...'

QUESTION: 'Ron, you said that the President had approved the operation. Was the specific point of an embargo presented to the President and did he specifically approve that?'

ZIEGLER: 'That was the judgment made by the commander,

General Abrams, to place the embargo for the purposes which he has referred to there and which I have conveyed to you. And it was his decision to lift the embargo. I believe Secretary Laird pointed that out this morning also.'

QUESTION: 'Did General Abrams have the authority to place that embargo?'

ZIEGLER: 'Yes.'

QUESTION: 'Without asking formally for approval?'

ZIEGLER: 'Yes, he does ...'

QUESTION: 'Did the President's approval of the operation include approval of the embargo?'

ZIEGLER: 'I answered that question earlier....'

Monday, February 8, 1971, morning—

QUESTION: 'Ron, the United States participated in the 1962 Accord on the Neutrality of Laos. How do we describe our participation in the invasion of Laos today with that policy or that agreement?'

ZIEGLER: 'The State Department has addressed itself to that. I have nothing to add to what they said in a very, I think, extensive statement this morning ... We feel that because of the North Vietnamese occupation of territory in Laos—and I am relating now to the southern panhandle of Laos—and their long-standing aggressive actions within Laos, that the steps which the ARVN [Army of the Republic of Vietnam] have taken with U.S. air power support, which we have referred to, is consistent with international law.'

QUESTION: 'Do you mean it is consistent with international law to invade a country? ...'

QUESTION: 'Did the United States initiate this operation?'

ZIEGLER: '... This was an ARVN-initiated operation. The U.S. air support, of course, was approved by the Administration and naturally by the President.'

QUESTION: 'Did the United States initiate the discussion of such an operation at this time?'

ZIEGLER: '... The basic consultation and decision, I think in terms of time, it can be said was arrived at in January of this year and proceeding accordingly up until the operation which went into effect last night.'

QUESTION: 'Ron, did the President order Thieu [President

Thieu of South Vietnam] to go in there? Order him to go in there?'

ZIEGLER: 'That would be an incorrect assumption.'

QUESTION: 'Just when in January? Could you be more specific?'

ZIEGLER: 'I don't want to be any more specific than that, Don ...'

QUESTION: 'Did he give the final go-ahead this weekend?'

ZIEGLER: 'No, that is not correct. The final assessment was made prior to this weekend.'

QUESTION: 'Did he contact directly at any point either President Thieu or Souvanna Phouma?'

ZIEGLER: 'In relation to President Thieu, of course, the on-going operations in South Vietnam call for continuing consultation with the South Vietnamese government through both diplomatic and military channels. That process, of course, was in effect and followed as is the normal course of events as it related to this particular operation.'

QUESTION: 'What about Souvanna Phouma, the second part of the question?'

ZIEGLER: 'I responded to that question the other day. President Nixon had no contact with Souvanna Phouma ...'

QUESTION: 'May I take a third stab at a question I have asked twice before? Did the United States initiate the discussion of undertaking this operation at this time?'

ZIEGLER: '... U.S. involvement in these consultations related to the air power which would be provided. From that standpoint, we were involved in that decision and in the discussions with the ARVN relating to the operation.'

QUESTION: 'Ron, can I try it another way? Was the directive to carry out this operation drawn up in Washington?'

ZIEGLER: 'It depends on what you mean by "directive".'

QUESTION: 'I am talking about Joint Chiefs of Staff directive.'

ZIEGLER: 'I am not going to get into the process of how an operation finally is put into effect. However, I will say that the planning for this occurred in South Vietnam. We, of course, were involved here in Washington as a normal course of events on a major operation.'

QUESTION: 'Was that planning in Saigon carried out as a result of the Joint Chiefs of Staff directive?'

ZIEGLER: 'I am not prepared to answer that question.'

QUESTION: 'Did this operation, the incursion into Laos, require an execute order in Washington?'

ZIEGLER: 'Of course.'

QUESTION: 'Can you tell us when that took place?'

ZIEGLER: 'I am not prepared to give a checklist as to when that occurred ...'

QUESTION: 'Ron, you say you can't tell us the geographical limits of this operation, but you refer to the Laotian panhandle in southern Laos. Can you tell us if the President has set some geographical limits on it without telling us what they are, if you can't tell us what they are?'

ZIEGLER: '... I am not prepared to talk about the operation in those details, obviously.'

QUESTION: 'I am not asking you what the geographical limits are. I am asking you if the President has set some geographical limits.'

ZIEGLER: 'I am not prepared to answer that. ...'

And so on—and on—every morning and every afternoon of almost every working day—issue after issue—crisis after crisis for as long as the Administration stays in power and the press continues to pry and the press secretary to defend.

Comment by one in a position to know (possibly enraged by too many internecine battles) on a particular Problem of Presidents:

'The State department is a total disaster. It is still filled with a group of extreme radical liberals who barely tolerate most Presidents and this one not at all. Their arrogance and obstructionism are beyond belief. It makes it impossible to deal with them on any basis of equality. They are controlled or they control. There is no middle ground.'

AID BILL TIES UP SENATE. THREE MEMBERS DELAY ACTION ON CAMBODIA ... LAIRD'S REMARKS ESCALATE DEBATE ON BOMBING POLICY ... DECLINE IN OUTPUT GOES ON. SLIDE IS WORST SINCE '61 ... CAMPAIGN TACTICS DEFENDED BY AGNEW ... MASS SESSION SOUGHT FOR CHILD PARLEY ...

*Alex Butterfield, deputy to Bob Haldeman, who occupies the
office next door to the Oval Office, handles the flow of mail
and papers to the President's desk. The President receives three
folders filled with communications every morning. One, marked
'F.Y.I.' contains principally National Security Council matters
and reports from the Domestic Council. A second is labelled
'Action' and contains the various options on the major problems pending that day. The third, marked 'Signature', contains
bills from Congress, special messages and greetings and the like.
The President has Butterfield witness his signature, although
there is no constitutional requirement for this—'It's the tradition that seems to have grown up in the office and we carry
it on,' Butterfield says. Muzak burbles along quietly in the
background in Butterfield's handsome yellow-walled office, as
it does almost everywhere throughout the East and West
Wings.*

Bud Krogh, member of the staff of the Council on Domestic
Affairs, former staff assistant to the President for legal matters,
particularly in the area of crime, drugs, law enforcement and
security, is tall, blond, pleasant, honest, earnest and absorbed in
his particular job—one White House staff member who has no
particular personal axe to grind but is simply devoted to the job
he has to do and anxious to get on with it.

'Prior to the reorganization of the Domestic Council I worked
closely with the President on such matters as I have mentioned
and also on the control of demonstrations. This is no longer
such a problem and hopefully will not be in future. There was
a time, you know, when we had some large demonstrations here
and it was a matter of deciding how people could march and
have reasonable protest, yet not come within range of the Mansion in such a way that they would endanger either it or the
First Family.

'This meant working with the Justice Department, the police
department in the district, the FBI and the Pentagon, since the
White House was really the focal point of all these demonstrations. We had to determine arrest policies, lines of march, at

123

what point a demonstration could be considered out of hand, how it could be policed internally and all these other matters of keeping it under control. The President finally decided, prior to the demonstration last May, that they could use the ellipse south of the White House grounds as a site and at the same time protect the Mansion. That demonstration was held there and from now on that will probably be the pattern if we again get requests for such gatherings. [It wasn't, in May 1971.]

'More recently I worked on the D.C. crime bill and the court reorganization bill, which have expanded crime control and enforcement. I have also been very much concerned with the problem of drugs and that continues to be my major interest now in the reorganized Domestic Council. I have also been involved in the control of gun sales and the thefts of explosives. In addition, I am involved with the concern we feel here over what the federal role should be in campus disorders. The explosion at the University of Wisconsin is the one which really pushed us over the brink in reaching the decision that while we should not dictate university policy, still when a crime is committed at a university it is no longer a university responsibility to punish the crime. The FBI should have primary jurisdiction when there is an explosion in any building partly or wholly funded by federal money. The FBI now has the right to go in, although theoretically, of course, it would not go in if it were not requested to do so.

'We have also been concerned with additional manpower for the FBI. The President said last July that we have just got to have enough men to do the job. As a result, one thousand men have been added to the FBI. I remember that J. Edgar Hoover came over and told us at that time that every agent then in the FBI was carrying twenty-seven cases per man, in contrast to a normal load of eighteen per man, and that most of them were working between an hour and an hour and a half overtime every evening to get the jobs done.

'In the area of narcotics, we have sort of made D.C. the crucible where we determine what can be done in handling both the crimes of the drug traffic and the crimes which are ancillary to the drug problem, such as addicts holding up people for the purpose of getting money with which to buy drugs. We have concentrated on a massive infusion of extra policemen and

124

also on expanding narcotics treatment. In addition we have inaugurated the street lighting programmes which you see around here at night, the soft orange lights on F Street and Fourteen Street, which greatly increase illumination, and also the grey-blue lights around the Federal Triangle. The street lighting programme is being extended up Seventh Street, Fourteenth Street, and along New York Avenue as the main crime areas.

'Essentially, the control of crime has to be something that comes from the people, from their simply being completely fed up with the situation. We don't get any more cries of "police brutality", or "racial discrimination" in the enforcement of the law around here. That has melted away. It has been overwhelmed by the cry for protection which comes from 99 per cent of the black community, who are just not going to stand for any more street crime if we can possibly control it.

'Interestingly enough, this office has also been expanded to include transportation policy and so we have become involved with the Amtrak programme and how to make it economically viable. We are also working with Housing and Urban Development on the model cities programme and community programmes. But it is principally in the area of narcotics that we are most concerned. Problems of the heavy drugs, heroin and things of that sort, are concerning us very much. We are trying to work out the optimum national programmes, to recommend new policies and to reinforce present policies.

'The President has a great desire to do something dramatic to stop that kind of crime—the crime associated with the drug traffic and with its side effects.

'There are all sorts of moral questions involved in the methadone treatment of heroin addiction, such as whether the government should be involved in addicting people to cures that are themselves drugs, even though they block the effects of heroin and keep it from physically and intellectually destroying the people who use it. It is a real intellectual challenge to come up with a new programme in this area.

'Congress is very co-operative in the drug area because narcotics is an extraordinarily popular issue right now. This is true even though its dimensions of course are nowhere as great as the problem of alcoholism. But alcoholism has become somehow accepted as a part of our society, something we can live with while we try to control it and correct it. The danger in drugs is that Congress can make mistakes in its legislation unless it is well-informed on the subject. Last summer, for instance, there was discussion of punitive action to be taken against Turkey to make it reduce the crops of poppies being grown in that country to produce morphine and opium. This showed a very poor understanding of Turkish politics, because the poppy is apparently a cultural as well as commercial crop in Turkey and has been raised there for hundreds of years. For the Prime Minister to reduce the crops on a schedule dictated by the United States government would destroy his government in Turkey. There has to be some way to find compromises which will consider their problem there and also the control of the whole situation worldwide.

'We have also been participating in narcotics talks between the United States and Mexico and the United States and France. We had to build a record to show that narcotics was spreading to France as well. I remember one French government minister remarking that the French didn't need drugs, they had sex and wine to keep them happy. But we were able to show him that the drug traffic was spreading into France too, and they have now become concerned about it and anxious to stamp it out.

'I report back on these things and if action is necessary at a top level such as a letter from President Nixon to President Pompidou, then I do what I can to make sure that this comes about. This has now become an important part of foreign policy.

'Basically the job here is to try to be a detector of the best information and the best talent so that they can be focused on a problem and a decision can be made, particularly in these areas which are of such concern to a stable society.'

'They were here before we got here and they'll be here after we leave. They aren't impressed with anybody—' the permanent secretarial and administrative staff of the White House headed by Bill Hopkins, a White House figure since the last year and a half of the Hoover Administration. There were 50 people on the staff when he came. There are 250 now, including the tele-

phone operators, file room, correspondence room, duplicating room, message service, telegraph and travel service for the staff and the gift unit. Secretaries usually work on a fill-in basis where needed, the rest perform assigned duties. Incoming mail is heavier now than at any time he can remember. Gifts to the President and First Lady are numerous too, and go directly to the Secret Service for safety check before being sent on to the recipients, a practice dating back to Franklin Roosevelt's days.

He finds the Nixon Administration like the Eisenhower, 'much more interested in the movement of papers' than its predecessors of the last forty years. Blandly, silently and efficiently, he and his staff watch the papers, like their originators and their recipients, come and go.

Leonard Garment is small, neat, cultured, sophisticated, a former law partner of the President's in New York who goes gently about the government doing good in a quiet, astute and effective way. He once played the clarinet in Woody Herman's orchestra and still enjoys a good jam session. He has a formal title but he is one of those men whose work is about one tenth above water. He doesn't make waves, but beneath his outwardly placid surface much activity goes busily on and much constructive good comes of it, both for his country and for the Administration. His comments on his job, on the President and on the staff are characteristically perceptive and to the point.

'My official job, I suppose, is special consultant on the Domestic Council, but I am somewhere between a counsellor and an assistant. Most of my time is devoted to human rights, civil rights, minority economic problems. I try to work with the executive and the legislative sides to help in the general area of poverty and racial difficulties, including not only blacks but Indians, Mexican-Americans and others.

'Basically, I suppose, I simply present another point of view, another place where people can make their appeals for help, a letter drop, a friendly ear if not always an effective helping hand. I am also a gadfly, sometimes a critical voice in Administration internal debates on these subjects.

'Another area of my interest is the routing of problems to make sure they get to the right people. I also have quite a bit to do with the arts and humanity side of the cultural effort of the government. I'm trying to make recommendations on the National Endowment for the Arts which will make it more effective and have helped considerably in that area, although that is not the most politically sensitive area of my activities.

'I've probably been involved more with school desegregation in the last year than with any other single thing. I believe the Administration is following fundamentally a very sound policy, one that has been designed to understand the problem, to do what is needed and to correct it. We are trying to avoid actions that would increase tension, to ease some of the fever, to try to bring the problem, which is staggering in its size, under control.

'Part of the problem, of course, has been a high level of rhetoric and expectation relating to the civil rights legislation of the fifties and sixties. We find that these problems sometimes take more time, that they do not yield to immediate easy answers. This naturally increases frustration and heightens the level of anger and resentment which we find among the minority groups, particularly the blacks. We started two years ago in a tough situation, but we are now in a quieter time, having made some substantial progress—although we have only begun to scratch the surface as far as improving the economic and commercial situation of the minorities. We find that we have to avoid substituting the balm of words for the reality of workable programmes.

'Some of the more radical elements, of course, feel that this Administration is not doing things as rapidly or efficiently or gratifyingly as the previous ones, but statistically we are doing damned well as compared to the Kennedy and Johnson administrations. Actually we have surpassed them in statistics. But statistics, however much repeated, do not really convince people who do not wish to be convinced, or are so upset emotionally that they cannot be convinced. Expectation and hope are sometimes not related to reality. This is partly our problem.

'I have the feeling that now is the time for the President to make a speech on this subject. I have a feeling that we should be trying to state things that are not too well understood about what we are doing.

'The thing about the President that I have always liked is that he is open and flexible. I personally feel that people approach a greater wisdom if they are a little humble about what they know and don't feel they have all the answers. I think this is true with him. Since '63 when I first knew him, his ability to roll with the punches and with changing events has substantially increased. He has a deep patriotism, a deep concern for the preservation of national values, for preservation of peace and opportunity for all people in the country. He is quite open to the flow of ideas and I think he has learned a lot.

'I think the staff also has learned a lot in the last couple of years. It is a bunch of relatively young and capable men. We came into the most complicated job, in this serene setting, and I have a feeling that we have all learned a lot, that some people are ten years smarter than they were two years ago, for such is the pace here. The staff was a good one to begin with, and in a way it has moved around and has been much more effective in the past year than it was before.

'This is like a free-form basketball game with no end lines and the court as wide as the nation. We have to know each other's strong points and weaknesses and know how to hand the ball to one another. I think this is being developed very well.

'As for the President's "remoteness' and "inaccessibility", I think the White House bureaucracy, to call it that, is a scapegoat. It is not necessarily the case. The charge of remoteness is a measure of how insistent are those who want to get things directly to the President or get close to the President or the staff. However, of course, it is a psychological matter: if people feel something is remote then it is remote.

'Somebody has to sort out the demands and the requests and decide whether it is more important to spend three or four clean days trying to decide a major programme like whether to withdraw troops from Vietnam than it is to set up meetings on any one of fifty urgent problems which clamour for attention from the President. This sometimes causes conflicts between those who think the meetings are more important than the quiet times.

'I think that as far as we are concerned here in the White House, after the first year or so of sitting around and wondering what it's all about, looking at the picture of Eisenhower or Thomas Jefferson or Lincoln on the wall, things really begin to get into shape. Then after you've been invited to all the parties you want to go to and attended all the formal ceremonies you think would be thrilling, you begin to get to the point of wondering and thinking about what you want to leave behind you. At that point the appointive bureaucracy of the White House begins to work together, they really become the President's men. They decide they *do* want to leave something behind, and so they settle down and make a sincere attempt to do it. I think that is the point at which the staff is now.'

Earnest young staffer, forehead creased with worry: 'We literally have to fight for everything we get from the media. The day we stop fighting we won't get elected. It's a sad fact but it's a hard, cruel world. It's very hard to get press and TV to treat us objectively, let alone give us a plug.
'I'd say our relations with Congress are getting more stable, although they're very quick to gossip up there if they think we've done something wrong. If we screw up some little thing here it gets around the Hill like that! [snapping his fingers]'
Older staffer, mouth twisted in an ironic smile: 'The President never gets anything but the most grudging acknowledgment from the liberals and the media. Imagine if Jack Kennedy were making these overtures to Red China that the President is making now. They couldn't contain themselves. They'd be masturbating.'

Bobbie Kilberg is in her mid-twenties, dark-eyed, black-haired, pretty, very intelligent, very earnest, very intent, full of 'Jesus Christs' and 'God damns' and 'sons of bitches'. She is a member of the Ripon Society, a small group of young Republican liberals who occasionally lecture the national Administration on what it should do. ('The Ripon Society has been going since September 1966 and has some three thousand dues-paying members, although the effectiveness and circulation of its ideas is much more extensive than that. There are eleven chapters around the country. We think we are constructive and we are going to stay Republican. We are going to back progressive Republicans in '72. Our purpose is to keep a moderate-progressive tone in the Republican Party. I think we are constructive and I think we will keep going.')

Mrs. Kilberg was a White house intern in the Johnson

administration, coming to the White House in March 1968. She was appointed to the Ehrlichman staff in March 1969, and by that time, having worked with LaDonna Harris, part-Indian wife of Senator Fred Harris (Democrat, Oklahoma), she was fired up to do something about the Indians. She has been the White House expert on Indian affairs.

'On January 26, 1970, the Vice-President called a meeting which included seven Indians and six or seven people from the government. He asked the Indians to come up with recommendations that could be sent to Congress. Mrs. Harris submitted recommendations which were sent to Cabinet officers and they were asked how they were going to implement these suggestions. We got answers that were completely unacceptable. So we put out option papers and started our own drive to get decent recommendations. Finally, after consulting various agencies and Cabinet members, we arrived at seven proposals, for bills to go to Congress, and for two or three administrative actions that could be taken.

'The only action taken so far has been to return Blue Lake in New Mexico to the Taos Pueblo Indians, which was passed by Congress and signed into law by the President a couple of months ago. We also now have an arrangement where an assistant secretaryship in the Department of the Interior has been set up and an arrangement has been made to give the Indian tribes the option to take over their own programmes and affairs. This is something of a double option, in that if the government finds that the tribe is incompetent to handle its affairs it can take the programme back, particularly in case of malfeasance of some kind, or incompetence; and at the same time the Indian tribe, if it wishes, and if it finds that it is not competent to run its own affairs, can hand the programme back to the federal government.

'We have done our best to consult with Congress on this because we have learned that if you want to get funding from Congress, you don't run around them. You try to work through them. Congress has established an Indian Trust Council Authority which provides independent legal counsel for land and water claims of the Indian nations. Let's face it, they've got screwed for centuries. They need help in getting economic development and control of their resources, and we intend to give it to them.

'In Congress, our relations with the House have been rather good. There has been no problem in getting sponsors for legislation. The Senate has been sheer disaster. They seem to feel that they were not consulted, a general feeling that the Senate has been ignored and not given proper place in all this. This has been complicated by the fact that Clint Anderson [Clinton Anderson, Democratic Senator from New Mexico] was against the Blue Lake proposition and has been for many years. This has created a lot of difficulties. Senator Allott of Colorado has also been opposed because the Senate Interior Committee, which he heads, rejected the bill. However, it was brought to the floor just the same and was passed over them by fifty-one to twenty-six. I don't think they've got over the shock of this yet. Normally when a bill is rejected by a committee it does not reach the floor. In this case we took it right away from them.

'The Indians have begun to have a constituency in Congress, although they are only one million people all told. Right now they are a very popular cause, but it is going to evaporate, I'm afraid, in the next year or so. Such things as Alcatraz, Plymouth and Denver, where they have made disturbances on government reservations and Army installations, have begun to create a ground swell of public feeling against them. I'm afraid they are going to become even more militant, and this in turn is going to create more of a reaction against them. For one thing, the government simply does not have the money to alleviate all their problems even though they've been shat on all these years, and it's a matter of trying to convince them to go a little more slowly until the funds can be found.

'Fortunately there seems to be a very strong bipartisanship regarding the Indian which includes such people as the President, the Vice-President, Senator Goldwater, Senator Griffin, Senator Harris and all of the leading candidates for the Democratic Presidential nomination. We hope to improve our relations with the Senate and are being aided by the fact that the Bureau of Indian Affairs in the Department of the Interior has reorganized itself. It was one of the most awful and controversial bureaux in the government. But we have managed, with the President's help, to get in a group of people in that agency who are very militant young Indians who are neither Republicans nor Democrats, but are simply devoted to the Indian cause. They have turned the BIA upside down, which has quite startled some of the staff people here in the White House, who wonder how they got through without their noticing and being able to stop them.

'The Indian problem is complicated by the fact that sometimes their interests are hard to define. There are very separate, distinct tribes with separate cultures. You have an urban-rural split, a split between activists and non-activists, a split between the old tribal chiefs who are very conservative and don't like change and the young Indians who are very impatient to have something done and more sceptical than the blacks about the federal government. This is because they have been lied to and lied to over the years. For instance, they are convinced that if they take over the schools in their reservations they will lose federal grants, even though we tell them repeatedly this will not be the case.

'I spend most of my time on the phone just trying to convince people that the government means it. Their problems are a whole different bag and a very difficult one. There are Indians who have relocated in the city who find they can't make it there and who become just like any other American citizen, getting relief funds in the city. But they find that the distribution of such funds is largely controlled by blacks, chicanos and such and the Indians get the short end. They find they have to fight for funds. That's why we are setting up Indian centres through the OEO to help in the distribution of funds to aid the urban Indians, but it is very, very slow going to get the funds. The OMB is cynical about it but willing to try and so we are moving forward on that front.

'We've had to sell the White House staff on the Indian programme. We managed to sell the package to them because we simply took control of it and rammed it through. Anything you do around here, there has to be twenty-five people checking on it, but if you can convince them of the logic of it, they are willing to buy it. However, I think that in the Indian part of it, we got it through because I don't think anybody really knew around here that it was going to go through and so they didn't pay much attention.

'We are aided, of course, by the President's own interest. He got in the Taos Indians for a briefing on the Blue Lake situation and since that point we have got a lot of help from people on the staff. It isn't so much that people are opposed to things, it is just that they are extremely busy. *Extremely* busy. It's very hard to get people to concentrate on things and pay attention to what you're doing.

'The President has been wonderful about it. He is willing to listen and to get new ideas. He's a wonderful guy and is willing to listen to anything that's rational and reasonable. He's the main reason I'm sticking around here, even though I'm a Ripon member and member of the governing board. When I find the President willing to buy ideas, then I am willing to stay. I felt upset for a while when I first came into the White House, then I felt upset again directly after this last campaign. But I think that since then things have changed very substantially. The Administration is now beginning to move more effectively back to the centre in revenue sharing and things like that. There is an organizational shift in the government which will be one of the most important changes.

'Social programmes have just gone wild and are going to have to be controlled. If you pour money into them, you can't guarantee it going to the people who need it. Therefore welfare reform is absolutely imperative, and I think the Administration is coming to a reasonable position on that. John Ehrlichman has made it clear that there's a place in this Administration for people of all opinions and there are several other Ripon members here. Ehrlichman has never asked me to do anything I couldn't do. Len Garment is one the most liberal influences around here and I work directly for him. I feel they very sincerely want liberal Republicans around here, just as much as conservatives. So I think I will stay on.'

Three months later word got out that Bobbie Kilberg was leaving to go to work for the law-firm Arnold & Porter, that den-mother of leftover liberals from both Democratic and Republican administrations. She told me cheerfully that her leaving had nothing to do with her ideas and pointed out that her duties would be divided between two girls, one black, the other white, both liberal. 'There are still quite a few of us around here. We haven't given up. We're still around.'

Another candid staff member, musing on internal problems of the White House: 'I think Haldeman does a really terrific job for the President and I think Ehrlichman does too. I have always found them to be very fair in their dealings with me, even though I think both are limited in their view of the President's image and the image of the Administration. As a matter of fact, I think probably that is the chief criticism to be made of this staff: that they are inexperienced in national politics, that they actually came in thinking that the President could just get along without Congress, that members of Congress would jump to do his bidding and that he really could dominate the legislative branch.

'This was a very naïve concept, particularly when the Democrats were in control of Congress, but it is typical of these men around Nixon that they did not have that political background. They were old friends of his and old campaign buddies, but they did not have the expertise in Congress or Washington politics which he has needed.

'By the same token, curiously enough, possibly because his own Congressional career was limited to four years in the House and only two in the Senate, he himself has a rather incomplete knowledge of Congress and its working. I really think an attempt is going to be made to correct this, but partly it is his own nature, which tends to be secretive and shy and lonely and does not make it possible for him to function too well in that context.'

The principal members of the staffs of George Shultz and John Ehrlichman meet at seven-thirty every morning of the working week in the Roosevelt Room of the West Wing. It is a jovial meeting, at least when outsiders are present, full of jests and jollity, along with an occasional pointed remark about the opposition. On this particular cold December morning, the Ninety-first Congress was stumbling towards a disorganized and ignominious close as liberal Senators, who claim to despise the filibuster, joined with conservative Senators, who frankly say they love it, to paralyse their august institution with filibusters on top of filibusters on top of filibusters. For an Administration trying to find its way through the murk and salvage—unsuccessfully, as it turned out—major pieces of its legislative programme, the prospects were confusing where not downright dim.

The meeting opens with Shultz, Ehrlichman, Virginia Knauer, Peter Flanigan, Leonard Garment, Bob Finch and ten or twelve others coming in, exchanging greetings, helping themselves to coffee and sweet rolls from a table in the corner. Presently all are suitably replenished and ready and the meeting begins, Shultz at one end of the long table, Ehrlichman at the other.

Shultz inquires about the status of legislation on the Hill and Gene Cavan, a member of the Congressional liaison staff, responds by reading a statement by the president pro tem of the Senate, Allen J. Ellender (Democrat, Louisiana), asking indignantly if the Office of Management and Budget is trying to subvert what Congress is trying to do.

'Of course, of course,' say several people, laughing.

Cavan says he held a series of meetings the previous afternoon with people such as Chairman Russell Long (Democrat, Louisiana) of the Senate Finance Committee, Senator Mike Mansfield of Montana, Senate Majority Leader, and Senator Hugh Scott (Republican, Pennsylvania), Minority Leader. He reports that the consensus is that it will be parliamentarily possible to move ahead on the family assistance plan as soon as 'the three-headed monster' (the combined trade-Social Security-family assistance bill approved by the Finance Committee) comes to the floor.

Cavan says his contacts are agreed that it will be possible at that point to move an amendment substituting the Administration's FAP for the committee version. Mansfield has said he will support it and 'we can expect others' votes to go with us, following his lead'.

'Do you need any in-puts from this group?' Shultz asks.

Cavan says he thinks so, but things are changing so fast in the Senate at the moment that it is difficult to say. He will have to let them know later.

'They think we have the votes to carry FAP,' he says, not the first or the last to make the mistake of predicting the Senate, and there are expressions of pleased surprise around the table.

John Ehrlichman, wearing glasses and looking snug and trim and spick-and-span, says he thinks 'we had better get our ducks in a row' on various pieces of legislation in these hectic closing days of the session. Friendly members of the Senate 'are going to want some signs from us' as soon as possible.

He says the manpower training bill has now come down to the White House and the President 'wants to force an up-or-down vote on his veto. We are getting a lot of mail from mayors and other municipal people who are under the impression that this is a sort of WPA that will absorb all the unemployed. We should meet this issue head on and put out a statement that will get rid of that idea once and for all.'

A staff member questions whether the veto should be announced Wednesday or Thursday in the midst of the hubbub surrounding the visit of British Prime Minister Edward Heath. He thinks the veto might be lost or overshadowed by the visit.

Ehrlichman thinks there may be a point there, and emphasizes that the President's veto message 'should make very clear our reasons for the veto'. He adds that the Vice-President is going to be meeting with the Republican governors in Sun Valley, Idaho, over the weekend and notes that some of the governors are out with a statement saying they want some ten billions' worth of revenue sharing.

'Somebody should position the Vice-President to make clear that the amount is not $10 billion,' Ehrlichman says with a pointed humour. 'It just ain't and he should make clear our position on that.'

He then inquires, 'Could you get the Department of Agriculture to counter-punch Jean Mayer?'

(Jean Mayer, former adviser to the President on nutritional matters, has just held a press conference charging the President with lack of leadership on food stamp reform and saying that he is apparently 'making a mockery' of his pledge to eliminate hunger in America.)

'Do you want a low counter-punch?' someone inquires.

'Yes,' Ehrlichman says. 'As low as possible.'

Everybody laughs.

Peter Flanigan is called upon and says he has received a memo from the Treasury offering to discuss proposed fiscal legislation with the leadership on the Hill. This in effect, Flanigan says, would give the leadership 'a veto over legislation'. He says he is 'not so sure we want to do that'. Everybody agrees.

Ken Cole, Ehrlichman's deputy, reports on the White House

Conference on Children currently in progress, and says there is a group of delegates who want to have a plenary session at the end of the week. He says there is no reason to have such a session, which would very likely be just a platform for malcontents seeking headlines, and 'basically our position is not to give in unless there is some major reason that develops why we should'.

'The bleeding hearts may get turned on by this,' he remarks, 'but I think the Administration can stand the pressure.' (It did.)

Shultz remarks that two of his children went to the conference last night 'and when they came back I asked them what was happening. They said a lot of old people were sitting around talking about kids.'

Everybody laughs.

Virginia Knauer reports that the National Archives 'wants to publish a consumer guidelines pamphlet'. She says she thinks 'the White House should grab this and publish it themselves. The guidelines will complete all of the President's recommendations and they ought to come out of here.

'We should alert everybody to the danger of Archives running off with the ball,' she says firmly.

Everybody agrees that the matter will be looked into.

There is further desultory chit-chat of no particular significance for a minute or two, and then, shortly before 8 a.m., Shultz adjourns the meeting and its members go off to face the Congress, and the day.

The press (male, veteran): 'I think Nixon is weakening. I think he has lost ground. His participation in the '70 election started it and it's continued since. Of course, the Democrats don't have anybody visible who can make any kind of race, so maybe Nixon can still come back enough to win. But for the moment, I think he is exhibiting all the signs of a one-term President.

'In fact, we may be entering an era in which all we're going to have is one-term Presidents—in which the problems are so insoluble that people are going to elect a man hoping he can handle them and then throw him out after four years when they find he can't, hoping they can find somebody else. This may be the way the United States is going. Not a pleasant prospect.'

BOMBING STAND HIT BY SOVIET. U.S. WARNED ABOUT
THREATS AGAINST HANOI ... NIXON VETOES PUBLIC JOBS
TRAINING BILL ... SOVIETS SLOW ICBM BUILD-UP ... AGNEW
DEFENDS TACTICS TO GOP GOVERNORS ... THE GALLUP
POLL: NIXON'S POPULARITY HITS LOWEST POINT [52%].

As stately as a minuet, as rigidly programmed as a space shot,
the state visit has become frozen into the pattern of the Presidency. Like his recent predecessors and his successors, Mr. Nixon
must greet, wine, dine and confer with a steady procession of
world leaders. The routine is almost unvarying, and the visit in
December 1970 of Prime Minister Edward Heath of Great
Britain is a typical example. From the President's viewpoint, in
the documents drawn up and presented to him by his staff,
this is how it looked:

ARRIVAL CEREMONY FOR
PRIME MINISTER EDWARD HEATH
OF GREAT BRITAIN

Thursday, December 17, 1970
10.00 a.m.
The South Lawn

THE PRESIDENT:

10.00 a.m.   You and Mrs. Nixon at edge of terrace for honours,
announcement, and 'Hail to the Chief'.

Down walkway, up driveway to arrival area.

10.01 a.m.   Prime Minister Edward Heath—standard arrival.

Ambassador Mosbacher will introduce the Prime
Minister to you and Mrs. Nixon.

You and Prime Minister Heath to platform. Mrs.
Nixon to right of platform.

10.03 a.m.   National anthems and 19-gun salute.

Inspection of troops—you and Prime Minister
Heath guided by commander of troops.

Return to platform—U.S. Marine Drum and Bugle
Corps passes in review.

10.10 a.m.   You deliver welcoming remarks to Prime Minister
Heath (suggested remarks attached).

| | Prime Minister Heath responds. |
| 10.15 a.m. | You, Mrs. Nixon and Prime Minister Heath will then ascend the right outside staircase to the south portico balcony. |

You will pause at the centre of the south portico balcony for a photograph and then enter the residence via the Green Room door. The remainder of the British party will then follow.

You will enter the Blue Room and form a receiving line along the south wall facing the Christmas tree. The remainder of the British party and other dignitaries will enter the residence by the same route, be received in the Blue Room, and be served refreshments in the Red Room.

| 10.20 a.m. | Return to Oval Office for private meeting with Prime Minister Heath. |
| 11.30 a.m. | Upon the conclusion of your private meeting, you may wish to invite members of the British official party who have been meeting in the Cabinet room into the Oval Office to meet briefly with you and Prime Minister Heath. |

Press Plan:
There will be full press coverage of the arrival ceremony.

FOR IMMEDIATE RELEASE AFTER 8 p.m.
THURSDAY, DECEMBER 17, 1970

President and Mrs. Nixon will entertain at a state dinner tonight, Thursday, December 17, 1970, in honour of the Right Honourable Edward Heath, M.B.E., M.P., Prime Minister of Great Britain and Northern Ireland, at the White House at 8 p.m.

Dinner will be served in the State Dining Room with the guests seated at an E-shaped table. The Johnson china, vermeil flatwear and candelabra will be used. Nine tall epergnes and five low vermeil vases will contain Christmas bouquets of holly, white snapdragons and carnations, red roses and carnations, white pompon chrysanthemums and gypsophila. Red poinsettias will be banked in the curves of the table.

The menu is: Fillet of Dover Sole Véronique

Supreme of Royal Squab
Wild Rice Amandine
Timbale Printanière
Bibb Lettuce Salad—Brie Cheese
Bûche de Noël

The wines are: Schloss Johannisberger, L. M. Cabernet Sauvignon and Louis Roederer Cristal.

The guests will be entertained during dessert with Christmas carols by the Army Chorus.

Following dinner, coffee and liqueurs will be served in the Red and Green Rooms, after which the guests will adjourn to the East Room for a concert by Garrick Ohlsson, pianist.

DINNER IN HONOUR OF
THE RIGHT HONOURABLE EDWARD HEATH
PRIME MINISTER OF THE UNITED KINGDOM
OF GREAT BRITAIN AND NORTHERN IRELAND

The White House
December 17, 1970
8.00 p.m.

Dress: Black tie ... long dresses for the ladies.

Photograph: At 7.40 p.m. you and Mrs. Nixon will come to the State Floor to have a photograph taken with a group of new social aides ... location is south end of the East Room ... after photo is taken, return to the Family Quarters.

Prime Minister Heath's Arrival: Standard Procedure—8.00 p.m. ... at north portico entrance ... Prime Minister Heath; Ambassador and Mrs. Mosbacher
—You will greet ... Mrs. Nixon remains in Yellow Oval Room
—Photo coverage of greeting

Yellow Oval Room Group: Standard Procedure
—Rogers, Annenbergs, Freemans, and Sir Alec Douglas-Home

will assemble just prior to the 8.00 arrival of Heath and the Mosbachers

—8.07 p.m. ... you present your gift to Prime Minister Heath (exact replica of the ship he is building for himself) ... official White House photographer and one photographer from British Embassy will be present

—Colour Guard will request permission to remove Colours at approximately 8.10 p.m. ... all guests depart except Prime Minister Heath

Grand Entrance: Standard Procedure

—Approximately 8.12 p.m. ... descend Grand Staircase preceded by Colour Guard ... Prime Minister Heath to your right; Mrs. Nixon to your left

—Pause at foot of staircase for official photos ... Prime Minister Heath to your right; Mrs. Nixon to your left

—Colour Guard reforms and procession moves to red carpet facing East Room ... pause during fanfare by trumpeters, Ruffles and Flourishes, and announcement ... take receiving line positions (Prime Minister Heath to your right; then Mrs. Nixon)

—Follow Colour Guard into East Room when 'Hail to the Chief' is played

Receiving Line: Standard Procedure

—Take position just inside centre door of East Room ... the chief of protocol will present your guests

—After receiving line, follow guests into State Dining Room

Dinner: Standard Procedure

—E-shaped table

—Army Chorus will sing Christmas carols during dessert

—As you lift your glass after toasting Prime Minister Heath, the Marine Orchestra will play 'God Save the Queen' ... at the conclusion of Prime Minister Heath's toast, the Marine Orchestra will play 'The Star-Spangled Banner' ... toasts will be piped to the press and to members of the official British Party who have been invited to the 10.00 musicale ... transcripts will be released to the press

After Dinner: Standard Procedure
  —Guests proceed to parlours for coffee, liqueurs, and cigars
  ... after-dinner guests join dinner guests in parlours
  —You and Mrs. Nixon and Prime Minister Heath are
  escorted to the Blue Room

Entertainment: Standard Procedure
  —Enter East Room through centre door and seat Mrs. Nixon
  in first row
  —Introduce entertainment (pianist Garrick Ohlsson) ... background information and suggested remarks are attached
  —At conclusion of performance, you and Mrs. Nixon go forward to thank performer
  —Photo opportunity for official White House photographer
  only

Departure: Standard Procedure
  —You and Mrs. Nixon and Ambassador and Mrs. Mosbacher
  escort Prime Minister Heath to the north portico
  —You and Mrs. Nixon are escorted to the Family Quarters
  —Champagne will be served to the guests who remain

NOTE: Lists of the dinner and after-dinner guests are attached.

SENATE MEETS IN SECRET. SEEKS TO END CRISIS CAUSED
BY FILIBUSTERS ... ARMY WILL DESTROY GERM WEAPONS
IN EARLY 1971 ... BRITAIN'S HEATH GOES HOME PLEASED
WITH TALKS IN U.S.

He is young, shrewd, sharp: more knowledgeable and more
philosophical that most who fit that description—and they are
many—around the White House; able to sit back and appraise
the operation with the candour and objectivity that the operation needs.

'Probably 1970 is the best thing that could have happened
to us, because if we had won that election we would have sailed
into '72 thinking that everything we were doing was right, while
ignoring various problems in the country and various weaknesses in our own approach.

'The fiasco of the President's God-awful final speech on election eve came down basically to the fact that when it was originally taped in Phoenix there was no thought of its being replayed, so it wasn't lighted or recorded or photographed very well. The staff was warned of the poor nature of the tape, but it was finally decided to go ahead and use it anyway, because there was a great time pressure involved—or so it was thought. NBC had agreed to set aside fifteen minutes in their L.A. studios that night if the President wanted it, but the President had an engagement in Riverside.

'So after lots of conferring it was decided by one or two top members of the staff that the Riverside engagement had to take precedence. So the lousy Phoenix tape was used, and you know the effect it made alongside Muskie's calm and statesmanlike address for the Democrats.

'I doubt if the matter was ever brought up to the President when the decision was made, so I don't think he can be blamed for it. And while disappointed in the result, I don't believe he has punished anyone who was concerned, and has not even reprimanded them very strongly.

'This indicated, I think, a real weakness of ours, which is that we are so dedicated to getting him where he is supposed to be on time that we are not flexible enough to take advantage of the opportunities that arise, or to do the things we should do to put him and the Administration in the best possible light. This really is one of our problems, but I think we are getting better and I think you are going to see some major changes in that area before too long.

'Another of our weaknesses is that we perhaps do not give the President a chance to react as *humanly* as he might want to if all the facts were presented to him. This is related to the fact that he has not fought perhaps as hard as he should have for his programme—which ties into what you tell me about the criticism of some old friends that he seems inhibited by the press and does not want to be as tough and as ruthless as necessary. I think this has been true in his pushing of the programme, but partly it is also due to the failure of those of us on the staff, and perhaps him personally, to realize that you have to state something to the country—and then keep restating it —and keep on hammering on it all the time. You can't just state it and then walk away assuming everyone in the country will instantly recognize how intelligent, noble and just you are.

'Most of us who came here in the staff were new to Washington and the government. We just assumed that if you had a good case and you were sincere and honest, as I think most of us are, then if you just stated it to the country, the country would accept it and would understand it and you wouldn't have to keep reiterating it. This isn't true. I think you will find from now on that the President is going to take a more aggressive stand in backing his programme and is going to keep hammering at things. I wouldn't want to see him do it in any bitter or unfriendly or exaggerated way, but I think he can do it firmly and positively and persistently, and that is what I think he is going to do from now on.

'Also the staff itself is beginning to open up—Haldeman, for instance, is going to go on the *Today* show, which is practically unheard of. [And is still unheard of, as of this writing, in July 1971.] And others are going to be more active. Ehrlichman and Shultz are going to hold some regional meetings in cities such as Memphis to explain the Administration programme on revenue sharing and the family assistance plan. This too will have an effect on the Administration's success in Congress and generally with the country.

'There was a lot of internal worry about the drastic government reorganization he has proposed. This has to go through Congress, and consequently it may not even get passed, but he believes it is right and he is going to go ahead with it, even though some people on the staff recommended that he wait until '72, when hopefully he will be re-elected and can do it in his final term.

'But it is going to cause a great rumpus, because each of these agencies and departments now has its own constituency and the committees of the Congress in fact are organized on departmental lines. If, for instance, there is no Labour Department as such, then the need for a Labour Committee of House and Senate disappears and this could mean a restructuring and abolishment of those committees. All of this will cause practically a revolution in the government. It will cause great opposition. I don't know what will come of it, but he believes we should make the attempt: somebody has to and we we are going to do it.

'I think Nixon probably has around him the best possible people for the jobs that need to be done. I try to look at it as objectively as I can knowing them as I do. It seems to me that really Haldeman is about the best executive and staff director I have ever known. Finch is an excellent idea man—he is no good in an administrative capacity, as he proved at HEW, but in the field of ideas and political sensitivity he is very good. The campaign of 1972 is already beginning to shape up with Mitchell doing the campaign planning and Finch doing the campaign sounding-out. He is moving around the country already beginning to sound out people, just as Mitchell is beginning to put together the organization. They complement each other very well.

'By the same token I think that John Ehrlichman is about the best you can find in that particular area of domestic policy. And George Shultz is an ideal choice for head of the Office of Management and Budget.

'The President has recently said to both Shultz and Ehrlichman, "Look, stop worrying about matching this dollar against that dollar. What we have to do is calculate the end result of these programmes and try to make them work for the good of the country. You can get too involved in the details and lose sight of the final objective. I want us to take a broader view of some of these things."

'Essentially, the President likes to have people that he likes around him. He seems to find it hard to work with people that he does not particularly care for. That may be a weakness but that is the way he is. You will find that he has a pretty good idea of who performs on the staff and who doesn't, and you can judge by how close people are to him whether he feels easy with them and feels that they are doing their jobs. He is very thoughtful, very easy to work with and goes out of his way for small personal touches.

'I think that you are going to find that the Administration will change substantially in the next few weeks and months. We are going to be much more conscious of how to present our programme and much more effective, I think, in doing so. Whether we can get Congress to go along with us is another matter, but at least we will make an aggressive statement of our aims and go after them. This should put the President in reasonably good shape for 1972.

'It could be that your friend who thinks we are entering an era of one-term Presidents may be right. I hope not, because if so, then that means it's too big for anybody to really control, and I think if we reach that point, then we have just reached a point of going downhill.

'Largely I think we've created these problems for ourselves in this country because we have played to special groups and given special constituencies an interest in various programmes. They therefore have a vested interest in keeping the programmes and the expenditures going, which makes it very hard to cut back and control. Nonetheless, it has to be done. I think that the President is going to make a real attempt. I think that people are going to give him credit for it and this will help in '72.'

Top officer of one of the independent agencies, explaining how you get the President—any President—committed to something: 'If you can slip an idea past the staff and get it approved for inclusion in the State of the Union or some other major speech, the President is then locked into a given position on it. Sometimes he didn't even intend this when he spoke, but once it's in there, you can always point to it when you get into an argument with the staff or the OMB and say, "See, the President wants it." This becomes a pretty potent weapon.'

OKINAWANS BATTLE GI'S, BURN CARS. ISLANDERS RESENT
U.S. 'ARROGANCE' ... EGYPTIAN OFFICIALS SEEK RUSSIAN
AID ... U.S. REPORT ON PORNOGRAPHY OUTSELLING THAT
ON RADICAL SPEAKERS ... A-SUB BASE IN CUBA HELD NEARLY
READY.

Dr. Walter Tkach is chief physician to President Nixon and was formerly assistant physician to President Eisenhower. He has two assistants, a Navy doctor who is a gastrointestinal man and an Air Force doctor who specializes in ear, nose and throat. Dr. Tkach, a general practitioner, maintains a small clinic on the ground floor of the White House for members of the staff. He is another of the many in the White House who spend much of their time just waiting until they are needed by the President. But, as he found out with President Eisenhower's heart and ileitis attacks, when the call comes the White House doctor had better be ready. In the meantime, his duties consist principally of routine checks on his famous patient and some extensive planning for the many trips the President and Vice-President undertake.

'In addition to the physical security of the President or the Vice-President that the Secret Service has to worry about, we here have to worry about their medical security. Whenever a trip is planned, one of us from this office advances it. We go out, check over the route the President will take, check the place where he is going to stay, where the nearest hospitals are, the quickest way to get him there if an emergency occurs, the doctors available in the area to help out. We have a list of all the top medical men of this country and of any country abroad where he or the Vice-President might be travelling. Their medical dossiers go right along with them when they travel. We know before they leave Washington exactly where to find emergency treatment if they need it.

'One of us also travels with the President or Vice-President, and a basic amount of medical equipment goes along also. The principal emergency we have in mind is a heart attack or something requiring sudden use of oxygen, so the principal things we take are an oxygen machine, a defibrillator and of course major items of medication.

'I find that President Nixon, like President Eisenhower, is a good patient. When his doctors make a decision, he, like Ike, generally abides by it. Not always without a little grumbling, he's only human, but he sees the sense of it and goes along.

'I would say he is perhaps the healthiest of the four Presidents I have known with some degree of closeness, starting with Eisenhower. I see him about twice a week for a routine blood pressure check, which so far has always been O.K. The main thing that worries me is that he finds it difficult to get as much exercise as I would like him to have.

'He'll bowl once a month, maybe, but that's not enough. Nor does he do enough walking or enough swimming. I'm sorry the pool was taken out to make way for the new press quarters, because that's excellent exercise and it's too bad he can't do it.

'He does get tired, because he works so hard. He seems to be working all the time, if not in the Oval Office, then in the EOB or in the Lincoln Study upstairs. I think all Presidents ought to get entirely away from the job at least once a week, but Mr. Nixon doesn't do so, either because he can't or he won't.

'Be it ever so humble, there's no place like the White House, but it's a hell of a place to live. You're in a cage.'

Social commentary: the gently sceptical look on the face of the stately, white-haired, tuxedo-clad old Negro in the head usher's office when the very young, very bell-bottomed young Negro messenger boy, his frizzled hair three times the size of his head, comes by with the morning mail ...

Ken Cole, deputy to John Ehrlichman, is another of those young, handsome, earnest, hard-working types that abound in the White House these days. He is a little touchy on one of the principal criticisms from old-line Republicans.

'I know very well that there are charges made that certain elements in the staff are leading him in a "liberal" direction. I think he is still pretty much in the middle. Actually the studies presented to him don't lean one way or the other. We try to give him three or four options and he chooses the one that benefits more people, in his estimation—also, naturally enough, taking into consideration the political effects and whether it is feasible to get the proposal through Congress. Therefore you will find a somewhat zigzag pattern, without any leaning, really, towards either liberal or conservative side. He makes a selection of where the merits appear to fall.

'This is partly due to the fact that so much effort is made to balance the papers that are presented to him so that he really has a chance to make up his own mind. We are really not trying to persuade him, we are simply making sure that he gets all the facts. He does ask advice on lots of things and sometimes this gets to him in a position paper. Sometimes he will make phone calls or ask members of the staff. Sometimes he will ask us to make a sounding as to what we think about it or how people around the country think about it. But basically he makes up his own mind.

'He doesn't always do what we think he ought to do'—grin—

'but I think this system works awfully well, in my judgment. It has helped the President make some awfully difficult decisions.

'We have such a mix here on the staff, so many different people who feel differently about things, that I think there is a better representation than there has ever been before, particularly with relation to Congress and the White House and how things should be done.

'As for the President's alleged isolation, after all there are only so many things you can do in a day. We do our best to sort out what is important to him and to get on with that. People get through to him when they need to get through. When it is necessary, it is possible to make things happen. Of course, the Cabinet and the agencies do an awful lot of pushing and shoving trying to get the President's attention, and naturally we have to protect him from some of this. The President is trying to wrench the business-as-usual approach out of government and make things happen again. We do our best to help him.

'As for Agnew, I have been working much more closely with him lately and I think he is a hell of a guy. He is terrific. He is such a human being, very bright, grasps things more quickly and forcefully than most men I know. I think he is going to be a very good and real help in pushing the family assistance plan, revenue sharing and other major programmes. He got positioned badly earlier. The media reaction to some of the things he said positioned him badly and it takes a while for him to get over that. However, the Vice-President can do a terrific-job for us and I think he is going to. I think he already has, in fact.'

White House staffer, resigning to return to a great profession whose present direction troubles him: 'I am very much disturbed by the leftward trend of the media in recent years. There are very few voices left on the other side now. I think the media bears a heavy responsibility for creating the very troublesome situations in which we live. They have pandered to the violence, they have affected foreign policy in ways that have not been good for the United States and in general they are responsible for many of our present troubles, in my estimation.'

The 'Plans Committee' meets every Saturday morning and it is, as Dwight Chapin had told me, the public relations council of the White House—the image factory. It is held in Herb Klein's office, and he asked that the specifics of its discussions be off the record except in limited paraphrase. The committee works from a formal agenda which it sometimes adheres to and sometimes does not. Its debates range from solemn to profane as it struggles with the problem of how best to present more favourably an Administration that nine tenths of the White House press corps is absolutely and adamantly determined to present in a harsh, suspicious and hostile light.

On this day the first item on the agenda was a memo from Bob Haldeman—signed with a large and imperial 'H'—requesting the consensus on 'possible Presidential participation in a satellite conversation with Prime Minister Heath'. The consensus was that this would be great if it could be tied to a major event, otherwise it would look contrived and phoney.

Second item was a request by the Canadian photographer Karsh to take pictures of the President. Decision was deferred.

Third item was requests from various magazines for information on the President's reading habits. It was agreed that this must be handled with great care, because if the President were disclosed to read anything even remotely frivolous somebody would be sure to pick it up and make it the basis for snide criticism that would be used against him forever after.

Fourth item was the possibility of the President appearing on various types of informal television shows other than straight press conferences or talks. This too was considered a matter for further study.

Next came a discussion of the proper time for airing the President's State of the Union message to Congress in January. Should it be at noon, Washington time, the traditional hour? Or should it be in the evening when it would reach the widest possible television audience, a practice increasingly followed by occupants of the White House? The discussion grew heated as the traditionalists battled the let's-make-the-most-of-it group. Finally someone remarked with some disgust that he thought the idea was to strengthen the President's image and help him get re-elected, and he didn't see why in hell it was so important what Congress said about his timing. It was the President's right to go up there when he pleased and talk when he wanted to. It was finally decided to place all the options before the President.

[In the event, he talked in the evening in prime time, which is exactly what all astute Presidents since the advent of television have done and will continue to do.]

Sixth item on the agenda was 'how to counter the theme that the President is heartless and cold', and the discussion very quickly got down to a specific: the recent episode in which a little black poster girl had been turned away without having her picture taken with the President, an incident that had brought in its wake great and probably abiding rancour in the Negro community. Those who deplored the incident's effect on the President's image were explosive and blasphemous in their criticism of the way it had been handled. Those who were responsible said crisply that the President was working on a speech and it was decided it was best not to bother him: 'It was a judgment.' (It was admitted, however, that it was a judgment the President had known nothing at all about until the media went into full cry that night. It had not even been brought to his attention at the time.) Those who were responsible said defensively that the President can't see everybody who comes in. Those who objected said he had damned well better take half an hour, if necessary, to be photographed with a little black poster girl—especially since just a few days later he had been photographed with a little white poster boy. Those who were responsible said well, anyway, the little girl and her parents were going to be invited to a Sunday worship service in a couple of weeks, and maybe he could be photographed with her then. Those who criticized said that of course an apology could be made after an incident like that, but if it were made weeks after the event, 'Nobody will hear, nobody will know and nobody will give a damn.' Those who were responsible reiterated in a tone that showed they were not to be budged: 'It was a judgment.' And that ended that.

The discussion began at nine-thirty and ran to twelve-twenty. It was laced throughout, on every topic, with the Administration's obsession with the media—understandable, but in its way as crippling as the media's obsession with the Administration. There were several in the meeting who remarked with considerable asperity that criticisms could not be evaded or avoided, that they would come even without fair grounds for them, that they were part of the burden this Administration carried and so to hell with it—let the President do what he thought best and stop worrying. But the dominant mood was a fretful obsession which, translated into action down the staff, successfully seems to thwart any Presidential action or reaction that might be based on the simple justice of a situation, or the simple response to it that he might make if he were given the option that really counts most in the image of a President—the option to be human.

CONGRESS RECESSES, KEY BILLS DEFERRED. WELFARE, AGED AID SEEN LOST ... CONGRESS VOTES CAMBODIA AID ... NIXON DIRECTS CABINET TO PUSH MINORITY PLAN ... U.S. FIRM ON RAID OPTIONS. ROGERS PEGS VIET BOMBING TO GI'S SAFETY.

He is back in private law practice now, but like Bryce Harlow and Pat Moynihan, Murray Chotiner is never far from the Nixon White House. A political associate since the President's early days in public life, he looks exactly what he is—a political associate. There is about him the aspect and the air of one who has handled many campaigns, made many deals, attacked and been attacked by many enemies, entered and survived many battles. Against the youthful earnestness, brisk efficiency and glittering good looks of many of the Nixon crew, he stands out like some battered, experienced old badger, claws extended and always at the ready. He is giving behind the scenes advice on how to run the re-election campaign in '72 and if he has his way, it will obviously be a rough one.

'You ask me what the issues will be in '72. The war should be in excellent shape. The boys are coming home, the Vietnamization programme is moving forward. If we go on as we are now doing to wind it down, the public is going to realize that the President did have a plan to end the war, and that he has succeeded.

'The economy, of course, also is a big issue, but as present signs magnify themselves and prove out, the interest rate is going to go down, inflation is going to drop and the stock market is going to go up. Housing starts are increasing, the auto industry is gearing up for a better year. The unemployed are going back to work and there will be a noticeable upswing. By '72 we should either have good times in which people can see that he is cleaning up the mess that he inherited, or really bad times, in which case there wouldn't be any hope for him. But I am sure that we will be having good times.

'He also has cooled off the temper of the campuses and the streets and I really don't see how you're going to beat him. What are they going to run on if they don't have an issue? If you don't have one, you're dead. If there is nothing to complain about, they're going to have nothing to go on. About all they can do is say that they can do what we're doing, only better than Nixon. But that is hardly a real issue or a real campaign.

'The Democrats have a real disadvantage because there is nothing they can really advocate. They had the government since 1960 and all the crises and errors that we have had occurred in their administrations. So it is very hard for them to complain about what has been going on. Also, they don't have any outstanding personality. There is no one to get a glint in the eye of the public. They just can't get a glint in the public's eye. Teddy Kennedy gets a rather bloodshot look—because everybody knows about him. Muskie is not exciting. The same thing applies to Birch Bayh. McGovern doesn't turn anyone on at all. Proxmire is a lot better but still not very good. Jackson won't get moving, he's too opposed by some of his own people on ideological grounds. If we get any kind of team at all on our side, we'll be all right.

'I think Agnew should be on the ticket. The Republicans can lose an election if they sit on their hands. Agnew is one who will get them off their hands and get them working. He represents what a lot of people have been thinking and I don't think the President is unfriendly to him at all. The President remembers that there was a movement in 1956 to remove him from the ticket. He has a good memory and is a sensitive person and he sympathizes with the Vice-President now in these publicized efforts to get rid of him. I don't think that these people who are writing that the President wants to get rid of Agnew have checked with the White House, because I don't think that is true. There are a great many Republicans who might even vote against Nixon if Agnew were dumped from the ticket.

'I think the President is amazing in his self-control. I have seen him over the years when he has been up-tight about things, but somehow he has learned over the years to control and subdue his emotions. After losing the Presidency in '60 and the governorship of California in '62 he seems to have become completely relaxed. That seemed to settle something inside him.

'It's amazing to me how a man like President Nixon, with all the problems he has and with his past history of political defeats, can sit back with his feet on the desk, so to speak, and be as relaxed as he is. But now he doesn't have to shoot from the hip—he doesn't have to make snap decisions.

'He is such a blotter from the standpoint of absorbing facts that he can go to Camp David or his office here and within a short time he can have a picture of something in his mind. I remember the one time I went to Camp David with him, we left 3 p.m. Saturday afternoon. We went to church services up there on Sunday and then came back Sunday afternoon, so it was only about twenty-four hours, but it permitted him to just relax and get away. It gave him a chance to think, and even though those of us with him were not aware that he was working very much, I felt that he was thinking through his problems and that he got a great deal out of it.

'I think the President should get away just as often as possible from the White House. What a President needs is time to think. There is no vacation for the President—when he is at San Clemente or Key Biscayne or Camp David or here or anywhere he is on duty all the time. But I think he is taking things in stride now. He is more objective, he is more certain and in control of both himself and the situation.

'The White House staff operates efficiently. I think sometimes they are a little overprotective, but as far as his being isolated, that's malarkey and a lot of baloney. I don't see any isolation. I think people who want to get answers can get them either from him or from Bob Haldeman. And when he wants to see any of us he can. So I don't think there is any real isolation.'

ROGERS CURBS ROLE IN MID-EAST FORCE ... TWO JEWS SENTENCED TO DEATH IN LENINGRAD : NINE GET PRISON TERMS ... PRICE INDEX CLIMBS .3 PER CENT, SECOND SMALLEST RISE OF YEAR.

Comments on the academic life, as seen from 1600 Pennsylvania Avenue—

By the Administration's favourite cartoonist, on some of his Cambridge neighbours who came to the White House in the Kennedy, Johnson and Nixon Administrations: 'These professors get down here and find out they can get laid every day in Washington and they're never the same again.'

By the Administration's favourite brain, met mid-corridor with his hands full of documents for the President's approval: 'You can't possibly despise the so-called intellectuals more than I do, Mr. Drury, because I have lived and worked with them all my life and I know what phonies they really are. Your fictional portraits are much too kind, believe me.'

The Nixon method of formulating foreign policy positions, as described by Dr. Henry A. Kissinger, special assistant to the President for national security affairs, begins when potential crises first appear on the horizon. A memo is sent around to the effect that the President has expressed concern on such-and-such a problem. It is the desire to put before him certain options for meeting the problem, usually within six weeks from date. The problem is considered by the geographic or country group involved, which consists of representatives of the State and Defence departments, the Joint Chiefs of Staff and the CIA.

That group in due course sends its recommendations to a 'senior advisory review group' consisting of the Undersecretaries of State and Defence, the director of the CIA, the chairman of the Joint Chiefs of Staff and Kissinger, who presides.

At that point, Kissinger says, he challenges everything and 'fly-specs to a fare-thee-well to try to work the bugs out of it, because it simply is not worthy to be presented to the President until everything has been thrashed out.'

The recommendation then goes to the National Security Council, which Kissinger also heads. The NSC meeting opens with an intelligence briefing on the problem, usually given by Richard Helms, director of the CIA.

Then Kissinger says to the President, 'Mr. President, you have the following choices.' He never, he explains, gives the President his own opinion on which of the choices he favours.

'I don't want to, because for one thing, if I did the bureaucracy would keep a check list on my successes and my failures, and I don't want that to happen. I also scrupulously refrain from giving him my advice for the most important reason of all: if I were to try to slant things according to my own personal views, and he ever found out I was cheating in any way—that would be the last time he would ever seriously ask my advice on anything. I just don't want to jeopardize the position I have with him by doing that sort of thing.'

When I said good-bye to Henry Kissinger, who says little pleasantly, he explained that he had been delayed a bit in getting back to his office to see me because the President had called him in to ask what he thought about a matter that had been discussed at the National Security Council meeting that morning.

He had been so scrupulous about not expressing his opinion to the President, he explained, that the President had called him in to find out what it was.

Manolo Sanchez, native of Spain, four-year resident of Cuba, American citizen since Inauguration Day, 1969, has been the President's personal servant for nine years—the coffee-server, the briefcase-carrier, the attender to little details, the smoother of the Presidential day. His English is sometimes hard to understand, but his enthusiasm for his boss and the First Family shine through as glowingly as his appreciation of his adopted country. 'It is unbelievable to me, what has happened since I left Spain in 1956. I walk in the hallways at the White House, I look at the people, I can hardly realize where I am. My wife and I, we voted for the first time last November and we were so excited we couldn't sleep all night. We kept saying, "We're going to vote, we're going to vote!" Americans, you know, you take it for granted being here. But when you adopt this wonderful country, when you make a choice—*then* you know what being an American means....

'The President is so gentle, so patient. When I first came to work he would never get angry if I make a mistake, he would just keeping saying, "Don't worry, don't worry." My English was not so good then, you know, so I kept wondering about what is this "Don't worry." Finally I asked another Latin-American and he told me. And all the time I *was* worry about "Don't worry!" ...

'The President eats very light breakfast, very light lunch. Before he is going to have a press conference or some big speech, he eats very, very lightly all day long....

'He tells me sometimes, "Don't get mad. Don't ever get mad. When you get mad, things go twice as bad, you can't think." ...

'I only see him really upset once—when President Kennedy was shot. For a couple of days, he was—I have never seen him like that. But he doesn't worry about himself—he never worries about his own safety....'

SOVIETS TO TRY NINE MORE JEWS IN HIJACK CASE. ISRAELIS APPEAL FOR PAIR ... SOVIETS REJECT PROTESTS, CALL REACTION TO SENTENCES 'BIT OF HYSTERIA' ... SOVIET SCIENTISTS SUPPORT ANGELA DAVIS ... NIXON SIGNS BILL EXPANDING U.S. BIRTH CONTROL PROGRAMME.

JULIE

The interview was set for 3 p.m. when she returned from practice teaching of the fourth grade at St. Anthony's School. I went in the east gate to the regular East Wing reception area where Helen Smith, Mrs. Nixon's press secretary, came down and took me over to the Mansion. We went up to the second floor into what is known as the West Hall. The last time I was there was when I attended a Lyndon Johnson press conference a couple of years ago and he invited me and several others to come up for coffee afterwards. That was in the morning around eleven o'clock, in the summertime, and we had a very pleasant visit. The same sofas and chairs were there and the same white telephone hanging on the stand beside the same chair that Lyndon used. However, the bank of buttons, probably twenty-five or thirty, which Lyndon was so fond of, is no longer there. Instead there is just the white telephone.

Julie came down the long centre hall from the East Wing, which is beautifully decorated with many sofas and comfortable chairs along the hallway, lighted chandeliers and many pictures loaned by the Metropolitan Museum and others. She came in as natural and cute as a little button, said hello and asked me to sit in a chair beside the sofa. She said this was the room where they sit to relax in the evenings because the yellow-decorated Oval Room along the hall on the right side is much too formal for family gatherings. She said this end of the hall is where she and Tricia sometimes eat dinner and watch television. She said her father does not watch television in this room and in any event does not watch it while eating dinner. 'But Trish and I do.'

How was her father standing the grind of the Presidency?

'What amazes Mother and Tricia and me is that he doesn't seem overburdened by it. He wanted it so much that he seems to just take it in his stride. He seems to carry all these things and not worry too much about it. Dwight Chapin has told me that when the staff is feeling rather low, he is apt to feel rather high and relaxed, and so that seems to lift up their spirits. The only time I have really seen him worried was during Cambodia, when he felt that he had to do what he thought was right even though some major members of his staff were against him on it. After the speech we all gathered in the solarium [the casually furnished family playroom on the third floor] and I remember that he was quite worried about it. But that is the only time I have seen him really disturbed by a decision.

'He is serious but he is never gloomy. I think that if a man tends to be gloomy, the Presidency brings out all the bad sides of his character. So I'm glad he isn't gloomy because if he were it would be kind of rough. He's always telling us not to worry, to turn off the television, don't read the newspapers and don't get upset by what people say about him, because that's all part of the game. Of course, you have to have a lot of self-confidence before you can ever run for the Presidency. But when you have it, I guess you also have the confidence to just keep going once you get in here.

'I do like campaigning myself and I enjoy politics. In '68 Tricia and I were in thirty-seven States. David also enjoys it a lot.

Did she think David would run for President some day?

A quick smile.

'Oh no, I don't think so.'

Then a thoughtful smile, head on one side.

'Of course, I think he'd be good at it, but you know, politics is such a demanding career, and you just have to devote your life to it, and I don't think he really wants to ...'

And then more thoughtfully still, the smile returning.

'Of course, he's very interested in politics and really enjoys it ...'

How does her mother stand the pressure?

'Mother stands it very well, and I think in some ways her part of it is harder than my father's. He gets the reward of making big decisions but she has just to take the criticisms along with him and she doesn't get these kinds of rewards. I really think that in her case the press doesn't give her praise for what she deserves and what she does because they think it will help him if they do. This doesn't bother her, but it bothers me....

'I never get over the feeling of being excited by the White House, particularly when you drive in or drive past. I remember before we moved in here that when I would drive past, I would think, "What's really going on in there?" And it still really hits me that we're living here. I'm just as excited about it still as I was when we first moved in.'

She asked me if I had seen some of the other rooms on the second floor and I said no, I hadn't. She took me down the hall to the small, intimate Lincoln Study where her father has the big, comfortable armchair he brought from his New York days, and where he likes to sit and think, listen to stereo and write on his yellow legal pads, one of which was on the desk beside the chair. There were several hundred stereo tapes, many books on shelves, desk and floor, logs in the fireplace. She said he always likes to have a fire.

'In fact, when Prince Charles and Princess Anne were here in July we went to a ball game and it was so hot sweat was literally running down our backs. When we got back here we were supposed to have an early supper with him before they got on their plane. When we came in the Family Dining Room he said he would like to have a fire. Of course, it was air-conditioned. The Prince and Princess didn't say anything but he went ahead and had a fire, so there we were in July with a fire going.'

She said the room was called the Lincoln Study because it is right off the Lincoln Bedroom. I asked if I might see that: a huge room with sofas, chairs, an enormous bed with a very ornate and elaborate headboard. She said Mrs. Lincoln bought the bed for her husband but that he had never slept in it because he thought it was too ornate. It is obviously made for a man of great height. She then took me across the hall to see the Queen's Room and said that five queens had stayed there over the years, the most recent Queen Elizabeth II.

We then walked back down the hall to the sofa in the West Hall and chatted for a few more moments, during which she remarked that she thought the White House machinery was just 'too big'.

'It's such a bureaucracy, you can't get through. You can't get things done. It seems to me that people who need decisions get stopped at the first desk—things don't really get through to the people who really can make the decisions. I suppose it's inevitable, but still it seems to me that it's just too big.'

She said that she has a poodle, while Tricia has a Yorkshire terrier and her parents have King Timahoe. She said that this is because the very first dog they had when they were married was an Irish setter, and one of the first presents her mother ever gave her father was a paperweight in the form of an Irish setter, which he still has on his desk.

She was completely charming, unspoiled, spontaneous and uninhibited: a delightful daughter for any parents to have.

We then talked briefly about *Advise and Consent*, which she had recently read, and she asked some questions about it, and about the new book. Then she took me to the elevator and I went down to the ground floor and back out through the long central hallway to the east gate, and so out into the sharp and biting winter winds.

(JAMES) FARMER URGES NIXON TO SPEAK OUT ON RACIAL ISSUES ... REDS HIT TOWN IN CAMBODIA .. MORE JEWS FACE TRIAL IN RUSSIA ... (DEMOCRATIC CHAIRMAN) O'BRIEN HOPEFUL FOR '72: NIXON HAS 'FAILED TO WIN TRUST.'

FIRST LADY

She is really a very lovely and striking woman, particularly her eyes, dark and deep-set; dresses very simply and smartly; has a very pleasant manner, although I got the feeling that she was somewhat tense at the beginning of the interview and was watching me very closely to see the general tenor of my questions and whether they were going to be hostile to her husband in any way. After a bit she began to relax, but every once in a while there would be a very careful, studying glance to see what I was leading up to, or how I was reacting to something she had said. This undoubtedly comes from years of having to defend him against interviewers and is a rather unhappy sidelight: but, I suppose, inevitable considering the political life they have been through and the incessant attacks they have had to take for twenty years.

'We just use the west end of the house, mostly the West Hall, where most of our family life is concentrated. We feel like we're living in a museum to some extent, particularly when we come up the driveway and there's the house in front of us and I think, "That's where I live!" Sometimes I find it hard to believe to this day.

'Dick never really gets away from his work. Things come up constantly. I would prefer that he take time off, but it just isn't possible. We did go over the other night and bowl for a little while: then he went back to work again. That's the first time we've been able to do that in about a month, and that isn't enough. But I just don't know any solution for it.

'He is so thoughtful of all of us. He is always planning little surprises and little gifts for us. He has a marvellous sense of humour. He is not a cold man. I have never seen anyone more thoughtful than he is. He gives an awful lot of time to our girls and me and he is always doing something nice for others, or asking me to do things for them, or asking the girls to do things for them.

'He always thinks of us. He does the little things that mean so much. He also is very thoughtful of our feelings about the criticisms he receives. When he gets some good editorials or comments in the morning, he will frequently have them Xeroxed and sent over to the house to us so that we can have a bright spot in the day, too.

'I think we all feel that California is truly home, but Florida is nice for a weekend. As for my own exercise, I swim and I like to go bowling when I can. When we are at San Clemente or Florida I like to walk along the seashore. For instance, when we were at San Clemente last week I walked two and a half miles down the beach to the Marine station. It began to get dark and

I really had not told anyone particularly where I was going—I just sneaked out and went for a walk. When I got back I found that Dick and Tricia were beginning to get quite worried. But the Secret Service is very good and always watches over us, and this time, although I didn't see him during the walk, when I got back, he stepped down from the bluff along the top and I knew that he had been following me right along all the time. They are awfully good about being there but keeping themselves unobtrusive. Of course, the constant surveillance does cramp one a great deal, but they couldn't be nicer or more devoted . . . but even so, just to have someone around all the time is bothersome to all of us . . . but, of course, there's no help for that.

'When I go with Dick on cross-country tours I see a lot of projects in the field and I report to him just as I do when I am going by myself. I remember when we were in Goose Prairie, Illinois, during the campaign, they were saving this last little strip of natural countryside with a combination of private funds and government funds and I went out to see it and attend the ceremony. It was just a small area but it meant a great deal to them and in a larger sense to all of us, and I was pleased to do it and be there with them.

'As for the social and ceremonial duties here, I have done it for so long that it hasn't been a real chore. I think I probably enjoy that part of it most, as a matter of fact. Before visitors come here on state visits I get briefing papers so that I know the points they are interested in, although as a matter of fact so many of the people who come here now as heads of government were well on their way to becoming so in the days when Dick was Vice-President. Therefore we know many of them already and it's easy to talk with them and make them feel at home. When it comes to planning parties, state dinners and so on, I sit down with the social staff and we discuss in advance what the menu is going to be, the entertainment and so on. The staff is excellent, but in the planning stages I often have to get into the act because I know some things from other administrations that they don't know and I find them making errors from time to time which need to be corrected.

'I like to do a lot of entertaining. We like a lot of young people in the house. We do a lot of family entertaining here, in addition to all the official entertaining that we have to do ...

'I'm not surprised you have heard King Timahoe barking, because he really likes to get out and run and it is impossible to let him do it as much as he would like. So he keeps complaining. The girls have always had dogs and each of them has one now. We also have always had cats, but our last cat died at a very great age a while back and we just felt that the White House was not a place for a cat. So we don't have one now.

'I really have so much to do with all the people I see on different problems and projects that I really don't know where the days go. I spend about four hours a day on my mail and I like to, because I really learn a lot from the mail. We get quite heavy mail most of the time and of course it zooms up substantially whenever there is a major national issue under discussion. When Dick was in the Senate I used to go down as a volunteer to his office and help answer the mail, and I still like to take a real hand at it now.

'I've always been interested in what he was doing. That's why we've been so close for thirty years.

'The trips overseas have been interesting and fascinating particularly my own trip to Peru. We had a rather wild ride getting in on a cargo plane and I think that this was one of the most exciting things about it.'

Was she amused by Tricia's avoidance of the press, particularly concerning her engagement? She smiled.

'We're all like that. I knew Trish would be like that, but she goes right ahead and does what she wants to do. She doesn't let the criticism get her down and I don't think she's going to. She just made up her mind that she's going to lead her own life even though she is in the White House, and she's going to do it ...

'Dick is a very dedicated person. I don't think that anyone who doesn't have the dedication he has could have gone through what he did go through to get where he is. He knows what he is going to do and he is going to accomplish it if he possibly can. He can't be deterred by anyone once he sets his mind on doing something.

'He and David are very close. They watch football games together and other sports events and they really have a good time together. They have played golf together and I would say that in a sense he has been a real comfort to Dick.'

Did she think David would go into politics someday? She smiled.

'I think he has a tremendous interest.'

Then she laughed.

'It scares me! ...

'Dick has a marvellous sense of humour—what you might call a situational humour. He always begins his speeches with some little note on something that has happened. I remember when we had the Republican National Committee reception over here, he spoke and cracked jokes and people were surprised because they didn't know he had this kind of humour. Frequently on the platform when he's campaigning, he likes to make some situational joke. He does this all the time but sometimes it doesn't appear in the newspapers, because of course it's not part of the prepared text of the speech. And also'—thoughtfully—'some people just don't want to write about it because they think it makes him seem more human and likeable.

'He is very spontaneous about things like that. For instance, he sat down and played the piano at the Christmas party for the children that we gave here—played Christmas carols. He always thinks like *that*'—she snapped her fingers—'about spontaneous things that he can do. I think the proof of his warmth is that the children gathered around him and put their arms around him. Children know.

'They don't cuddle up to people unless they have something going between them.

'He's very thoughtful about phone calls also. He will call someone on some very special day. He uses the phone a great, great deal. I don't use it so much nor do the girls. It is not unusual for him to talk with the girls from his office several times a week. When Julie is away with David he almost always calls her on the weekends.

'He usually starts the day breakfasting with someone, the Cabinet or Mike Mansfield or someone else he wants to talk to, and he keeps going pretty much all day long. He will sometimes come over just in time to dress for dinner. In fact, that's one of my big worries—that he works so hard and so long.

'He really sees a lot of people at San Clemente and I think it's a good thing that he has a place out there, because in a sense,

I think it has brought the country closer together to have a so-called 'Western White House'. It indicates that all parts of the country are important to the President, not just the White House here in Washington.

'He has exquisite taste in everything. He can look at something, some item or some planning for something, and point out the errors in it right away, if it's not right. And he's always correct, too, I must say!

'He always has time for the girls and me. Two or three times a week we all eat together privately in the Family Dining Room. We have a good visit, we eat a good meal, we have music and candles with dinner and everything is very nice. Then he has to go back to work.'

SENATE FREES OLD-AGE BILL FOR PASSAGE ... SOVIETS TO SPEED LENINGRAD APPEAL ... ISRAELIS APPROVE TALKS. EGYPT GREETS CABINET VOTE WITH CAUTION ... U.S. TO AUTHORIZE NON-ATOM BUILD-UP.

TRICIA

We talked in the Yellow Oval Room on the second floor, which she said was her favourite room in the house, both because of its elliptical shape and because of the colour, which she described as 'bright and cheerful and fun'.

She is surprisingly tiny; beautiful peaches-and-cream complexion; sparkling dark eyes, very beautiful blonde hair; has a way of cocking her head on one side and smiling a bit as she thinks of an answer, which is very like her mother and sister—perhaps more like her mother. Charming, as are all the Nixon ladies.

I began by saying that I wanted to congratulate her on her success in escaping the press and preserving her privacy in the White House. She laughed merrily and thanked me for it.

'I just made up my mind that I was going to lead my own life and so I do. They keep after me but I've managed to do what I want to do. I think that's important and I've succeeded in doing it.

'I don't often go to the formal dinners here because I find them rather boring—partly because at the table, you only have two people to talk to, one on each side, and if they're dull then you're stuck for the rest of the evening. At the type of party where you can circulate around and talk to lots of people, you're apt to find someone, or perhaps many people, you can relate with and enjoy.

'Living in the White House, of course, is a fascinating thing for me because I majored in history and I'm very familiar with the history of the house. Just being here is an historical experience. It can't help but have an effect upon those who live here. At first I thought a little bit about living in an apartment. Then I thought, no, I would live here, because I thought that if I looked back afterward and I hadn't done it, I would think, "Whatever got into you that you didn't take advantage of that historic opportunity? You'd be crazy not to do it." So I do live here now. However, in a way it's like living in some sort of institution. I never feel quite at home in the White House and I don't think most people do.

'I do think my mother has tried very hard to make it warm, and I think she has succeeded very well in the West Hall and here on the second floor in the family rooms. However, there still is that feeling of a museum which you can never quite get away from.

'To really relax I go out of the White House—I go to friends' homes or to their apartments. For one thing, here you never know who you're going to run into in the hall. For instance, last night my father was having a dinner downstairs and I had some friends upstairs on the third floor in the solarium, thinking we were going to be perfectly private and have a good time and not bother his party, and vice-versa. But apparently someone down there asked about the solarium and he said, "Let's go look at it", and next thing we knew, we were being invaded. But they were interesting people and we had fun, so it was all right.

'It's not dull living here, that you can be sure. It is not dull....

'I'm not the greatest sportswoman in the world and I don't do a great deal to relax in the way of sports. But I have tried ice skating and last weekend they tried to get me up on skis, which I find I enjoy a little bit. I love the beach and I particularly love San Clemente because we have beach there as far as the eye can see. I don't like Florida as well because I don't like tropical climates. California is sort of intermediate and I like it much better. Probably'—laughing cheerfully—'that will make us lose Florida next time, but that's how I feel.'

She asked if I had seen the film *Dr Zhivago* because her dog, a Yorkshire terrier, is named after one of the characters. I said I had seen the movie. She said she reads a lot and sees a good many movies.

'We show quite a few here in the White House. My father is very patient and very loyal to a movie. He's the last one to walk out on one if it's bad. The rest of us keep saying let's go, come on, this is lousy, but he says no, let's wait a bit and maybe it will get better. He is a perpetual optimist about everything, including people.

'It always amuses me and sometimes annoys me when the press writes critically that "the President left the party at 11.20", let's say, and left the guests dancing downstairs in the East Room. Well, sometimes he has gone to see Dr. Kissinger and they had business to transact at that hour. And other times he has just been tired and felt he had a right to go to bed. I think that's perfectly understandable.

'How do I regard the press? Well, I think they're a necessary evil—no, I won't say that, because they aren't really evil. They have their job to do and I suppose that without them the public would not be informed, and in a way a President could not really do what he wants to do because he couldn't get public opinion behind him. However, I do think that sometimes the questions in the press conference are not so much questions as they are an indictment. I don't think that is so good ...

'How do I regard my parents? I suppose that's the most impossible question for any child to answer. I am glad they are my parents. I love them. They've been very understanding and patient with both Julie and me. They've always been there when it counted. It's true my mother has always said she felt guilty because they had to be away so often when my father was Vice-President, when we were growing up. But in a way that's contributed to our independence too.

'If ever there was a disciplinarian in the family—and there never was very much of a one—it was my mother. My father is a real soft touch, from everything to letting the dogs come to the table and feeding them when my mother doesn't want him to, to everything else. He has always been there to give advice but he has always waited to be asked. He has felt that we were on our own, in a sense—that we *should* be on our own. He has encouraged us to acquire independence and lead our own lives. We have always known he would be there when we needed him, and that has given us a great sense of security, because we have had our independence but at the same time we knew that the parents were there.

'It is a very wonderful thing to know that your parents trust you, and Julie and I have always had that. There have never been any very strong rules in the house, no saying when we had to be in in the evening or anything of that sort. We have really had a very wonderful upbringing, I think.

'As for how my father is standing the Presidency, I don't think I have ever seen a person more dedicated than he is to his job. I think that lets him carry the terrible burden that he has to carry. If he didn't have the conviction that he was contributing something to the country, and the feeling that he can accomplish something for all Americans, I think that it would be almost too great for him to bear—I suppose too great for any President to bear, because they all must have felt that. I think that keeps him going.

'Actually, though, he is just the same sort of person he was when he was Vice-President—fun-loving, with great areas of humour, a very relaxed person, at least outwardly, and very easy to get along with. He is sort of the favourite father of my friends because he likes to listen. He likes young minds around him and he wants to find out what they are thinking. We really have had some lively discussions here in this house, with a lot of give-and-take, when my friends have come here and we've got into arguments about things.

'I think both generations have learned a lot from one another in this house since we have been here.'

SENATE VOTES RISE IN SOCIAL SECURITY ... INDOCHINA TROOP CURBS APPROVED ... PRESIDENT SIGNS JOB SAFETY MEASURE ... ISRAEL: STRENGTH KEYED TO SUCCESSFUL TALKS.

In early December a recommendation arrived at the White House from some downline functionary in the Department of

Health, Education and Welfare that the President veto a bill
to provide permanent financial assistance and medical care for
a former employee who had been hopelessly injured in the
government service. The recommendation was based on a highly
technical point, and it advised that the President hand down his
veto on the day before Christmas. Such 'private relief bills', as
they are called in Congress, are routine and the veto might well
have slipped through automatically in the shuffle of papers sent
the President if an alert staff member had not caught it.

The staff member does not quite believe that the recommen-
dation for such a veto of such a measure at such a time was
made maliciously by someone in HEW. But he is not entirely
sure. It would have meant some jolly headlines and television
broadcasts for Mr. Nixon if it had not been stopped.

Eternal vigilance is the price of being a Republican President.

At year's end the staff, reacting officially to criticisms of Presi-
dential 'isolation', issued statistics:

In his first two years in office he travelled 185,000 miles, visited
17 countries, talked with governors more than 150 times, enter-
tained more than 13,000 guests at 132 dinners, welcomed another
40,000 to breakfasts, luncheons, teas, coffees, receptions. He
signed 776 bills, issued 131 proclamations, 121 executive orders,
sent out almost 6000 telegrams. He met with businessmen 150
times, labour leaders 30, racial minority groups 30, campus rep-
resentatives 50. He held 12 formal news conferences and had
more than 200 personal and telephone conversations with indi-
vidual members of the media.

The statistics were received with a shrug in Washington, for
still, to many, there remained an inescapable and unshakeable
feeling of isolation, based upon an old political truism: a spon-
taneous visit to Congress or a hearty slap on a Congressional
back a couple of times a year is worth any number of rigidly
scheduled appointments behind the guarded gate.

And this, unfortunately for him in many ways, is not a slap-
on-the-back President or a slap-on-the-back Administration.

On the late afternoon of New Year's Eve, with most of the staff
gone home, he did one of those spontaneous human things he
can do—when the staff has gone home. Moved by a sudden

impulse, he left his office and walked to the press quarters. There he found four reporters, two photographers and two broadcast network technicians still on duty. 'Darkness,' as the AP's Frank Cormier reported, 'had fallen and snow was falling even more heavily.'

The President said it was a social occasion, invited the surprised newsmen to his office in the EOB, poured martinis for those who wished them, had Manolo Sanchez serve drinks of choice to the rest. He said he mixes the finest martini in the world and offered his 'secret formula' to those who wanted it. He himself, 'sipped sparingly on a single glass of white wine'.

As Cormier and UPI's Helen Thomas reported the conversation, it was a curiously wistful mixture of nostalgia, boastfulness and practicality. It was also the conversation of a man who just wanted to relax and act like a human being and found himself with one of those rare opportunities when he was free to get away and do so.

Asked if the Presidency were different today from the 1950s when Dwight D. Eisenhower was in the White House and he was Vice-President, he said the fifties were quieter, the Chief Executive had fewer complex problems, there were fewer splits in the body politic, especially in Congress.

Asked if he ever worried about major decisions he had made, Cormier reported, 'Mr. Nixon turned to the language of sports. No, he said, suggesting for example, a duffer golfer should always forget his last shot—especially a bad one—and concentrate on the chore immediately at hand.

'In golf, Mr. Nixon suggested, too much looking backward can lead a duffer to string together a series of bad shots.'

He made the comment after remarking that his own decisions —citing his move in launching the Cambodian strike—could not lead him to second thoughts.

Helen Thomas noted that he had remarked, somewhat tartly, that he was not isolated—he knew what was going on and 'can't be hoodwinked'.

He described his staff as having the highest IQs since the group that surrounded the late President Franklin D. Roosevelt in his first term—'all those fellows are champions when you get in the ring with them.'

He denied that Henry Kissinger and Secretary of State William Rogers were rivals for his ear in decision making and described them as 'very intelligent men who work well together'. He, he said firmly, makes the decisions.

He also denied stoutly that he personally felt lonely in his job. 'That's a lot of nonsense that the Presidency is the loneliest job in the world.'

Later that night, back in the Mansion, he and Mrs. Nixon rang in 1971 watching Guy Lombardo's orchestra on television. Later he called several special friends: evangelist Billy Graham, comedians Bob Hope and Jackie Gleason, actor John Wayne. Then the lights went out in the family quarters and the Nixons slept, while across the nation the New Year's parties roared and in Washington the heaviest snowfall in years kept hissing gently down, softly, inexorably, to cover the silent floodlit house and the ghostly deserted streets of the uneasy, imperial city.

PRESIDENT IN EXCELLENT HEALTH, DOCTOR SAYS AFTER CHECK-UP ... YEAR-END GALLUP POLL: NIXON 'MOST ADMIRED'.

3. All Around the Town

The weather is bitterly cold.

In Lafayette Park across Pennsylvania Avenue from the White House the wind is driving the leaves across the huddled grass. In front of the northwest gate the Hare Krishnans dance, jumping up and down and banging their drums with an extra zeal contributed by the biting flurries that whip their orange scarves about their heads and hike their orange skirts. The impassive guards watch from the control box. Presently the pseudo-Tibetans leave, defeated by the pseudo-Tibetan weather ...

Past the east gate a wild, dishevelled, grey-haired man, talking violently to himself, walks by the impassive guards, who follow him with their eyes but do not move their heads as he rages on down the street, propelled by some vicious internal anger ...

The fat, squat, stumpy young woman, almost as wide as she is tall, who has been wandering the shopping areas of F Street and Connecticut Avenue for the past few days, walks stolidly past the northwest gate. She is dressed in dungarees and a dirty blue sweater. Passers-by look startled, shake their heads with puzzled smiles. The impassive guards watch but do not move as they read the enormous cardboard sign strapped across her back:

'I WAS TAKEN FROM CANADA BECAUSE I CAN PROVE JOHN F. KENNEDY, ROBERT F. KENNEDY AND MARTIN LUTHER KING WERE MURDERED BY THE FBI AND THE CIA ...'

At 'the other end of Pennsylvania Avenue'—as it is described in Washington, though Pennsylvania Avenue stretches far both east and west beyond the embittered mile that Washington means—sit the 535 men and women who possess the final power to make or break Presidents.

Some strong, some weak, some noble, some ignoble, some old and calculating and crafty from many years in office, some impatient and angry with the arrogance of the young and newly elected, they wait in the arena for each succeeding Daniel. Sometimes, if he is strong, if he belongs to their majority, they will get along with him well—for a little while. Sometimes, if he is strong but does not belong to their majority, they will still get along with him well—for a little while. But sooner or later they will snarl. Sooner or later the first claw will come out. Sooner or later they will turn and rend, whoever it is.

The event is perhaps inevitable, under the American system, and perhaps it is best for a democracy that it should be so.

But it does not make life easier for Presidents, who come and go beneath the generally restless, and frequently downright hostile, gaze of the Congress of the United States.

It is ten in the morning, and once again, as on so many occasions before, the Senate Foreign Relations Committee has a date with a member of the President's Cabinet. Almost always it is the same member, the Secretary of State, or his Tweedledum in foreign policy, the Secretary of Defence. They follow one another around and around as through a revolving door, surfacing for a few hours of heated argument as they are whirled into the committee room, vanishing for another spin and then reappearing within a few days, or weeks, or sometimes only hours, to face the committee again. In recent years, spurred by Vietnam, the tone of the committee has been consistently displeased, disgruntled, uneasy and suspicious regardless of Administration. It is nothing new for its members to joust with the Secretary of Defence, as they are about to do this morning, but it is instructive, for it says much about the position and the response of the Nixon Administration as unlucky inheritors of the errors of the recent past.

The committee meets in its rather small brown-panelled hearing room in the New Senate Office Building. Plaques of various areas of the globe adorn the walls. In the opening moments before the session begins, television cameramen prepare their equipment, still photographers position themselves, members of the press gather at their tables. In the audience a number of long-haired, bearded youths and their blank-eyed girl friends shove and jostle for position with sedate and more elderly types. Capitol police stand along the walls looking nervous. But the mood is interested and attentive, and there is no evidence of any real problem.

Shortly before 10 a.m. the chairman, Senator William Fulbright (Democrat, Arkansas), enters with his usual smug, superior and supercilious look. He is accompanied by the recently defeated Albert Gore (Democrat, Tennessee), whose expression is peaked and bitter. A moment later Secretary of Defence Melvin Laird sweeps in accompanied by the Joint Chiefs of Staff, glittering in their uniforms and medals. They move to the witness stand, take their seats, smile amiably at the Senators, who smile amiably back, everyone aware that they are about to engage in another of those bitter tugs-of-war that make the Nixon Administration's road in foreign policy so difficult.

The issue is the Administration's request for authorization of additional aid for Cambodia. Israel is in there too, but of course Cambodia is today's red flag for the committee.

Fulbright opens the proceedings by complaining in his customary petulant tone that the committee is probably not going to have very much time to question the Secretary. The Secretary explains politely that he is hosting a lunch for Israeli Defence Minister Moshe Dayan at 12.15 p.m. and so must leave in time for it. This allows the committee approximately two hours in which to give him a good going-over, but Fulbright is still disgruntled. Finally he agrees that it is really very unfortunate, but of course the Secretary will have to keep his date with General Dayan.

Fulbright notes that the House has passed the appropriation for this new aid before it even passed an authorization bill. Would Laird recommend that the Senate do the same?

Laird replies that he realizes Congress is desirous of an early recess for the Christmas holidays, so 'whatever route Congress decides to take, I support as Secretary. I realize these are two equal branches of government, and whatever you wish to do, we are very desirous to co-operate.'

'Since you left the Hill [where he was a Congressman from Wisconsin for sixteen years]' Fulbright says with an ironic little twinkle, 'I think the legislature is not so co-equal as it used to be.'

They join in the jolly laughter of two implacable antagonists just before the battle.

Fulbright informs Laird that his committee staff has secured figures which show that it is possible to give to Cambodia, under already authorized appropriations and from the President's emergency funds, a total of $350,000,000. He wants to know why it is necessary to have new legislation when all this is available. At this point Senator George Aiken (Republican, Vermont) enters, looking every inch the white-haired, homespun New England sage. He takes his seat at Fulbright's right as the ranking Republican member of the committee.

Laird replies that the reason for the new request for Cambodia is 'simply a matter of being out of money'. When Fulbright continues to pick at it, Laird starts to say blandly, 'As far as the funding of Israel is concerned—'

But it doesn't work.

'That's another matter,' Fulbright says quickly. 'Israel is already authorized.'

Immediately thereafter it becomes apparent that the committee is out for bigger game than either Israel or Cambodia, as Fulbright asks, 'Did you personally review the [intelligence] photographs of the Son Tay [prisoner-of-war] camp?'

At this reference to the empty-handed raid on the presumed American POW camp in North Vietnam, Laird tenses a bit and remarks that the photographs 'are on my desk'.

'Will you make them available to the committee?'

'I will be glad to discuss them in closed session with the committee.'

'It will be extremely important if you could make those photos available to the committee,' Fulbright persists. 'Is there any reason why they cannot be made available to the committee?'

'I see no reason,' Laird finally admits, grudgingly.

Fulbright asks who made the final decision to launch the raid. Laird says the final decision was 'made by me, of course, with the authority of the Commander in Chief'.

Fulbright wants to know why the leaders of the raid can't be brought before the committee. Laird says, 'several committees of Congress have requested their appearance and I am studying these requests.'

'However, *we* have a resolution concerning the raid before us,' Fulbright points out smoothly. 'These other committees do not have, as I understand it. Therefore, why can we not have these men before us?'

'The resolution you have deals with the heroism of these men,' Laird says with equal smoothness. 'I think Admiral Moorer [Chairman of the Joint Chiefs of Staff] and others can testify as to their heroism. This resolution, after all, deals with their heroism.'

'It also deals with the purposes of the raid,' Fulbright reminds him sharply.

'The President said last night in his press conference that everything would be made public about this raid.'

Fulbright asks again why the leaders cannot appear and Laird reiterates doggedly that 'we have several other requests for these men to appear'. 'Is any request more urgent than this one?' Fulbright inquires.

Senators Stuart Symington of Missouri and John Sherman Cooper of Kentucky come in, both looking tired and worried, to take their seats along the rim, Symington, the Democrat, to Fulbright's left, Cooper, the Republican, to Aiken's right.

Laird remarks, again rather doggedly, that he tries to keep his Congressional relations on as fair and even a basis as possible, and notes that the other committees have authority over military matters.

For the first time Laird gets a little help, as Cooper remarks that 'if we are going to investigate the raid, then we should separate the resolution into two parts and have an investigation.'

At this point Senator Frank Church of Idaho, looking perennially youthful and cherubic, comes in and takes his seat between Symington and Gore.

Fulbright remarks that he can only repeat the President's promise of full disclosure, and does so, adding that it is 'very important whether we knew or didn't know that there were prisoners there, or whether there was some other purpose for the raid'.

'I know you have made that charge—' Laird begins.

'I haven't made any charge,' Fulbright interrupts. 'I have simply raised the question.'

Laird maintains there was 'significant intelligence information to indicate that this complex was used for American POWs. ... We do not have a camera developed that can go through thatched roofs to find out what is in there.'

At this there is hearty and scornful laughter from the press tables and the audience.

'You either had faulty intelligence or you knew they were in there,' Fulbright says sharply.

Laird tells him heatedly that he doesn't think Fulbright has any information or any intelligence to support what he is suggesting. Fulbright keeps trying to interrupt with 'Intelligence— intelligence—'

Fulbright subsides, looking surly. Church looks sceptical, Symington watches with a patient, rather sad smile.

Laird remarks that he would be perfectly willing to start his prepared statement on Cambodia. But Fulbright wants to skirmish a bit more on the POW raid and does so. Finally Laird tells him that he is 'very sorry you have questions in your mind and raise questions in the minds of others' concerning the purpose of the raid.

'It is the purpose of this committee to raise questions and not to rubber-stamp the Administration,' Fulbright snaps. He says it is his information that the CIA was not involved in the raid, that it was based solely on Department of Defence intelligence—which he refers to, scathingly, as 'this perfect intelligence'. Laird snaps back that the CIA 'was fully advised'.

Clifford Case of New Jersey, looking tired, sad and careworn, as he always does, comes in and takes his seat on the Republican side.

Laird offers to give the committee a briefing on intelligence at a closed session, but Fulbright decides he has had enough and turns to quoting the President's press conference remarks on his 'understanding' of the bombing policy in North Vietnam.

After some seesawing, Fulbright finally observes that 'maybe we are quibbling over semantics'.

'That might be the case,' Laird agrees. 'I am sure the North Vietnamese understood that we would stop the bombing on the basis of certain actions that we were going to take. And not only North Vietnam but the Soviet Union understood this as well.'

He admits that 'it is not a great number of planes that have been shot down, but they have made some violations of understandings'.

Fulbright says he will suggest that this Administration, 'like the last, is trying to bring about a settlement of the war based on the application of superior force. Is that not a fact?'

Laird begins reciting the various things the President has offered in the Paris negotiations. Fulbright chokes him off summarily with a tart, 'We are aware of those things. They have been published.'

He then jumps to the subject of the Army gathering dossiers on suspected subversives and inquires in his customary nasty-nice way, 'If I should happen to vote against this appropriation, would this be added to my dossier?'

Quick and reverential, laughter wells up from the audience and the press.

Laird assures him that he has 'been made aware of certain activities' and has been taking action 'to see that this is under proper supervision, and cut back'.

'Would you let me see my dossier if you have one?' Fulbright inquires.

'I would be happy to,' Laird says. The obedient titter swells again.

Laird then asks if he may proceed with his prepared statement on Cambodia and Fulbright tells him to put it in the record and summarize it. Laird reads from an obviously prepared summary of his prepared statement and the room settles down a bit. Claiborne Pell of Rhode Island comes in and takes his seat next to Symington, his dark, heavily lined visage serious and intent.

Albert Gore, looking sour and waspish, leans forward and asks if Laird thinks widening the U.S. commitment to support the present government of Cambodia can contribute to negotiations to end the war.

Laird starts to discuss the Vietnamization programme and Gore interrupts, 'It is my purpose to withdraw all troops from Vietnam!'

'It is our goal too,' Laird replies. 'We can reduce our presence in Southeast Asia if we give these people the tools to do the job. I don't want to debate old questions, Senator.'

'Now will you answer my question, Mr. Secretary?' Gore demands.

'I thought I had answered it, Senator.'

'You didn't touch it top, side or bottom,' Gore says sharply. And repeats that he wants to know how widening our commitment can contribute to negotiations.

'I wouldn't accept the premise that we *are* widening our commitment,' Laird replies with equal sharpness. He says he believes the United States is reducing its commitment and its involvement will be lessened by increasing military assistance while at the same time reducing military presence.

'You say our involvement is being lessened—' Gore begins.

'It *is* being lessened, Senator Gore!' Laird snaps. Gore sits back in disgust and says, 'No more questions, Mr. Chairman!'

Frank Church wants to know whether the Vietnamization programme will be affected if Cambodia falls.

Laird says it would certainly have an effect but that he doesn't believe it would mean the failure of Vietnamization.

'If it should turn out that more American money won't save Cambodia, what would you recommend we do?' Church inquires.

Laird says he believes it would be very harmful for us if the Vietnamization programme were to fail. And Church asks patiently again what he would recommend.

He says he would recommend greater use of South Vietnamese forces—adding quickly, 'Of course, it would have to be at the request of the government of Cambodia.'

Church wants to know if there is a 'contingency plan' to send in U.S. troops if the Cambodian government appears in danger of falling. Laird says contingency plans 'are a matter I don't cares to discuss with this committee at this time'—adding at least five times that there is no contingency plan, 'no *approved* contingency plan', at this time on this subject.

Laird says the air war is being 'substantially reduced' as compared with 1969 and early 1970. But he says if there is a target 'and it is a target as far as personnel and supplies is concerned, and in an area that can be hit without damage to civilian centres, we do it'.

Church concludes and Case inquires in a sombre tone what the future shape of the Cambodian programme will be—'at a higher level than this year?'

Laird admits that it will be at a higher level—somewhere between $695,000,000 and $800,000,000 this year, and larger than that next year. 'If we reduce American military presence we'll have to have a substantial increase in the military assistance budget' and also in economic assistance 'if the Nixon Doctrine is to be viable'. The U.S. commitment to Cambodia, he says, is solely in the area of military assistance to improve Cambodian forces.

Case remarks in his hushed cathedral tones that, 'We can't look at this as something we can turn on or off like a water faucet. Once you get into this thing, you have to carry it on.'

Aiken inquires gently, 'Is Cambodia the home of the white elephant?'

Everybody laughs.

Symington remarks that he saw the President on television last night and, 'It seems to me we're escalating the war over North Vietnam. It is clear to me that we've now decided to escalate the war over North Vietnam.' He inquires if there isn't some way the United States can get some of the on-hand ammunition in Vietnam, and some of the Communist supplies captured in Cambodia, into Cambodian hands instead of trying to manufacture new ammunition for them 'when there are ample supplies on hand'.

Laird says some of the captured ammunition has been made available to Cambodia.

Symington returns to the 'understanding' about bombing and Laird, his tone somewhat indignant, remarks that 'the North Vietnamese can't have it both ways. They claim we violate understandings when we bomb the North but then they claim there is no understanding when they infiltrate in the South. If there is no understanding, they can't claim we violate it. Either there is an understanding or there isn't. It works both ways.'

It is now almost noon, and after a little more wrangling the Senators let him go, having underscored again the sometimes rather wearing self-righteous attitude of the Senate Foreign Relations Committee, which sits in smug safety and picks away at policies for which it has no direct responsibility and to which, given the constitutional prerogative of the President, it apparently nowadays can contribute only annoyance.

Postmaster General Winton ('Red') Blount (pronounced 'Blunt'), of Alabama, wearing a sports jacket and slacks on this particular day, is a tall, rangy, red-faced Southerner with prominent ears, a kindly expression and a ready smile. His office is high-ceilinged, rich, dark-panelled. A cheerful fire burned in the fireplace. It was perhaps the most luxurious office I had seen so far in Washington, including the rather cold and empty Oval Office of the President.

I asked him if there had been any interference with his office by the White House staff, or any friction. He smiled.

'This is a pretty big government. In my case we have 28 per cent of all government employees right here in this department and we do need help with things. Sure, the White House staff is extremely important. I find that it is enormously helpful to me and it helps all of us to do the job for the President that he wants done. Part of the problem is that there are so many people who want to see him and just so many hours in the day. The President in effect has asked the Cabinet to take over their particular share of running the government. The Cabinet officers also contribute to his decisions in other areas.

'People get concerned because the President doesn't follow the precise advice they have given him. I don't follow the precise advice my wife gives me. I don't feel blocked off from him. It is the job of his staff to be protective. I see him whenever I want to see him.

'Of course, I will say that sometimes you get individuals who have an overview of their own importance. They think they are running the country, when actually the President is running the country. I'll admit some of the White House staff seem tough, but it's a tough world we live in. I'd much rather work with bright tough people, even if they are difficult sometimes, than with a bunch of dummies.

'In the post office here we have a $10-billion-a-year business, with 700,000 employees, which comes into daily contact with over 200 million citizens. This is a nationwide utility and there is no reason, given time and sufficiently dedicated people, why we can't run it as well as anything in the business sector. We are an operating department as opposed to a policy department such as State. The challenge is to get people to do the job that is going to be needed here under our new reorganization plans. On the whole the plans are good, but Congress put in certain limitations and we have to work with them to achieve the goals we must achieve. Never before in the government has there been the kind of wrenching change that is going to occur in this department.

'I think this is going to be a very partisan two years coming up, with the opportunities for constructive achievement on the part of the President rather difficult in a Congress controlled by the opposite party. It's going to be very rough. But this is a political ball game here and that is how you have to play it.

'The President is held in high regard in the South—probably stronger than in the rest of the nation. The big challenge to him is the economy—the pocketbook issue is the dominant issue. In the first two years he allocated his time to Asia and brought about a fantastic change in Vietnam and a fantastic success in that general area. Economic problems are just as tough and just as much of a challenge, so that now he is going to be spending more time on them. The President is a tough guy himself. He is going to apply himself and things are going to happen.

'If George Wallace runs again he will get far less response than he did in 1968. He can't generate the same enthusiasm and support, and I believe it will be hard for him to come up with the same drive another time.

'The government is a very big and very difficult thing, but it is manageable and I think it can be done. Many of its institutions, such as the Post Office, are far out of date. I think we here are going to be an example to the rest of the government. If we can reorganize and do it all right, then others may be encouraged to do the same. We are about to pull the Post Office Department kicking and screaming into the last third of the twentieth century. I think many other areas need the same thing, and not only in Washington. State legislatures also need to be brought up to date—they are thought of very badly by the people in general.

'It is important for people to have confidence in their government and in its efficiency, and I think we can achieve this by reorganizing and restructuring. The Congress itself is obviously archaic. I was astounded by the way they operate up there. God, I've been shocked by it! They really need some reforms on Capitol Hill. If the reorganization doesn't work here, then the effort to do it in other areas and institutions of the government is going to fail. But if we can do it here, then they will say, "By God, we can do it elsewhere." '

He is one of the more influential and active younger members of the Congress, a Republican, involved in the Republican leadership, dealing daily with the White House. He is diplomatic but not too happy.

'Many of the people at the White House are able and not arrogant, and are trying to do a good job. This is particularly true of the people who have formal liaison with Congress. But it may be that the so-called "palace guard" around the President contains some troublesome and difficult people. I think this comes about because people who are effective in Presidential campaigns tend once they get in office to be very protective of him and insulate him from Congress, and I think also even from his own Cabinet. These are people who don't know the Congress. But there are some improvements. The appointments of Clark MacGregor and Don Rumsfeld as special advisers indicate that he is going to have some people around him in the White House who really do know the Hill.

'I think that Nixon's own attitudes are complicated by the fact that he really has a rather limited knowledge and memory of Congress. He was only in the House four years and the Senate two years before he became Vice-President. His experience in the House became a source of great publicity because of the Hiss case, but it was not exactly the experience of a typical Congressman. As Vice-President he was not intimately involved with the work of the Senate. Therefore his real experience up here is really quite limited. Also, people who have served in Congress and then become President often have more problems than those who have not served here, because somebody who has served in Congress seems to come out thinking that he knows it all.

'Nixon does take advice from the leadership to some degree. But one of our problems is that there is not enough consultation with us before major decisions are made, so that we have a chance to put in our point of view and get it considered. We are quite often upset with what happens because we find that they have decided something down there and we are expected to carry it out. They don't give quite the consideration to Congress as a co-ordinate, separate and equal branch of the government that they should give in order to maintain harmony.

'When we do have a chance to give advice, I don't think our advice is ignored. I get the feeling it makes some difference.

'As for this session of Congress, I feel things will go better on the Republican side as you get closer to the election. It is then that we begin to realize the importance of hanging together rather than hanging separately.

'I think Agnew is a fine person but as of now he would be a handicap to the ticket in 1972. However, I think that if he will drop some of the things he has been pushing and emphasize more positive things in the government, he will come through in fine shape and there will be no difficulty about his renomination.'

He is stately, he is saintly, he is Republican, he is every inch the Senatorial Statesman. He is back and forth between support for the President and active opposition, usually in company with some younger colleagues. He is a real gentleman, though he sometimes gives the White House fits.

'Although I have been opposed to the President on such things as the ABM, Cambodia and the nomination of Justice Haynsworth, there's been no change of any kind in my personal relationship with him. I see him often and for rather lengthy meetings. He is perfectly accessible to me and has asked me several times to come down to talk to him. It is an easy relationship and I think both of us enjoy it.

'As we get closer to the election, partisanship is going to be more obvious than it has been up to now. I think that Congress on the whole believes the President's record has been good— not *very* good, but good. The tone of the '70 campaign was not any help to him up here and the reaction in the Senate has been adverse towards the manner in which the issues were established in the last campaign. It has caused the Democrats to be much more critical than before.

'There is continuing criticism of the White House staff. They do not come to Congress on specific issues as early as they should. There was some thought that having been in the Senate and the House, and Vice-President, Mr. Nixon would be very able in politics. But there has not been the communication between Nixon and Congress that you would expect. This has been reflected in various departments and agencies of the government, not only in the White House. People have become hard to get hold of when you want to discuss things with them.

'Of course, I realize the President can't spend all of his time talking to all of us up here, but on the main programmes, if he could start to work them out and discuss them up here first, and then take them to the country, he would get along better.

'As for Vietnam, Vietnamization is the programme we have and I shall support it now and do all I can to make it work. I think in foreign policy the President has done well, better than we expected up here. I think he has made the right decisions on the SALT talks and I think he made the right decision to keep our troops in Europe with NATO, considering the Middle East and Berlin situations. I don't think renewed bombing in Vietnam is escalation. Rather I think it is part of troop protection.'

HILL PASSES FOREIGN AID, EXCISE TAXES ... TIRED CONGRESS TAKES THE HOLIDAY OFF ... SOVIETS SPARE TWO JEWS FROM DEATH SENTENCES ... MUSKIE NOT INVITED TO AIR LAW SIGNING.

He is young, intelligent, shrewd, Republican. He, too, has complaints.

'Two years ago I thought relations with the White House were fairly good. I thought there were some difficulties but I thought they could be worked out. Two years later I find it a little harder to be tolerant. I've got to confess that I find some difficulty in getting through the barriers to the President, although I have talked to him a number of times. I think he desperately wants help from Congress, but I think because of the staff, at times he is not able to get it. I think we need a President's office in the Capitol where he can come up and be available to members from time to time. The distance from here to the White House has not become smaller. It is getting longer, year by year.

'However, as we approach the Presidential election year I think the President will find more success with Republicans up here, because every political realist on the Republican side of Congress knows that his destiny is tied up with that of the President.'

Senator Mike Mansfield of Montana, leader of the Senate Democratic majority, is one of the nicest men that ever lived, sincere, earnest, equable, intelligent, fair. He criticizes with reluctance and with a genuine attempt to be objective.

'I think Nixon needs to work more closely with his own leadership. He and I have a good relationship, but it is inevitably one of opposing political friends. I think he does discuss legislation and his proposals generally with the Democratic leadership. I in particular am often asked to have breakfast with him, usually just the two of us, after which he will call in Henry Kissinger to elaborate for perhaps fifteen minutes on foreign policy matters. He is quite frank with me and I try to be as frank with him as I can be. We have a good relationship and a frank one. He considers my advice, as he does that of many others, but of course he has to make up his own mind.

'I have never criticized him personally and I wouldn't criticize any President personally. The office is so rough that you've got to recognize the fact and be somewhat considerate of his problems. I would hope that he maintains a very close relationship with his own leadership in the next couple of years, so that he can get from them a feel for the Senate in relation to himself and his office.

'For instance, my feeling is that he should have called in at least his own leadership on Cambodia, if not all of us. He should not have called us in on the raid on the POW camps. I find no fault with that raid itself, other than the worry I expressed at the time, which was that if it had been successful it might very well have brought reprisals against the other prisoners.

'Most Presidents find it difficult to get along well up here— even President Johnson, who did not take the advice of his friends concerning Vietnam.

'One of the peculiar things about the Presidency is that some people think that because of the experience they may have had up here, they know what it's all about. Then they get in office and find that it's a hell of a lot more difficult than they imagined it to be.

'One of the problems nowadays, if they have an arm's length relationship with Congress, is that things move so rapidly—too much happens too soon—there's no time to think through these matters and get the advice they ought to have from Congress. There also is a tendency to misinterpret what people in Congress do. There has not been a realization down there at the White House what people like Cooper and Church are doing to help the Administration. Not to thwart it—not to frustrate it—but to be helpful. I don't know who is responsible for this. But somebody down there has not understood these things.

'More reliance ought to be placed by the President on people like Cooper, George Aiken and others like them. If the President turned to people like that and discussed things with them personally, rather than through some staff member who gets between him and his friends up here, things would move better for him.

'I hope this will not be a partisan session ahead. I would dislike the feeling that people were putting the party ahead of the nation. As for me, the nation comes ahead of party. That is the only basis—the only basis—on which I can operate.

'I think the Senate has acted quite responsibly up to a few days ago. Since then we have not acted as well. I have never seen such a situation as now exists. Filibusters on top of filibusters and filibusters within filibusters—God knows where it's going to end.

'As of now, the President would be in a horse race in 1972. He'll have to do something about the economic situation. And Vietnam is still a hidden issue. Much depends on the talks in Paris in the meantime.

'Muskie is way in the lead at this time for the Democratic nomination. He might hold that position successfully, but there are others who will be active. Yet for now I would say he is so far out in front that he would be hard to overtake. I think Humphrey would be available but he is not going to break his neck trying to get it.'

CONGRESS ADJOURNS TODAY ... COMPROMISE EXPECTED

Clifford M. Hardin, Secretary of Agriculture is a tall, square-faced, grey, fifty-five-year-old former Chancellor of the University of Nebraska, quite serious but with a sudden smile that wrinkles his face and eyes—almost automatic, but pleasant and not too forced. He is quiet-spoken, wears a wide tie, smokes a pipe. He offered coffee, cheese and crackers at ten in the morning and generally was very amiable and relaxed.

'There have been problems with the White House staff, principally in the area of decision making, but they have been smoothed out as far as I am concerned. I recognize the intelligence of the people there and recognize their problems, and they have recognized mine and have done their best to change procedures so that there is better understanding and better communication. I understand why some people feel that they may have been a little bit overbearing in their attitudes about some things, but as soon as a problem has been called to their attention they have tried sincerely to correct it. At least that has been my own experience.

'I think Cabinet meetings are helpful to the President and us because while they are not decision meetings, and sometimes don't give even have a formal agenda, they do give us a chance to exchange ideas on an informal basis, which gives us a chance to get his thinking and for him to get ours. I think it is very important that the people in major positions around the President have this kind of informal understanding, because then, even if we do not see him frequently or on a too regular basis, we at least know generally what his thinking is and we can proceed in the confidence that we are going generally along the lines that he favours. I think things are now going along in pretty good shape as regards the Cabinet and I think we will continue on that basis.

'Things are relatively quiet over here in Agriculture because while we still have major farm problems they are not the political storm centres that they have been in past administrations—at least not so far. Agriculture is still in transition, responding to new technologies which are creating larger and fewer units employing fewer people. That is really what is behind all the farm programmes. Often in the past recommendations and legislation have been directed towards the symptoms rather than the basic issues. I think we are trying to direct our efforts towards some of the basic problems that face the farm economy. Productivity has regularly increased but the individuals involved have not benefited as they should because they are operating in the open market. This is one of the main concerns of the President. One of my major responsibilities has been to try to put a greater stress on farm exports.

'We are also involved in environmental questions and in this area recent public interest, and indeed public emotion, have caused some old-line programmes to be shunted aside while the stress has been placed on air pollution, sewage and chemicals. Let's don't forget that a lot of real bread-and-butter work has been done in this department over many years, particularly in the area of preventing soil runoff into lakes and streams. This runoff of silt is seven hundred times all of the dumping from all of the sewage systems in the country. We have several more years of work ahead of us in this area but I think we are developing some good ideas on it. We are also involved in extracting water from sewage by running it through a field of growing plants. This brings it out fresh at a cost of five dollars per acre feet, compared with fifty dollars per acre foot when this is done by a chemical method. We are also working on trying to incorporate sewage sludge back into the soil in a way that will be beneficial to crops, after it has been treated.

'Our surpluses now are less of a problem than they have been in the past, but of course big crops can be recurring at any time. The subsidy programme is in reasonably good shape at the moment but we still have to keep fifty million acres out of production to avoid demoralizing the market.

'Congress is reasonably co-operative on farm programmes because we did not take in an Administration bill for Congress to pass: we simply brought in the situation, presented it and consulted with them for a solution. We held thirty-odd seminars with the Agricultural Committee of the House, meeting every Monday night for months before we worked out the legislation. We developed a good programme because Chairman Poage [Democrat, Texas] wanted a bill and not an issue, and we

190

wanted a bill and not an issue, and so our differences did not blow up along party lines. There was a little politicking at election time, but on the whole the approach has been non-partisan and bipartisan on the farm programme and we have moved along relatively smoothly.

'The President is amazingly relaxed and on top of the job. Many times we have come away from Cabinet meetings commenting on the fact that he still has his balance and his enthusiasm. He knows where he's heading and why. When he is slapped around by the newspapers he doesn't let it bother him. He simply goes ahead and does his work. He's being analytical about it and not desperate. He doesn't complain. We have not heard him once complain about the pressures of the job.

'I have not run into opposition from the bureaucracy in this department, certainly not in the area of holdovers who are deliberately trying to sabotage. There is a bureaucratic tendency to oppose change which seems to run through all departments, but I feel I have had really wonderful support from the staff that did carry over. At first we had a couple of problems in a couple of agencies but I brought them in and said, "Now, look: you can either get the job done with the people you have, or we will start making changes and making political appointments." They got the message and since then we've moved right along without any trouble. This is a rather quiet office here because I have worked it out so that not all of the emergencies end up here. I have delegated a good deal of authority to assistant secretaries and they have moved into the job and seem to like to operate that way. I'm convinced that's the best way for an executive to work. Of course, I'm conditioned by my background as a college official, but I think that's the way that works best. The President works this way.

'We are also involved in the food stamp programme and the food distribution programme, and I think that in eighteen months we have done more to feed hungry people than has ever been done before in this country. We have doubled the programme that we found. Of course, we have a lot more to do, but we now see our way clear to eliminating hunger as a problem in this country. I think we will be pretty well along in this regard by the time the four-year period is over.

'The school lunch programme we don't have complete control over, it's simply a matter of keeping on the pressure and trying to educate people to do it the right way. All we can do is withdraw funds, as a means of bringing pressure, and that is really no solution. So we try to encourage the school districts to produce a good system of school lunches. We have succeeded in many places. There are now less than ten counties in the entire country that don't have a food distribution system, while the number who do not have school lunches is somewhat larger but decreasing. The President made a pledge that he was going to abolish hunger in this country, and we have the job of making good on that pledge. I think we've come a long way and that we are going to go farther before it's over.'

He is in his mid-thirties, dark, stocky, round-faced, soft-spoken; a former White House staff member who left because of a gradual disillusionment with the way the political side of the operation was being run, particularly in the area of press and Congressional relations.

'I am really disturbed by the general inflexibility of the staff and its unwillingness to allow the President to deal with Congress in a spontaneous fashion ... although, of course, if the impetus for this kind of approach doesn't come from the top, then maybe one shouldn't blame the people down the line too much.

'I feel the President could do a great deal with a few corny gestures towards members of Congress—that is, what people who don't understand the human nature of politics might consider corny. Sometimes a quick handshake, or a call about some personal matter, or a joke about some problem in a man's district or state can really make a member feel good towards the President. I think he should do more of this, particularly with his own Republicans. After all, as somebody has said, "You want to keep your own troops turned on." I don't think the President has succeeded in doing this.

'In the same fashion, I find quite disturbing the attitude of the President and the top staff towards the press corps. Even if they are bastards who are constantly looking for excuses to attack the Administration, still I think they could be mollified a bit by personal contact. I feel that the President is basically shy about this, having been hurt so often by the press, but even so, he should be able to overcome this to some extent and be a little more cordial towards them. The attitude is reflected all through the staff, particularly in the press office. It makes things more difficult than they need to be for the Administration, in my opinion.

'At the same time, of course, I will concede that the press is so hostile that the Administration has simply got to be right on everything. It can't afford, for instance, to have a phoney witness in the Berrigan case. It can't afford any personal or economic scandal on the part of any member of the Administration for the simple reason that the press tolerance which is accorded to Democrats simply does not exist towards Nixon. Now, I know Ed Muskie, for instance: he's a man of somewhat limited grasp and somewhat limited intelligence, who is frequently banal, indecisive, short-tempered and generally inconsiderate with the press. But somehow there is a built-in tolerance towards Democratic candidates which prevents the press from letting these things really get out to the public with the sort of consistent hammering they devote to Nixon's shortcomings. They are so anxious to find an alternative to Nixon that they will build up almost anyone and give him all the benefit of the breaks in the process.

'I think the people on the White House staff, the top people, are of generally high calibre, but I think Bob Haldeman has one weakness that affects the whole operation—he reacts too fast to the President's suggestions, or requests, or temporary explosions of annoyance, or desire for something to be done. Before he became President there used to be one or two around who were in a position to say no to him, or to suggest that he wait a bit and think something through. Unfortunately that is no longer the case. Now there is no one on the staff who can say, "Mr. President, are you sure you want to do this right away? Are you sure you really want it *at all*?" Because frequently, of course, he will change his mind about something, as anyone does—but by that time it's too late. Bob Haldeman has jotted it down and gone dashing off to get it done without even stopping to think, himself.

'If I were President, I would love to have Bob Haldeman doing the job for me, because he does it superbly. But he does have a too-fast reaction time, and this sometimes produces results that the President perhaps would not have intended at all if he had stopped to think about it more carefully. I have seen things occur as a result of what Haldeman had heard from the President—or what he thought the President felt about something—and sometimes these have been rather unfortunate.

'I think the President's chances of re-election are about even. But again, as I say, he can't afford any mistakes in any area, or they will be exaggerated and used against him in a way that could seriously damage his chances in '72.'

West Winger, commenting on Cabinet officers and the games people play: 'Red Blount, the Postmaster General, is a real tough guy. He doesn't stand for any nonsense from the White House staff.' [With a sudden grin.]—'Many a quiet cocktail hour has been spent by the staff trying to figure out how to purge Red Blount from the government. But he stands up to us, and the President likes him, and you can't help but respect him. There are some others like that in the Cabinet—not all, but some. They know that over here we play two games: One of them is called "How Close In Are You?", which means how close are you to the President—and a lot of people pretend they are much closer than they are. The other is called "The President Says" and that's the one we play with Cabinet officers. When you go to Red Blount, though, and say, "The President says—" he always replies, "Well, if the President says that he can say it to me, and when I hear it from him I'll believe it and then I'll do it." This makes him a tough cookie, whom we respect but find a problem sometimes. However, the President does like him, and he is very good. We can't play our game with him. So I expect he'll be around for a while.'

EGYPTIAN PRESIDENT OPPOSES AUTOMATIC TRUCE EXTEN-
SION ... KOSYGIN HITS U.S.-ISRAEL 'OBSTRUCTION' ...
(FEDERAL) BLUE-COLLAR PAY RAISE IS VETOED ... HILL
RESTRICTIONS WON'T BALK INDOCHINA MOVES.

William Ruckelshaus, chairman of the Environmental Protection Agency, is thirty-eight, dark-haired, square-faced, wears dark-rimmed glasses, is pleasant, intelligent, well-spoken, obviously competent.

'Essentially we have two problems in EPA right now: 'The first is to take this organization, which is made up of some fifteen component parts from three departments and two agencies, and blend them into a single functioning organization. We have approximately six thousand employees, some seventeen hundred of them here in Washington, the remainder in the field. Our principal acquisitions for this new agency have been the National Air Pollution Control Administration, which used to be in HEW, and the Federal Water Quality Administration, which was in a number of other agencies and finally wound up in the Interior Department before EPA was established. We also include various pesticide agencies which had been in HEW, Agriculture and Interior; the Radiation Control Board from the Atomic Energy Commission and HEW; and the Bureau of Solid Wastes from HEW.

'Our external problem is to convince people generally that we are really serious about this issue and that we intend to carry out our mission to clear up the environment as fast as we can in a responsible way. The main thing is to gain credibility for the agency and that is going to take a lot of doing, a lot of persuasion and probably some mistakes along the way. But I am hopeful we can work it out. Many people think we are organized to do more than we are actually organized to do. However, we are going to do the best we can with the materials and the means we have, and I am determined to see us succeed.

'Air and water are, of course, our two main problems, with air control being approximately ten years behind water pollution control. Actually we are really a couple of years away from an effective programme on air pollution even with the new legislation that we are working under.

'The approach we have elected to take is one of standard-setting, followed by enforcement. Once you set standards and then set a pattern for adopting them by the states, you have something to go on. After the standards are adopted by the states, they put each industry—whom we call "polluters" but they prefer to call "dischargers"—on a schedule to control their emissions.

'We set what we call air quality criteria for five major pollutants: sulphur oxides, carbon monoxide, photochemicals, hydro-carbons and smoke. Under our new legislation we set some standards in a given area within a period of thirty days. We publish in the Federal Register and then the states or anybody who wishes to has ninety days in which to comment, protest or agree. We then adopt a final standard which can be challenged in the courts if people do not agree with what we have done, feel we have done too much or have not done enough.

'The final standard then goes to the states. They have nine months to get an implementation plan devised to meet the standards, putting each "polluter" or "discharger" on notice that he has a certain schedule of time, say six months, a year or a year and a half, in which to eliminate the things he is doing that create pollution.

Four months after the states receive this go-ahead they sub-mit their pollution control plans to EPA. If we disagree with the plan, they have two months in which to submit a substitute. If they do not come up with a satisfactory one we work out one ourselves and declare it to be in effect.

'In other words, we move in if the states don't act, or if they don't act in a satisfactory way according to our view of it here.

'Consequently it is really almost two years before we will be in a position to make real progress. We do have some emer-gency powers, of course—we can go into court and get an injunction if there is some particular flagrant example of pollu-tion. However, we would prefer to work through the orderly procedures set out by the law, because that makes for better feeling, a sounder result and a more popular programme.

'I do feel the job can be done. I'm convinced our technology has advanced so fast that we just didn't pay much attention to what it was doing to us, and that we have got ourselves into kind of a hole. However, I think man is intelligent and can get himself out of the hole. And that's what we intend to do.

'The attitude of industry is varied. Some are very co-operative. Some are not. Some are going to have to be pushed, some are nervous about their public image and very anxious to co-operate. Those who are reluctant to co-operate usually are original pro-ducers who have to go through three or four middlemen before their products reach the consumer, and therefore are not directly subject to public reaction or public pressure. In the area of detergents, for instance, Procter & Gamble has a very high degree of concern with public opinion and is very co-operative, whereas Lever Brothers, which is based in England, fights every step of the way and couldn't seem to care less. Their attitude in England seems to be that they depend upon exports and therefore why should they cripple their manufacturers by imposing costly restrictions on pollution. One man said to me, "We'll just build the smokestacks higher and let it blow off to Norway."

'We do have an international office in EPA which I have established, and there are a number of international conferences going on and scheduled in this pollution area. The United States really has an opportunity to exercise leadership because the rest of the world is looking to us for it. With the possible exception of Sweden, we are far more advanced than any of the others in our attempts to control pollution. There seems to be a worldwide awakening about the environment. It is really incredible, the interest which seems to be manifesting itself all over the world. This means that we should get a lot of co-operation in cleaning up the environment, not only here but worldwide.

'In the area of pesticides, the environmentalists see it almost as a moral evil. DDT is a hazard to wildlife, admittedly, but not to man, as yet. We have reduced the uses by government order from 436 to 24, but in some areas such as cotton growing, no substitute has been found. Without pesticides the crop would be destroyed. Therefore pesticides do have some beneficial uses for society, and the same applies to herbicides and fungicides. Some of the problems in pesticides and these other areas of treating the insects and diseases of nature arise from the fact that scientists are not agreed on their effects either on nature or on man.

'In the area of radiation, however, all scientists are working from the same set of facts basically and consequently we are concentrating on short-term, high-level exposure. We don't really have adequate facts as yet on long-term, low-level effects. There are a few scientists who are much upset by the levels of tolerance set by the AEC and they are out attempting to stir up, and quite successfully, public opposition to building atomic power plants. This causes difficulty, because the power load in the country is getting so extreme that we are going to have to have some other source for it. This means that we will have to have some form of atomic power and the plants will have to be built. But they do have a good point in wanting to be sure that they are protected and not a danger to human beings or the environment as a whole.

'In the area of solid waste are a lot of problems which we are trying to work at, and with some success. The Resource Recovery Act signed by the President in October is a boost to attempts to recycle certain solid wastes such as glass, paper and so on. We are running one pilot project in San Mateo, California, in which the city is disposing of its solid wastes by burning them in a closed environment and we are finding that this will provide 20 per cent of the power needs of the community. This may be a very significant breakthrough.'

Clifford Alexander, lawyer with Arnold & Porter, was formerly chairman of the Equal Employment Opportunities Commission under President Johnson and prior to that was deputy special counsel to the Johnson Administration for minority affairs. He is a Harvard graduate in his thirties, a tall, good-looking, light-skinned Negro whose resignation, forced by the Nixon Administration a year or so ago, caused loud outcries in the Eastern press. He states his views clearly and forcefully, in a quiet and reasonable voice, in his office on the second floor of the old restored home on Nineteenth Street where Arnold & Porter have their offices.

'It seems to me that it is the responsibility of the President to set the tone for the nation on the Negro question. He has not delivered a major address to any group, or to the nation, concerning the black and white issue, which is perhaps the major problem confronting the country. There is no more serious situation in America and yet he has failed to speak out in a constructive and positive way. Everything he has said has been negative. For example, in his last press conference, his failure to react to a question about Martin Luther King and his statement that he was not going to force integration were just simply two more indications of this. The President is not setting the tone. He is not stating that the goal of the government is not just equality, but what is right and what should be done to bring the black people up to full equality.

'The black community, I would say, is more than 90 per cent convinced that we have a President not only disinterested in our problems but actively against our goals—which are basically economic achievement and the ability to get ahead comfortably in this country. The black community is depressed and worried, wondering whether it is possible now to make any such progress under present conditions with this Administration in control of the government.

'I think that it was very significant that in *Time* magazine recently, in an article on the black community, the Harris poll revealed that whereas JFK and LBJ had a sizeable percentage of the blacks for them, Nixon has only 4 per cent of black Americans backing him, and that practically none say they are ever again going to look at the federal government as an ally in working out their problems—*ever again*. The Administration's shortcomings and his disinterest are shown in the failure to have a black in the Cabinet, a failure to preserve certain blacks who have been in the government in their positions and to reappoint them. It is true that they reappointed the black mayor of Washington, D.C., in an attempt to create the impression that they are doing something, but there are other indications which refute this—my own experience, for example; the opposition by the Administration to extension of the Voting Rights Act; failure to stress increased funds for black education; and so on.

'The advice flowing into the White House on this subject is not really advice. It does not come from responsible blacks nor does it take responsible black opinion into account. Pat Moynihan is an example with his memo on "benign neglect" of the Negro problem. The black community really despises him. The genesis of their hatred for him may be right or wrong but it is there. It is callous, at best, to project this man as an expert on "urban affairs", which has now become the shorthand for the inner cities and the black community.

' "Benign neglect" has generally been adopted by the Administration as a matter of fact even though it denies it. Moynihan's memo also seemingly pitted group against group, because he said that the blacks should not get more than the chicanos or the Indian Americans, and so on. He referred to the govern-

ment outlay as a pie, and that is not sound analogy, in my
opinion. You don't look at it as a pie to be split up, you look
at it as making it the pie it has to be, to do the job that has to
be done. Not to take away from one group and give to another,
or to try to divide everything up equally when the need is not
equal and the problem is not equal. Advice such as that is the
kind that goes to a President who has no background himself
with the black community, who has no really deep commitment
to the black community and doesn't seem to have much real
understanding of the black community.

'Black advice at the White House is essentially non-existent.
There is really no in-put at the staff level or from the outside
leadership. Some of this, it is true, is due to the nature of the
black movement, in which the old-line groups like NAACP,
CORE and so on are being opposed by the younger black people;
and some of it is due to the self-seeking of black politicians.
However, there is sound advice to be got on the black problem,
and the Administration is simply not getting it.

'Very often those who make attempts to consult with the
Administration are turned away. This makes the younger
blacks feel that this man won't listen. For instance, a while
back, in fact nine months ago, the black members of Congress
made a formal request to the White House that they be allowed
to sit down and discuss things with the President. They received
a very snippy reply from John Ehrlichman two months later,
who replied with a listing of black appointments and various
ceremonies for black people which of course ignored the essential request of the members of Congress. Now, these are elected
members of Congress. They are not going to beg on their knees
for things, they are probably going to demand them, as they
have a right as Congressmen to do. But certainly they are going
to give the President a responsible view of the black community.
And he simply will not receive them, or his staff will not let
him receive them—which amounts to the same thing, because
if he really wanted to see them, he could do so. [Finally, on
March 25, 1971, almost a year after the original request, he did
see them for seventy-five minutes and declared himself much
impressed.]

'Also, there is the "Southern strategy", so-called, which has
been adopted by the President, which is an insult to the black

people. What he attempted tò do to the Supreme Court is an example of it. When you see somebody nominated for that court who has denounced you as an inferior being, you don't need to have it spelled out for you. My six-year-old son can see that without having it written out. It is quite clear the attitude that prompts such an appointment. And it has been tried, not once, but twice.

'Also there is an overemphasis on the Black Panther Party by Attorney General Mitchell and Mr. Hoover. There is a disregard for the meaning of the sanctities of the law. If we are a society premised on law, the point is not to gun them down for what they say. Let them spew their venom where they want to and when they want to, but get them when they violate the statutes and the laws. Don't assume that what they say in their rhetoric is going to be automatically followed by crime and try to get them first. This is not the way an orderly society functions.

'There is a general callousness and hatred towards the blacks which seems to come from the callousness of the people in the White House, the Haldemans and Ehrlichmans who have had no contact with black people in their life, who have no understanding of the black community, and who come up time and again with negative opinions about it.

'I must say that I am amused by the writings of Kevin Phillips, if this is the author of their Southern strategy, and he seems to be the one who talks about it most. If this was a trusted aide to the most trusted aide of the President, Attorney General Mitchell, then that's a pretty good indication too. His racism has spewed out of his pen and therefore is probably spewed out of his heart. I read his column because it does indicate where they're coming from, so to speak, but I find it pretty grim humour.

'The Administration has put out some cruel hoaxes on the blacks. One is in the matter of appointments. They have put out this booklet about Negro officials in the Nixon Administration and when you look at them'—and he exhibited the brochure with its many photographs and laudatory text—'you see that seven people in the State Department, for instance, all are junior diplomatic ranks, that many of the appointees are holdovers from past administrations, that there is a tendency to claim that certain people who are listed here as "staff assistant" on such-and-such a commission, or "staff adviser" on some other body, are really important, whereas anyone who knows government knows that these positions do not mean very much and that this is simply a show.

'In the government today, GS-18s who make the top money are 1.4 per cent black, while GS-1s, who don't make any money and are at the lowest levels of the government are 52 per cent black. Nixon has done nothing to indicate to the bureaucracy that other offices should be given to blacks and that the Administration really wants to emphasize the interest of the blacks. At least when [the Negro] Bob Weaver was Secretary of HEW in the Johnson administration it indicated to the rest of the government that the Administration really wanted something done. But in this Administration, promised high-level appointments have never taken place and no new ground has been opened up. Instead there has been an attempt to create with phoney numbers the impression that blacks are really being appointed to important positions. This is a fraud.

'They really don't have any use for us, when you come right down to it. The one effort they claim so much credit for, namely the Philadelphia Plan, started in the last Administration. They do deserve credit for pushing through Congress some legislative support for it, but after that great battle only forty-one jobs have resulted.

'The government has not used the power it has to withhold money from contractors if they don't abolish discrimination. It simply has literally not brought its powers to bear. When you see this in the Labour Department, you have to conclude that this is more than sloppy bureaucratic operations—it would lead one to think that someone is telling them not to do anything.

'They do a lot of talking about "black capitalism", yet when the Office of Minority Business was first announced and was put together out of parts of the functions of 112 different government operations, it was not given any funding and very little is going on there now.

'The leverage for a President who understood where the problems are and how to solve them is there if he would use it. But he is not doing so. He knows the business community and he knows very well that the top jobs are not being opened up in industry to Negroes for all the talk.

'This President and the White House crowd and the corporate group that they deal with are undertaking a slowdown rather than a speed-up in helping the blacks. I think the message that industry gets from government is that you better do nothing. So far their programmes seem to follow a pattern of about eighteen months or two years of lag to get to something, then a sustained interest for a little while, then a cutoff and a downturn. I think it is quite possible to see negative interest in the blacks rather than a positive one.

'It is time for the President to say that he believes in black capitalism, not only in the corner drugstore or the hot dog stand, but to urge Ford Corporation or Lockheed to bring blacks into high position in industry. These things are not taking place. Nixon is not doing anything about it. In Poor's Directory there are listed 2522 executive positions in major businesses in this country and absolutely zero of them are black. I see a flow of statements from lesser lights in the government about how much they like the blacks but I see no evidence issuing from the Small Business Administration, no new projects in the works, no appeals being processed, nothing being done. There is no pushing and shoving against the situation that exists.

'The White House has real economic power if it will use it. That is where the action is and he knows it, but he certainly is not doing it. At the same time private industry is no better— the television networks in particular are a travesty as they pretend to put blacks in high positions and think they can satisfy us with a few black faces in programmes, and nothing, again, emerges from it of any substantive or substantial size.

'There is a refusal to listen to people of responsible leadership in the black community, such as the black Congressmen I mentioned, and this means that the black community becomes increasingly disillusioned. I don't mean in the sense of saying it's "pigs versus blacks", which is an absurdity—black people want good law enforcement as much as white people do. But I do mean that the Administration is simply not giving a positive push to the needs of the black community and I don't see any signs that they will. I find it very hard to understand, since on a standpoint of practical politics if nothing else—leaving aside simple human compassion—you would think that they would see that it is to their political advantage to do something for this largest minority in the country. Yet they aren't doing it, and he is giving no push to it from the top.'

U.S. INVITES SOVIET SCIENTISTS TO ATTEND [ANGELA] DAVIS TRIAL.

In his first Cabinet meeting of 1971, preparing for a State of the Union message that called for a radical overhaul of the federal establishment, the President concluded with an impromptu rallying call to his Cabinet members:

'This country has served and worked well under a Constitution written two hundred years ago. Before the Constitution was completed, it was the result of a lot of thinking and much work and debate by a lot of men. We sometimes forget that it, too, was not a perfect instrument and thus we have amended it.

'The changes we are proposing in our bold domestic programme are the most basic changes offered to the country since that time. These, too, may not be perfect, but they provide the instrument for a dynamic programme by our people.

'The American people are ready for a change. They recognize the need to use the great talents, skills and tools we have to make progress as we go into the next hundred years.

'The programme we have is not one developed suddenly. It is the result of six months of intensive effort. When I first heard of some of the ideas at San Clemente, I thought, "My God!— special-interest groups will be so strong that we can't gain approval." I believe we can gain approval if we all solidify and work together on the offensive.

'This is a programme on which we should unite as a Cabinet and as government leaders and unite with the governors and the mayors and many in Congress who will work with us to bring this series of proposals and high goals to fruition. The goals we have are goals of the American people. The best brains we could find have gone into the development of the programme. I have observed and participated in government over a twenty-five-year span—first as a Congressman, then a Senator, then as Vice-President, and now—as President. I am convinced that this is the greatest effort I have seen and I believe it is the right* *effort, in that it will succeed if we come out solidly for it.*

'In the year 1971, we will present the American people with the most imaginative, bold, revolutionary programme in recent history.

'We hope this will be adopted this year. When it is adopted, it will carry the country forward for another hundred years.

'We have really got something we can be proud of. Let's make the most of it.'

He is a veteran of thirty years in Congress, a Democrat but always a non-partisan and objective one; a decent, fair-minded, blunt and honourable man. Asked for his analysis of the President, he shook his head and looked grim.

'One of his faults or deficiencies is that he seems to have a feeling of insecurity—a hesitancy about making decisions. In making decisions on major issues he seems to try to find some way to accommodate contending positions and opposing factions on all sides. By trying to accommodate all viewpoints he doesn't satisfy any.

'His intentions are noble and, like all Presidents, I know he would give anything to go down in history as a great President. But he's got a vacillating indecision about him, a complex or something. He doesn't hit hard and drive for what he wants.

'As for his State of the Union message, it would be wonderful if you could consolidate all these departments, but just how to go about it he leaves dangling. I'm afraid he's vacillating.

'On the war, he winds it down, yes, but he does it in such a way that nobody is really happy with it. He still is trying to please everyone. Now, I am not partisan, as you know. I like to help this country, particularly when she's involved in a bad situation like this. But I'm afraid that political expediency has dominated many major decisions that have been taken in the past couple of years by this President and this Administration.

'The basic question is: Are the American people still willing to make the sacrifices which are necessary to sustain the republic? I don't think this republic can be maintained if you don't pay the price for doing it. And I don't think the President is giving the leadership which will make the country do this.

'We have got so many obligations abroad, and to this country, and yet somehow we seem to want to meet them without making any sacrifice. I think the American people are willing to sacrifice, but they have to have the leadership that will show them it is necessary and will inspire them to do it. We're going to have to sacrifice if we're to maintain all the programmes and all the commitments, and the military posture that we have got to maintain to protect ourselves and preserve ourselves.

'Now in this coming election the President is going to be challenged by people in my party of whom I don't think much either. They are going to promise the people more and more and more with less sacrifice. Well, it can't be done. The problem is sheer survival. Now, he should reply to that strongly and firmly. But will he? I'm afraid that he's going to try to match their offers with competing offers, instead of saying to the country what has to be done. The American people will make sacrifices, but they won't make them unless someone provides the leadership. And he isn't doing it.

'As for our candidates on the Democratic side, all they offer is more spending, more giving, weakening our defence, more compromise, no firmness—retreat, retreat, retreat.'

Bill Rogers, whom I have known for many years dating back to the days when he was staff counsel of the Senate Investigations Subcommittee, has put on a little weight and turned greyer, as who has not, but is still the same handsome, amiable and very likeable gentleman he has always been. In the beautiful and impressive Secretary's office on the seventh floor of the State Department, he greeted me dressed in a conservative dark-blue suit and spent most of his time staring thoughtfully out the window while he talked with good humour about the many problems that confronted him.

He was not disposed to answer questions directly concerning his feeling about the influence of Henry Kissinger. Most of his talk was devoted to the ways in which he and his department have contributed to the President's thinking and to world initiatives in various major matters.

'The thing I have found here in the department is a great tendency to assume that if you say something, it has been done. My principal job here has been to urge people to get moving and get things accomplished. There is a tendency in foreign affairs to delude yourself that you are doing something simply by stating it. This is not the case. You have to make a decision. Therefore I think I have helped some in getting the department to take on a new look, because I've been constantly urging, "Let's do something, let's get moving, let's reach a decision on these things."

'For instance, one minor incident, but one which nonetheless could have blown up substantially, occurred a few months ago when I was overseas. A passport was denied Yehudi Menuhin on the ground that he might have lost his American citizenship by accepting honorary citizenship from Switzerland. He wrote me a very aggrieved letter and the department sent it forward to me with the notation that there was a grave legal question involved and they just didn't know what we should do. I said to hell with that, let me have a letter ready when I land in the United States telling Menuhin that it's quite all right with us for him to accept the honorary citizenship from Switzerland, it won't affect his American citizenship. When I arrived the letter was waiting, I signed it and six hours later it had gone off to him. He was happy and everything was smoothed over. Now, if we had delayed, the press would have really cut us up about it. That has been one of the main things I have done here, simply to force answers on things that are pending and *get them done*.

'The Leningrad trials of the Jews in Russia also represented a whole orchestrated programme with other nations that originated here in the department. I sent a letter to Gromyko, and other things were done to bring pressure to bear and focus world opinion on the Russians. If we hadn't pressed forward, forced the situation into the headlines, there would have been a big fuss here and it would not have been as well done as it was. The same way with the Middle East cease-fire. I have been criticized occasionally for proposing it, but in five months there has been no fighting, and at least we have been able to keep things from exploding again over there.

'Our two major problems in the department, of course, are Vietnam and the Middle East. We also have to figure out how to get along with Russia and the Chinese, but now that the Communist world is no longer monolithic this is an easier problem, although it still by no means can be termed simple.

'On Vietnam, we decided upon and recommended a process

of Vietnamization in my speech to the Associated Press in 1969. That was the first time an alternative to negotiations had been proposed, and it was proposed by me. We pressed that point of view and worked it out very closely with the President and he adopted it. How the President is influenced on things I don't know'—a broad smile—'but I felt strongly about this issue and said so.

'I always felt we should start and follow through on a policy of giving the Asians a chance to control their own destinies. We had to work out what we would do in the light of our past policies. A government like ours just can't change overnight, it isn't fair to the nations that rely on us. Responsibility is always there and you worry that your policy is not going to succeed. Sometimes you find that something you want to do would not work out till six months from now and would be too dangerous to undertake.

'Here in the department we formulate policy, announce policy and pursue it. I was strongly for pulling out the first 150,000 men from Vietnam, for instance. Everybody said that things like that can't be done. But you just have to go ahead and advocate it and see what happens. We think we have done it just about right, even though some in Congress continue to be very mistrustful on the basis of what has happened before. Cambodia found a great many opposed, but it was an essential part of the Vietnamization programme. There were lots of different ideas on how you do it, but I never had any doubt about the importance of cleaning out those sanctuaries.

'So far we've avoided pretending to do one thing and then doing something else, which I think is very important in maintaining trust in the United States. By setting a deadline of July 1 on Cambodia we in a sense tied our own hands, but this was good because we had to go along with it and have the troops out. This established our credibility.

'We have been very active here in the department in formulating the Vietnamization policy and we have played the role of being sure that we do things as we said we were going to do them. I met a lot of students during the Cambodia business and one day six or seven came into my office and asked to talk to me, so I let them. After they had finished I began to reply and they began interrupting me. So I said, "Now, I listened to you. Now, you let me talk and be polite enough to listen to what I have to say." I said that if our troops were not out by July 1 I would write them a letter and apologize and I said, "If we are out by July 1, why don't you write me a letter and apologize?" Of course, I haven't heard from any of them since.

'It is true that problems continue and the problem in Vietnam remains, although it is getting substantially better. I don't know anything to handle it that could have been any better than what we have done. I think the President has done a remarkably good job. Eastern Europeans, although they won't say anything on the record, will admit it behind the scenes when you talk to them.

'The Nixon doctrine of withdrawing from Asia to some degree and letting Asian nations maintain their own defence was first proposed by me on my first trip to Asia. I strongly supported it and you can take a look at my speeches, which show that I did. I said it and we are carrying it out. We were overextended with treaty commitments going back to World War II and Korea upon which we cannot renege. In the event of an attack by external forces upon those nations, we could either stand by or apply the treaty provisions. We said this could come about in the event of an attack by a nuclear power, which of course really means China. But there are other forms of aggression. In meeting them we can beef up their self-defence, we can supply economic and military *matériel* assistance, without supplying manpower. We reduce our presence militarily but we stand ready to aid in other ways.

'Our policy is understood in Asia, although of course it is not particularly liked, because our withdrawal has certain economic manifestations that sometimes affect their economic well-being, and this has to be adjusted to. However, through modernizing equipment and giving funds for things of that nature, we can beef up their economy and help them get over this crisis brought about by our withdrawal.

'In the Middle East, the initiative for the cease-fire which the United States took, and our attempt to get negotiations going, was a well-orchestrated and well-planned effort which arose on our initiative here in this building. I'm responsible for the cease-fire, I had the negotiation idea worked out, and when I heard Nasser on an NET television programme say that he would welcome a temporary cease-fire I got in touch with him immediately, and it began to develop.

'You know, peace and war have an inertia all their own. War is tough to stop and once peace gets rolling, people like it. They don't like to change over and start fighting again, and this helps. It seems to me in the Middle East we had to take the initiative and get things off dead centre. I had a long meeting with Tito to spread the word, and this also helped to get it to Nasser and to Egypt.

'The missile violations by the Egyptians and the Russians were unfortunate in that they slowed down negotiations. But in another way they were stabilizing, because now Egypt has better equipment, while Israel is content with the advantage over Egypt which the equipment we provided has given her. So a certain balance has been established. Egypt has a little more self-respect and the situation is somewhat more stabilized than it was when Israel had a complete whip hand.

'You ask whether I trust the Russians after their missile violations. Anybody who has my job who uses the word "trust" should be examined. I don't "trust" anybody in international affairs. That's why we had the U-2s going over the next day and why at the SALT talks we are trying to establish some proof of good faith before we commit ourselves. There are situations where trust may not be present, but where mutual advantage can keep things stable.

'An international treaty cannot be enforced. All you can do is try to work out an agreement. If you do, you assume that the parties would like to have it observed. But you say to yourself that maybe they think you're going to be deluded, so the answer to that is that you keep watching for any violation. If the agreement is violated, then you have to take other steps. Essentially the agreement is based on the feeling that both sides like to have peace. If they don't, then we can't have peace anywhere. But if they do, then we can work out these individual problems.

'I don't know that they do, but I'm prepared to say that maybe they do want peace, and therefore let's make an agreement and watch each side take steps to protect themselves against violation, and see if we can't work it out. Maybe Russia does want to fish in troubled waters—that could be. But do they want to fish in really troubled waters? You can't fish in a typhoon.

'I have some doubt that Russia feels she can gain anything by a major explosion in the Middle Eastern area. That would put her whole foreign policy in jeopardy, the policy by which she has aided the Arabs without ever directly getting involved herself. Because if Israel succeeded in driving the Arabs back, then either the Russians would have to come to the defence of the Arabs or the Arabs would say that Russia gave us promises and arms but didn't protect us when the showdown came. Of course, if Russia is willing to face us on that point, then we're in trouble. But I don't really think that she is.

'If, on the other hand, we can work out a compromise so that the Arabs can come off pretty well and save face, then they can say that the Russians did it for them, and the Russians could continue to play their game of inciting the Arabs to make trouble and upset things. But I don't think they could take the risk of letting things blow up altogether in that area, because they could not afford not to help the Arabs if the chips were down, or they would lose terrible face themselves. Actually I think, for all the rhetoric which is thrown against us by the Arab States, that they are convinced that we are working in good faith to try and get a settlement. Their government people will admit this in private, even though, of course, in public, we get the usual attacks from them all the time.

'All our treaty commitments are still firmly adhered to by this government. Our commitment to NATO is firm and we are going to stand by our other commitments also. Russia is obviously going to continue to try to create situations and troubles and we don't have any false illusions about that. They're proceeding to negotiate, but we are making clear to them that we are hardheaded about it. With Berlin, for instance, we are insisting that the Russians make real concessions or we don't have an agreement permanently about Berlin. We are prepared to maintain the status quo there forever, until we get some sense of real co-operation from them. And they know that.

'Come back and see me when you finish the book and of course if the Middle East has blown up by that time'—with a wry grin—'you can forget all this. But if everything is stable there, as I think it will be, then we can take some credit for it.'

And then, more seriously:

'In a sense we will never solve our problems. The whole job here is to live with the problems, to stabilize them, to prevent them from bursting into fighting and to put them in a form where they can be managed peaceably, or reasonably so, for the safety of the world and this country.'

MIDEAST TALKS RESUME. EGYPT SAYS ISRAELIS ARE NOT SERIOUS ... NIXON TO PRESS RAIL STRIKE BAN ... JOBS SAFE, NIXON TELLS HIS CABINET.

There was a request by the wife of one of the ambassadors from the black African states that she and her sister ambassadresses be permitted to give a reception for Mrs. Nixon on her fifty-ninth birthday. It was a pleasant and flattering thought, coming from an area where the Administration feels it must look for friends. The idea was passed along to the White House. Given the way the White House operates, it seems entirely safe to say that Mrs. Nixon in all probability never even heard about it. Presently the answer came back from the staff: thanks, but no, thanks, because 'the question really is, if you do it for the Africans, then won't you have to do it for the Asians and the Europeans?'

And suppose you did, in a world where America needs friends wouldn't it have been worth it in good will and good feeling?

He is a little less bouncy, a little less bubbly, not quite so voluble as he used to be: the years and his defeat for President have taken their toll. But Hubert Humphrey, once more a Senator from Minnesota, is the same good-natured and gallant battler he has always been. He is also a pretty good analyst of the man who barely beat him in 1968.

'My impression is that the President has done a great deal to reorganize the White House staff, to expand the White House facilities and provide himself with the special assistants and the necessary facilities to do the job. This fits in with my view of the President as an orderly man and in a sense a technician in government.

'I think, however, that one of the weaknesses of the Nixon Administration is Congressional relations. There is no follow-through. The President announces a programme and then generally there is a time lag of several months before a draft bill comes up to us and we can get to work. People are given the impression that simply because the President has announced it, it must be before us. So we come under criticism because we are not acting on the President's legislation.

'There is no real build-up behind his legislation for some time after it is proposed, and I think perhaps partly this is due to a staff problem and to his lack of drive in getting the staff to work on these things. Mr. Nixon is not the taskmaster and driver that Lyndon Johnson was or John Kennedy was.

'When I was Vice-President with Mr. Johnson, we spent a great deal of time following up every proposal with chairmen, subcommittee chairmen and important members of Congress. We had a chart on the wall in the Cabinet Room where we kept an up-to-date record of exactly where all bills were, what had happened to them, what was being done to them at the moment, where they were going next. We had an exacting, demanding procedure at the White House. This has not been the case with President Nixon.

'I am often in agreement with what he says. My criticism comes over what he does or does not do. There's a terrible lack of follow-through, as for instance when he speaks of the dangers of inflation. What he does *not* do is much more important than what he says about it. On the domestic side I believe he is now trying to reverse his field. He is very cleverly placing before Congress a number of proposals that attempt to meet and cancel the opposition in Congress.

'In foreign policy he has done much better. He has given a great deal of thought to it, he has reduced troops in Vietnam, he has started his Vietnamization programme, and I think that on the whole he has done well in this area. I do not agree with some of my Democratic colleagues that this could be a big issue in 1972, providing he continues as he is going. I think he is determined not to let the country go isolationist again, and I support him in that.

'I think that in many ways he is not a strong leader of the public, though he wants to be. But I do not think he is. He works at his job but he does not have the charisma of a Kennedy, or the trust of an Eisenhower, nor does he have the vigour of a Johnson. Johnson in his sheer power was a master of government. By sheer will and energy and manoeuvre he got things through. Mr. Nixon thinks in concepts rather than in details. The Administration is strong on public relations but it is weak on public performance.

'I think if the Democrats are moderate and creative and constructive and if the economy continues as it is, we can win in '72. But if the economy is stable, then I think we will have a difficult time. It is the trends which count, the way things change and develop. If the economy is coming back to full strength, then Mr. Nixon's strength will be coming back with it.

'I certainly intend to keep my options open as to running again myself. I plan to travel extensively around the country and if I find that there is a substantial interest in my candidacy, I certainly will not foreclose myself from doing it. I may very well be a candidate again and I will hold that option open for myself.

'Mr. Nixon is a man who learns. He has learned a great deal in the recent [1970] campaign and'—with a wry chuckle—'I have a healthy respect for him!'

His chauffeur has to take him by a different route to work every morning, the Cabinet officer says, to avoid the possibility of kidnapping. But that, he says with a grin, is 'just one of the penalties of the job'.

Dick Kleindienst, Deputy Attorney General, is in his mid-forties; large, round face, large blue eyes that can stare at one blankly but are usually full of considerable humour and life; very strong, very determined, a tough man. If he could get past the Senate, he could be a choice for Head of the FBI when J. Edgar Hoover leaves the scene.

'In a sense I am executive officer for the department under the Attorney General. I see that the policies of the President and the Attorney General are effectuated by the seventeen divisions of the department. We also administer all ninety-three U.S. attorneys in the country, all the U.S. marshals, the office of criminal justice, Congressional liaison office and so on. My day begins at 8 a.m. with a meeting of one or another of the assistant attorneys general or the bureau heads, usually without a formal agenda. At 9 a.m. I meet with the Attorney General and at 5 p.m., I meet with him again. That way I can capsule any problem that comes up for his attention. Also there are Attorney General's staff meetings from time to time to get everybody together. I prepare the programme for that. I also deal with Cabinet officers and with the top people of the White House when they visit the Department of Justice to discuss questions of interest to the President. Every Friday noon the Attorney General and the assistant attorneys general have a luncheon staff meeting. Frequently these include lawyers from the nine legal divisions of the department.

'In the area of civil disturbances, the President traditionally delegates to the Attorney General rather than the Secretary of Defence the responsibility of recommending when federal troops should be used and how they should be used to quell civil disturbances, both in the District of Columbia and in the states. We have a pretty complete operation now and I am, you might say, in a sense chief of staff of that operation.

'We haven't had the problems in that area that the Democrats had, such things as Watts, Detroit, Washington, Newark. Logically they would occur in a Democratic administration and logically they should not occur under our Administration, because the Democrats are obligated for a lot of their political support to the black groups, which vote overwhelmingly for them, and therefore they hesitate about putting things in order when these groups create disturbances. We don't have that kind of relation and therefore we are able to respond more promptly and efficiently without hanging back because of political considerations.

'When one of these situations has arisen it has caused a great outcry from the black leadership because of the pressure on the Democratic President not to do much about it at the start for fear he will be charged with "repression" and "attack on black rights". This has usually been accompanied by the threat that, "if you do take strong measures, we'll go back to our people and suggest that the Democrats are as bad as the Republicans and they might as well vote Republican". Ramsey Clark, the last Democratic Attorney General under Johnson, was particularly susceptible to this kind of pressure—as susceptible to pressure as anyone has ever been in the United States government.

'Our approach is based on plans, intelligence, quick response. We have people in place, we serve notice that disturbances are not going to be permitted to get out of hand and if they do get out of hand they're going to be stopped right now. The whole atmosphere on that changed at once on Inauguration Day, 1969. I was down here within a couple of minutes after the swearing in of President Nixon and I immediately put plans into operation to control any possible disturbances at Inauguration or after. There could have been disturbances on the first anniversary of the death of Martin Luther King and they did not occur. There could have been violent disturbances at the time of Cambodia and they did not occur. This is because we advised people in advance that preparation of federal troops was being undertaken, and we said to them in effect, "you can speak, but beyond that, when you get into violence, we are going to stop it right now".

'They can't threaten us because they vote against us anyway.

'At the same time, we have co-operated in every possible way with all these dissenting groups, working with them to determine how they can march, what units will be on hand to control violence and what elements in their own ranks can be depended upon to help us control violence. Our purpose is to make it easier for them, not more difficult, and the fact that we have made it easier is proved by the record and it is one reason why riots and disturbances have not come back. [This was pre-May Day 1971.] We've used a reasonable, even-handed approach.

'As for the campuses, I and others have been going all over the country speaking on campuses. I don't think we have affected that calming down too much. I think it has been calmed down by the calming down of the Vietnam War, basically. We found a completely inept policy of handling campus disorders under the Johnson administration when we came in. I think that his administration was one of the most disastrous in history.

'On the race issue as it involves these disturbances and law and order in the country, whether we get credit or not I firmly believe that we turned the corner to end the demonstrations. I think we have gained credibility in winding down the war, revising the draft and providing opportunity for young blacks to make their way economically.

'In the judiciary, we have appointed 115 federal judges in 19 months, which is a fantastic record for any administration and I don't know that it has been equalled by any administration. President Nixon has made it a fixed policy not to send in any name for a judgeship not deemed fitted by the American Bar Association. With the exception of Carswell and Haynsworth, we have not had any difficulty with the Senate as to judges.

'In the area of street crime and general city crime, twenty-three cities of a hundred thousand or more have been having a steady decrease in crime in the last two years. Statistics generally over the country have seemed to be going up a bit, but our statistics here in D.C., which is kind of a pilot project on what can occur, show that crime can be controlled and is being controlled. As a result of the President's recommendations here in D.C., which Congress finally adopted, the District police have been increased from twenty-seven hundred to more than five thousand, there has been a 60 per cent increase in prosecuting attorneys, the courts of the District have been reorganized. Previously the federal district court of the District of Columbia had thirteen judges and they handled two thousand felony cases in 1952 and they only handled two thousand in 1968, which showed no gain at all because the number of felonies actually committed went up from two thousand to twenty-six thousand a year in that period. We have now reorganized the District courts to provide a superior court and a supreme court somewhat similar to the national Supreme Court to pass on criminal matters here in the District. We also have increased the number of blacks in the District police from twenty-one per cent to forty per cent. We have a real police community relations programme, and our whole emphasis is on an even-handed enforcement right down the line. Within a reasonable time the District of Columbia should have the best crime record in the United States.

'As for political crime such as assassination and kidnapping, in terms of numbers and impact the effect on society is minuscule. It's only important as it is dramatic. When something big like Chicago occurred, Ramsey Clark initiated an investigation, called the grand jury, but when he got the results he didn't do a God-damned thing at all. In effect, he said he was not going to prosecute anyone for tearing up Chicago, and so when we came in we had to go ahead with the prosecution.

'Organized crime is another area where in motive power, determination and organization, more is being done by this Administration than was ever done before. We found that the resources of government were not being effectively used in this area because the various component parts were not working together. Frequently they weren't even speaking to one another. Now we have got the Justice Department, the FBI, the Internal Revenue Service, Customs Bureau of Narcotics and Dangerous Drugs and all the other enforcement agencies of the government working together in task forces to fight crime. There's a whole new ball game here and a whole new enthusiasm in this area because the Attorney General had the precondition that all of these people who are appointed on this are going to work together and if they don't they're going to get off.

'As far as fighting crime, if you use traditional techniques you're going to get no place. A gangster or criminal who is brought to the stand can always intimidate or buy other witnesses and just subvert the judicial process.

'Congress provided that we could go to electronic surveillance, which Ramsey Clark again refused to use before passage of the bill, and announced he would not use if the bill became law. This was an open invitation to them to know that the government was not going to do anything. We have straightened out that situation too. The Attorney General has authorized 250 electronic surveillances. He alone has the authority and he has to take it direct to the courts for approval before wiretapping and other measures can be used. This has brought the indictment in eighteen months of between five hundred and six hundred major criminals. It has been the first massive attack from the federal government. We now have task forces in twenty-three major cities and it is paying off very well.

'The court order which covers electronic usages requires that the Attorney General must state specifically what the need is, must specify what is going to be used. The court then grants authority for a given number of days. If you are not able to get what you want in that time, then you can go back and get the time extended. Upon indictment, all the evidence secured by wiretapping and other electronic means is immediately made available to the defendant and his attorney so that they know what is going to be used against them.

'In narcotics, the control of heroin is an organized-crime function which we have to work out with Turkey, where the poppy growing occurs, and with France, where the poppy is turned from opium to heroin at Marseilles and then is shipped to the United States. This is a major organized-crime activity because the money needed for this process is very substantial and so big money and big crime rings are behind it.

'In the area of dangerous drugs, barbiturates and the like, we have now instituted tougher controls on manufacture of these dangerous pills. With marijuana we are working out co-operative controls with Mexico, where 85 per cent of the crop is grown. This Administration has advocated diminution of penalties for first use from felony to a misdemeanour. The real effort now is to attack the trafficker and not the users.

'I predict that in a reasonably short time the narcotics problem will be stabilized and then reduced down to a normal irritant, rather than the major one that it is now. Congress has given every dollar we have asked for in this area. A great deal of this is due to the personal confidence that Congress has in John Mitchell and in this department. Congress has given us all the money we asked, clean across the board.

'As for street crime, there is a basic philosophic dispute in the Administration about whether to give money appropriated for crime fighting back to the states and local communities in block grants, or whether there should be one federal bureaucracy again to control what is done. What is really involved politically, of course, is whether the money is going to Democratic machines and Democratic cities or to state councils who will try to beef up the whole system in each state. The President favours the block approach through the state councils.

'Given a few years when the full impact of these revisions and these new programmes and planning and all this money can be felt all across the land, there's going to be a strong resultant effect on the statistics of crime. In the area of corrections in the federal prison system, that system is relatively a shining star compared to the antiquated and almost medieval systems of many of the states. The President has advocated a ten-year programme of correctional reform and has provided that every block grant to a state has to include a reform plan for criminals.

'These civil libertarian bastards complain about what we are doing, but the fact remains that we are clearing up many of these problems. One of the main problems is, of course, that of recidivism, which means the returning criminal who is discharged from jail and on present statistics can be expected, 75 per cent of all those released, to be back in jail again within five years for some other crime. What we have to work on is rehabilitation plans that will send somebody back to society as a constructive member. If we have eight years at this and get the money and support that we ask from the Hill, you're going to find a most substantial drop in the crime picture in this country.

'In the area of anti-trust we also have undertaken vigorous enforcement to stop this headlong rush towards conglomerates. The former Administration was obsessed with the idea that it needed new legislation in the field, whereas the President has ample authority now under present law. If we had continued the headlong rush that they permitted, within a very short time 85 per cent of the productive capacity of this country would have been in the hands of between fifty and a hundred companies. That was stopped six months after we got here. We have been engaged in a vigorous anti-trust programme, which is going forward with substantial success.

'In all of these areas you have to do it with vigour and determination and honest people who don't care for the political consequences but go ahead and fight crime.

'You can't do it with weak, opportunistic, chicken-hearted bastards.'

NIXON DECLARES CONGRESS FAILED ON KEY PROPOSALS. SAYS IT WILL BE REMEMBERED FOR WHAT IT DID NOT DO— WELFARE PLAN CITED. ALBERT REBUTS ATTACK. SAYS IT'S THE ADMINISTRATION THAT HAS FAILED ... SOVIET WARNS U.S. IT MAY RETALIATE FOR HARASSMENT. THREATENS REPRISALS AGAINST AMERICANS UNLESS JEWISH MILITANTS ARE CURBED ... SOVIET WARNING REJECTED. U.S. 'SHOCKED' AT 'THREAT'.

He is a rising star in the Republican firmament on the Hill, tough, ambitious, aggressive, challenging his elders, going after what he wants, demanding, scrambling, pushing, shoving, with a zeal for partisan battle and self-advancement that sometimes reminds his elders of the young Lyndon Johnson. So far it has paid off for him very well. His appraisal of the personalities at the other end of the Avenue is intelligent and astute.

'From a general standpoint, I think the President has done quite well working with a Democratic Senate and a Democratic House. Contrary to some reports, I feel that the President is accessible. There has been a great improvement recently in relations between the White House staff and the Hill. There was an early lack of communication which left bad feelings, but this has been improved, though we have not yet reached the millennium. It is still difficult to communicate with certain top members of the White House staff, and it is difficult to work together unless we know one another. I still feel it would be better if we could be thrown together in a non-legislative fashion, sit down and visit with the Haldemans, the Ehrlichmans and the Shultzes. I know they can't devote a lot of time to individual members nor can the President, but a little more informal contact and getting to know one another would be helpful.

'The President does recognize those who play a leadership role in his battles. I have received calls from him thanking me for my efforts, and also from time to time those of us who help him get what we call "R.N. notes".

'I think if the President followed his own instincts more in dealing with Congress he would be an even stronger President. Not only is this true of Congress, but of other things—for instance, when he got up in the night and went to the Lincoln Memorial after making his Cambodia decision. That wasn't programmed—that was Nixon. By his own nature, he's apt to let himself be programmed too much. He doesn't have to be programmed. He should let his own instincts control sometimes in how he reacts to things. I am hopeful that in the next couple of years he will be himself more.

'Of course, I realize the demands on his time account for some of this. He has so little time to do his own thing.

'I think he has mastered his worst fears about the media, although the White House is always aware that the media is there and that they are largely critical. I wish he would have more press conferences. I think that would give him a better contact with the public. If the people can read the transcript of the conference, and if they have seen the President on television, they can form an opinion for themselves regardless of what the media may say. They can see whether he is being direct or whether he is not being direct. I also hope he moves around the country more in the next couple of years. I think he should not be a prisoner of the Presidency and I think he is going to demonstrate that he is not a captive of the White House.

'It seems to me the New Left and the violent young are beginning to quiet down and that this particular era is about to end. I do hope, however, that we do much more in the Republican Party than we have done to attract the votes of black people, Mexicans, Puerto Ricans and other minority groups.

'In the next couple of years politics should be as much as possible disassociated from the White House. We are now in the home stretch of the President's first term and politics should be reserved for the National Committee, where it belongs. The campaign managers should not be in the White House. If they are, then the feeling spreads through the country that the White House is simply a political arm of the Administration, and that is not a good reaction to encourage.

'Very few around the President have had any political experience, have ever been on a ballot. Bob Finch is perhaps the only one who has. There has got to be some recognition in the White House staff that you can't push out someone appointed by Senator Russell, let's say, or someone who got his appointment through Senator Mansfield in a previous administration, simply to make room for a Republican. These things have to be done selectively in order to hold friends here on the Hill and to get things in line for the coming election.

'Of course, there is a feeling on our part up here that we deserve more attention than we probably do and there is a feeling on the part of some of the White House hierarchy that we are less important than we are. But it seems to me that we're all in the family. In a partisan sense, we have an obligation to work out the problems we have by getting to know one another better. I don't think, however, that "access" must necessarily be physical access to the President. It can be simply getting a Presidential decision or comment on something directly from his office, without having to go through a great many people or getting blocked all along the way.

'As for Agnew, we don't see him much. A few lame ducks around here are very annoyed with him and it is probably just as well if he keeps a low profile. If he does keep a low profile for a while I think he will be all right two years from now and will again be on the ticket. He did spend a lot of time up here in the early days learning the rules and the faces and the names and at that time relations were very favourable. Of course, he's pretty good at raising hackles and also at raising shekels. I think Agnew is a plus on the press. At least he can't be ignored and many people agree with him heartily. I think, however, he should be active in other areas this coming year for his own political good.'

JARRING EXPECTED TO FLY TO ISRAEL TODAY FOR PARLEY. REPORTED TO HAVE AGREED TO GO DESPITE OBJECTIONS BY EGYPT AND JORDAN. ARABS SAY FOE STALLS. BUT INTERMEDIARY IS SAID TO BELIEVE THE TRIP WON'T IMPERIL PEACE TALKS ... END OF GI COMBAT FORESEEN BY LAIRD. IN PARIS, HE ASSERTS TROOP ROLE IN VIETNAM WILL BE LIMITED BY MIDSUMMER ... NIXON NOW EXPECTED TO TRANSFER HIS EMPHASIS TO DOMESTIC ISSUES ... U.S. MILITARY ASSISTANCE FOR 1970 IS PUT AT 8 TIMES THE FIGURE IN BUDGET.

Arthur Fletcher, forty-six, Assistant Secretary of Labour, is an enormous Negro who got his degree in political science and sociology from Washburn University in Topeka, Kansas, went on to play professional football with the Los Angeles Rams and the Baltimore Colts, then became more and more deeply involved in civil rights, minority manpower problems, industrial and community relations. He is around 6 ft. 5 in. and proportionately broad, has an intense rapid-fire manner broken by sudden uproarious laughs. The first of these came when I told him I had already talked to Bob Brown and Cliff Alexander. He went off into a roar of laughter interrupted by astounded and delighted expletives. His comment when he finally calmed enough to be coherent was, 'They're light-years apart!' He then zeroed in on the standard Republican complaint about past Democratic administrations: the weakness of promise without performance.

'The Kennedy and Johnson administrations aroused high hopes among the Negro community, I'll grant you that, but the hopes weren't answered. They just weren't answered. Somehow, somewhere, along the way, they got lost. But those pieces of legislation, in any event, were not the answer. They were designed to remedy the social condition, while blacks all along have been well aware that their problem is not social but economic. That's the mistake that has been made too much by too many whites.

'I shy away from the term "liberal" whites. I would rather use "concerned"—many whites who might be conservative in some areas are more liberal when it comes to the Negro problem and are actively concerned in trying to better the condition of the black community. I find from Goldwater to Javits a hell of a lot of common ground when I start talking about bringing black Americans into true economic equality.

'Once we solve the economic problems, the black community themselves will find a solution to their social problems. They'll make the decision whether to move to better neighbourhoods, whether to carry their children to certain schools and so on. Give them the money, the economic standing and security, and these other things will take care of themselves as time goes by.

'I think this Administration is dealing with this problem better than any other administration. When I came in this department twenty-six people were in here, and no guidelines. All the emphasis was on conciliation of contractors who were not obeying federal regulations about hiring blacks, and the attitude also towards the unions was that the federal government should simply conciliate, it should not demand and insist. This brought about an attitude on the part of both contractors and unions that the federal government doesn't mean it—if they really did, they would punish and order, and instead they try to persuade and conciliate. Therefore contractors and unions considered that they could do as they pleased in past administrations.

'No administration had really tried to make it work until we came in. Now we have enough money to do the job—money in America is the alpha and omega—it's the beginning and the end, brother. Without money, you're not going to get the manpower to do the job. Now in the Office of Federal Contract Compliance, which I'm head of, we have the money to do the job, we have guidelines laid down, our twenty-six people are up to at least ninety persons, and our budget has been increased more than 45 per cent.

'The same thing applied to the Equal Employment Opportunities Commission. It was all talk, there was really nothing to it when Cliff Alexander headed it. There was no real enforcement, there was no effective administration or pursuit of black objectives. The black hope in this country was tied up in that commission and in the Contract Compliance Commission and neither was working. The Equal Employment Opportunities Commission had five commissioners in five years, practically a complete turnover from chairman to janitor. People were playing games with it and consequently the black community had no confidence at all in it. That commission too this Administration has now given power to, and given teeth to it.

'One thing we recognize is that when you get through talking about how liberal you are, and about how much you're going to do for the blacks, you better have the money to do it. We do have it and we don't have to apologize to anyone, as far as I'm concerned.

'Back in the days when the administration—the Democratic administrations—were getting our hopes all up, we were on the negative side of zero in the black community. People had lost confidence and we haven't really won them back yet—even though now we've got the money, the power, the manpower, the legal ability to go ahead and go to bat for them. The problem is that we came on the scene at the time the black community and concerned whites had lost confidence in our democratic process and its ability to help the blacks.

'We came into power a little bit ahead of our time, in the sense that people were beginning to think finally of how to make government work, not just talk, but work and deliver. Even now there is still a lingering feeling at the White House that to get legislation passed is to make it work. But that is not the case. The problem is to actually make it work after it gets on the books.

'The black community now knows how to demonstrate, and get attention and make a protest, and get legislation put on the books, but that does not actually make the legislation work. That's where the ball game is right now. If you haven't got the sophistication to make it work, then you hadn't ought to pass it. We have to make this great, big, sluggish thing known as "the bureaucracy" work and function for us.

'A black man in government today has a different mission than he did in the past, when he was just supposed to be a symbol of something and that's why he was appointed.

'Most blacks in the past came in the government and simply adjusted to the situation as it existed. They became captive political appointees and didn't do anything much. My job, as I see it, is that I'm going to have to attack some things. I'm going to have to change it and raise hell and talk to people and do everything I can to get them to see things my way. Under the Nixon Administration, I get away with saying today things that other assistant secretaries in past administrations would be fired for—or other assistant secretaries in this Administration, for that matter, would be fired for. The President has thrown the resources of the White House at my disposal. At the time of the Philadelphia Plan he threw all the resources in his power to get the job done. He did not flinch. When I explained what I was trying to do, he said, "Let her go, Arthur. Let her rip!" He himself knows the black problem is economic and that when that is solved a large part of the social problem will be solved also.

'So far it has been almost impossible for me to get the NAACP and other groups behind me. I need a constituency. Their attitude is that I am on a white charger but that I'm going to get cut off at the pass by the white government. I don't believe this is true. I need their support, and to tell you the truth, I haven't really got it yet.

'This matter of a constituency is important because those who come into the government from labour can be sure that when they take on a federal job or project, they're constantly going to be supported by a flood of letters from labour to the government, to their friends on the Hill and to the White

House. The labour man in government is in a position to blanket the White House with protests or support of some project that he puts into action. I can't do that. I couldn't get a hundred letters from the black community to get what I want done.

'The black community has a strange feeling that, "Well, this is the wrong Administration in which anything can be done, and so nothing is going to be done, and so I'm not going to support them." This is a tragedy of the first magnitude. I don't really know how we're going to deal with it. Hopefully by 1972 we will have some specifics and some case histories that I can go to the country and campaign on, for the President. I believe I can prove that we have delivered some jobs to blacks and to Mexicans and to American Indians as well. I am counting on increased support from the President, not less. If I have some cases to point to, then I can really deliver. We've got to get to the point where we're not just on the launching pad but we've got the missile in orbit, and then we can get some votes and really convince the black community to believe that something is being done for them.

'I'm trying to convince the President and the White House and Congress that the way to solve the economic problem is a ten-year plan to ease the situation and wipe out the gap between whites and blacks. That's why I'm at war with the unions, because they say, "We've got men on the bench and we're not going to share anything with the blacks." If we let them get away with it, the unions are going to monopolize jobs by giving phoney tests on qualifications and using other tricks to keep blacks off the payroll. Black American workers have been living in a recession ever since the Depression.

'We've got to get down to shared employment. A lot of the young blacks are rioting because they're unemployed. They need to be assured of a fair share and told that if they're able-bodied, they're going to be able to share.

'This is the first Administration that has employed a black person in a job like this and allowed him to really do the job. I'm doing my best and I think we're going to get it done.'

FED REDUCES BANK RATE AS CREDIT EASES ... SOVIETS SENTENCE TENTH JEW. ANTI-AMERICAN INCIDENTS RISE: U.S. PROTESTS ... AGNEW TO SELL PLAN TO SHARE U.S.

Frank Shakespeare, head of the U.S. Information Agency and
its Voice of America, is short, stocky, blond, with prominent
blue eyes and a quick, rather amused smile. He was with CBS
for eighteen years and loves to stride up and down his office
while he expounds. It is clear that he is adept at arguing in
the corporate jungle.

'I have not made changes in structure, so much as changes
in the thrust, of the USIA. I report directly to the President
and so we are a White House agency, reflecting his point of
view and his wishes in the way America is presented abroad.
We are banned by legislation from doing anything to influence
the ideas of citizens of the United States. We have no role
within the United States. We don't show the people of the
United States what we do, and this can cause certain misinter-
pretations of our role. We have a budget of $180 million a
year, and that is being increased in the upcoming budget.

'Our mission is several-fold. We are to assess the attitudes of
people in foreign countries about current or proposed or possible
United States foreign policy moves and then to present this
information to the President and the Secretary of State as factors
in their decisions. After a decision has been reached in foreign
policy, our mission is to distribute the information on that
decision throughout the world. Our mission also is to convey
the quality of American life and help the other countries understand America.

'We have two areas of operation: management here in Washington, and the field. In the field we have a public affairs counsellor who is one of the senior people advising each of the
ambassadors in the different nations. Usually he is the cultural
officer, so-called, and under him are libraries and cultural
centres, Fulbright scholarships, TV, radio and all other means
of transmitting ideas to the local population. Our staff may be
a small one in an African nation, which will have perhaps two
U.S. nationals and five or ten natives. In India we have forty-five
Americans and several hundred Indians. In Japan we have

thirty Americans and a hundred Japanese. And so on.

'I decided early in the game that I wanted to avoid making the mistake of sitting in Washington and trying to decide what would be the best thing to do in the field, so I decided that I would travel a great deal. I make perhaps four or five trips around the world every year. It seems to me I am always travelling.

'To free myself for this, I made the deputy director in effect an executive vice-president. All the heads of division under him report to him and he reports to me. This does away with the old system of my predecessor in which perhaps seventeen agency heads reported direct to him.

'We also decided that the man in the field would have the decision on whether he would use the material we sent to him. He's got to orchestrate—he's got to play the violins. It's up to him to decide whether to take a soft approach, a tough approach, to be anti-Communist in a strong way or a subtle way. We say to him, "you're there, you do it".

'The Voice of America has its headquarters here in Washington, and there, too, we try to have as much autonomy as possible. Of course, we make steady and regular evaluations of how effective our programme is, both in the VOA and abroad, and if somebody doesn't measure up, then we get somebody in who will do a more forceful and better job.

'We are the official voice of the United States. When we speak, this nation speaks. Therefore it must be very carefully done and very responsibly done. The VOA has to be fast, vital, informed. If the USIA is to be worth a damn to America, the people in it have got to become more creative. I am constantly saying, "You must be responsible, but also be creative." '

(He interrupted his explanation to take me to the screening room and show me a twelve-minute film, *Czechoslovakia, 1938-1968*. This was an extremely clever montage of screen clips and stills, with musical accompaniment, showing the domination of Czechoslovakia by the Germans, its struggle to achieve independence and finally the Russian invasion of 1968—a most effective and powerful film. He said it had been sent out without announcement to all the USIA offices around the world and they in turn had distributed it to their local contacts. In Argentina, for instance, it took over all the TV networks that day. The

Japanese ran it as the centrepiece of their regular half-hour evening news programme. France showed it after their formal news programme at eighty-thirty. In Peru, theatres ran it as a fourteen-minute short with introduction and conclusion. And so on.)

'As to whether people in the field can sabotage the programme, that is one reason I travel. You have to go to the field to detect whether there is any attempt to sabotage. We have to ride pretty tough herd on what goes on—and we do.

'The overseas libraries when we came in were overloaded with books on the liberal side. There was no real reflection of conservative thought. I took the position that people in the field should not burn liberal books, they should not take them off the shelves, *but* they should provide an equal balance of conservative thought. I said, "If you carry journals of one kind or another, you must have a reasonable balance." This was very, very tough to accomplish, but I have put it through and now we have a balance of liberal and conservative publications in our libraries abroad.

'I said we must do this because we have to have a representation of all points of view to give a fair picture of America. We have corrected the unbalance.'

He is a very senior Republican who has been watching them come and go since Franklin Roosevelt. The media, as he says, are constantly trying to promote a quarrel between him and the President. But he is more patient, more tolerant and more kindly than they would like him to be.

'I try to help all Presidents, although some'—with a little twinkle—'are easier to advise than others. I find Nixon very good to work with, but he has a tendency to get separated more and more from the Congress—and not only from the Congress but from others too. He hasn't had a well-co-ordinated establishment up till now. In some sense, of course, this is due to the fact that the government is just too big. The President doesn't have time to talk to every person who calls up. And yet when a member of Congress calls, some one of his new people says, "Just what do you want to ask? And *I'll* decide whether it's good enough. And then *I'll* put the call through to the President—if *I* think it is."

'This rankles, up here.

'Now, every President wants to be a great President, a good President, a constructive President, and Nixon is no exception to that rule. But every President also makes mistakes. Most of them think they don't but they're human beings, and they do. I can't think of anyone who is really qualified to be President.

'These next two years are going to be hard because the Democratic strategy is to get as many vetoes as possible—to make the bills just so expensive and so costly and so impractical that the President will be forced to veto them. Then they will be able to go to the country and say, "Look, he is against this, or that, or whatever." The Democrats are insisting on adding to every bill they can enough money to force a veto. They'll do that with every welfare bill that comes up and everything else they can. In this kind of situation, of course, a Republican President is more under attack than a Democratic President would be. It is a very difficult problem for Nixon to solve.

'I try to help him in every way I can but the media react in such a way against him that if I said, "It's going to snow next Tuesday," there would be some members of the media who would interpret it as an attack on the President.

'I think he keeps his cool with the media much better than he used to. But he never forgets them for a moment. He finds it difficult to forget. He is always conscious they are there.

'He has changed a good deal. He now advocates things to keep in the trend of the times that he would not have done ten years ago. It's a little bit like the story I used to tell about the man who saw the bulldozer rolling towards him down the road and he had two choices—he could stand there and get crushed, or he could jump on the back and try to steer it.

'The Nixon Doctrine is a good doctrine and I hope it will be carried further. Nixon has made South Vietnam safe and he is winding down the war and getting us out of there, so he is succeeding on that. On the whole I think he is doing reasonably well—as well as he can under the circumstances of a Democratic Congress and the issues which he faces.'

He picked up my ideas at the Congressional breakfast the other morning,' said Hugh Scott of Pennsylvania, the Senate Minority

Leader, 'and gave me a nice plug for them. He said Hugh Scott had pointed out that every time the Republicans propose a programme, the Democrats will exaggerate it—the Republicans offer $3 billion, the Democrats raise it to $5 billion, and therefore the Republicans can always be put in the position of opposing what is being done. But, he said, "We can't outbid the Democrats on that sort of basis, and therefore we should meet them in a competition of ideas. I believe in my six goals, and in the reorganization of the government and I think we should base our campaign on giving the country better ideas and programmes than the Democrats offer. I want you fellows to go out and sell these ideas on that basis."'

LAIRD CALLS WAR TREND HEARTENING ... JARRING CONVEYS ISRAELI PROPOSAL TO EGYPT ... U.S. AND BRITISH PULL OUT OF UN COLONIALISM UNIT ... U.S. PROTESTS HARASSMENT OF AMERICANS IN MOSCOW ... JOBLESS RATE UP TO 6% IN NATION: HIGHEST SINCE '61. DECEMBER RISE DASHES THE HOPE OF NIXON FOR DROP AT END OF GM STRIKE. 4.6 MILLION WERE IDLE. HODGSON SAYS THAT PEAK IS REACHED—ZIEGLER CITES A STEP TO PEACE ECONOMY ... BLAST DAMAGES SOVIET BUILDING IN WASHINGTON. NO INJURIES ARE REPORTED AS PRE-DAWN EXPLOSION OF BOMB BREAKS WINDOWS. A CULTURAL OFFICE HIT. STATE DEPARTMENT IN APOLOGY. GROMYKO MAKES 'STERN PROTEST' TO U.S. ENVOY ... SOVIET SAID TO ASK ANTI-MISSILE CURB. U.S. IS REPORTED TO HAVE REBUFFED PLAN TO LIMIT ABM'S TO TWO CAPITALS ... RUSSIAN SUB-TENDER THAT STIRRED CAPITAL QUITS CUBAN WATERS ... TWELVE FAST ATOM SUBS ORDERED BY NAVY.

He has been a governor, served in the Cabinet, worked long and hard and ably on the Hill for his constituents and the country: has come about as close to being a genuinely disinterested public servant as it is possible to find in a very human system in which self-interest and national interest inevitably go hand in hand. Like his fellow Democrat who commented earlier, he is in many ways a non-partisan, fair-minded, objective man. He speaks with a genuine concern of what he feels to be a fundamental handicap at the other end of the Avenue.

'My feeling is that Nixon has a basic weakness, and that is his failure to appeal to the best of America. He appeals to the worst. For instance, on the family assistance plan, which is a great move and I applaud it and expect to be active in helping him to get it through—if it can be got through—he is undertaking a very radical change. And yet how does he go to the country with it? He says in effect, "I'm going to get these bums off the relief rolls." He doesn't say, "I'm going to try to provide stability and something good for all Americans, which will help the country." His approach with so many people is so negative on these things. It's a very commendable operation, a landmark move by a President, and instead of saying he's going to correct the welfare system and abolish poverty as the main objective, he says he's just going to get the bums off.

'I think this basic weakness of Nixon comes about because of his failure to understand the great sweep of giving more leadership to the best elements of America and really bringing them together. I'm convinced you're not going to solve the black minority problem or any other until you solve the problem of the whole lower economic range of the country. You can't regard these various claimants as competitors. You've got to say you're going to solve the whole problem and take care of all the needs. He's divided the people, rather than brought them together. I'm convinced the American people have a lot of common sense. They want a leader to unite them and bring them together around their divisions by showing them positive solutions to things. He isn't doing this.

'The only leader we can have in this area is the President, but there is a great weakness and it goes all down the line. In the State of the Union message he talked about "people power" and kept using the word "revolution". He doesn't seem to have the depth to understand that he should appeal to youth on the positive side rather than the negative side. I think he imagines himself as a consummate politician and tries to be cute, instead of letting the best of his instincts take over. He tries to manipulate the American people. He's figuring where the most votes are, and I don't think that's the way to go about it.

'I feel the reorganization of the Executive Branch is long overdue, but, again, he has advocated broad policies without specifics. The specifics may come out three or four months from now, but the initial impact is lost because he fails to be specific. He doesn't follow through: he throws out an idea and doesn't back it up.

'I personally have never known a President to tell the truth, Kennedy or Johnson or whoever it may be. Presidents basically don't trust the American people. They feel they have to rationalize and dodge. These wise-guy Presidents surround themselves with bright young men who feel that they have to be cynical and smart and have to play a game with the American people: and finally the game becomes more important than anything else. Because a President very seldom gets into details, these bright young men around him feel great. With Kennedy they were on the liberal side, with Nixon they're on the conservative side, but they all have the same failure. They're able and they're dedicated and they believe they're serving a President well, but basically what they're really serving is their own egos.

'The President is trying to appeal to too many groups, as they all do. If you try to please everybody, you're not a good President. If he'd go ahead and follow his instincts and concentrate on what needs to be done without worrying about votes he could be a great President. I wish he would be.'

JARRING GETS PEACE PLAN FROM ISRAEL ... FBI PROBES ANTI-SOVIET BOMBING ... APOLLO 14 CREW EAGER TO BE OFF FOR THE MOON ... PRESIDENT IS 'OPTIMISTIC' ON HIS 58th BIRTHDAY.

There is a certain similarity between George Romney, Secretary of Housing and Urban Development, and John Volpe, Secretary of Transportation: the similarity of men who have long had their eyes on the Big Brass Ring but, in both cases, are in all probability never going to catch it. Both are successful former governors, Romney of Michigan, Volpe of Massachusetts, who seem somewhat submerged and lost-track-of in the rush of Washington. Neither likes it, obviously, and neither may stay for long. While they do, their support is dutiful, their comments of a pattern. Both are pleasant and able gentlemen, even though both follow the custom—most usually followed by those who still have political ambitions of one kind or another—of

234

having an aide sit in on interviews. It is an interesting sidelight that neither the President, his family nor the really disinterested men of the Cabinet—Red Blount, Bill Rodgers, David Kennedy at Treasury, James Hodgson at Labour—bother to have their interviews thus protectively attended. The practice is usually a tip-off that ambition and excessive caution still reside.

George Romney is ruggedly good-looking, outwardly relaxed, earnest; received me wearing sports slacks and a blue cardigan in his office, which overlooks unattractive southeast Washington and the lazy sprawl of the Potomac River. The tenor of his comments was not unexpected:

'This Administration is making more progress in housing than has ever been made in this area and I believe we are going to continue. One of our problems is to achieve credibility that our goals are being pursued honestly and earnestly. Of course, many of these goals have been around for a long time. The problem has been for government to get the housing starts up in order to ease the shortages. In prior years, new housing starts were never beyond 50,000. Last year they were up to 410,000 units of government and private housing. We hope to get starts up to 1,750,000 a year before too long.

'I am always struck by the President's breadth and depth of knowledge on these questions and his ability to articulate significant considerations in so many fields.

'He is much more effective in working sessions than he is in his public appearances, even though he is very good in those, particularly on TV. The warmth of his personality and his intellectual capacity do not come across clearly in public appearances as they do in private. He has a great desire to do what needs to be done for the country, and that deep sincerity sometimes doesn't come across on television. There is too great a tendency for some critics to overemphasize the political conditions that must of course enter into his decisions, and to overlook his basic personal dedication to them.

'I think he has moved the country from a very dangerous situation two years ago. He was confronted then with nightmares on the domestic scene, as he said, that had to be eliminated, and I believe he has gone a considerable distance to eliminate them. In the foreign area I think he has operated magnificently in winding down the war.'

John Volpe is a health bug who works out in the gym and sauna room on the top floor of his modernistic new department building every morning when he comes to work, and shows the results of it in his trim and efficient appearance. He is pleasant, forceful, intelligent—and diplomatic about his relations with the White House staff, which have not always been smooth.

'There is no question but that in this Administration, as in all others, there has been a shakedown cruise for a while to get things under way. There has been the gradual development of a team. In this process there naturally have been some frictions here and there. But the development of the Domestic Council has created a focal point for the decision-making process. It has created a tremendous potential to get answers more quickly for the President, and also to work in getting information back to the Cabinet from the President and the White House. Of course, even though we work well with the Budget, sometimes they want to cut and that hurts. But I think we have got sufficient funds for the programmes we think are important. Overall, we have a very fine relationship with the Domestic Council and the OMB.

'I think to some extent the President, like all of us, is a little frustrated that things don't move faster in some areas. When you sit in the top seat, as I found out when I was governor and as I know the President has found out in the White House, you don't accomplish things quite as rapidly as you do in business. You just have to take into account the fact that things don't move as fast in government.

'I find there is very little opposition from holdovers in this department to Nixon policies. I think Civil Service people as a class represent thousands of dedicated, clean, hard-working people who do a devoted job for the government. There are tremendous resources and reserves of real talent in the Civil Service and I have not felt any particular opposition in this department to programmes of this Administration.

'Our major concern right now is safety, on the highways, on the seas and in the air. We have a good record in that area and it is getting better all the time. We had a reduction in traffic fatalities from 5.6 per cent to 5 per cent for every hundred million miles of highway travel and this means we saved about eleven hundred extra lives this past year. We have reversed the trend towards higher slaughter on the highways. Of course, it is still a tremendous problem, but we are beginning to turn it around. As far as the airlines are concerned, I think we have turned a significant corner also. There's not been a single death on our commercial airways in 1970. The auto industry is co-operating in try to get better safety devices, we are getting more air traffic controllers, we are adopting educational programmes on safety in all areas that this department touches.

'We have spent enormous sums on public transportation to create the best highway system in the world, the interstate system. The federal government began in 1964 to take a definite interest in public transportation and in these last couple of years we have come a long, long way. We passed the Urban Mass Transportation Act of 1970 last year, providing a $10 billion programme stretched over twelve years which will help solve the tremendous congestion of traffic in our cities. Twenty per cent of our major cities need subways but above all they need good bus systems. There's been a drop of two thirds in the buses of the country. Our job is to upgrade, provide new systems and new buses, make it a public responsibility and get the job done.

'For the railways we passed the Railpax system and that is going to be a start in updating equipment, keeping key lines open. As we go along, the Railpax Corporation can add additional routes and enlarge the service. In time, hopefully, we will be back somewhere near the full rail network we once had in this country.

'The President seems to thrive on a very heavy work schedule. Physically, he is in excellent shape. Both mentally and physically he seems to have grown into the job as though he always belonged there—and of course he was very well qualified for it in the first place.

'We have a great President!'

LAIRD SEEING THIEU. NEW VIET AID FOR CAMBODIA ON THE AGENDA ... JARRING ENDS ISRAEL VISIT, EXPRESSES HOPE ON TALKS ... SOVIET IRE SPREADS TO NEWSMEN ... EGYPTIAN PRESIDENT TAKES TOUGH STAND ON PEACE TALKS.

One of the younger Democrats on the Hill in point of age, he is getting to be one of the more senior in point of service. In recent years he has become a consistent and leading critic of the Vietnam War. Yet he remains, as he has always been, a very fair-minded man.

'The case is not all in on Nixon. He has certainly changed his policy in Southeast Asia and has undertaken to wind down the war. It's a question of how far he intends to go, and how much, or whether, we are going to get involved in more Cambodias and Laos-type excursions along the way. He has to decide fundamentally how much he can afford to expose American troops to further Communist attack during the withdrawal period. He could conceivably decide to go back in full strength if he felt the circumstances warranted it.

'Domestically he has serious problems with the economy. I don't think he has been forthright about it—he has been reluctant to take any direct action, even in the area of simply urging, or raising the possibility of, wage and price controls. Basically the Republican idea is not to interfere with the economy, to let economic processes move along more or less untouched. But the government can use moral suasion to help maintain guidelines, if it will do so. Or it can use its direct authority and the force of law. Nixon has been very reluctant to do either. I think his capacity to use moral suasion in this area was greatly undermined at the very start of his administration when he accepted a $100,000 increase in his own salary and approved almost doubling the salaries of the Cabinet, members of Congress and other high government officials. When he went along with this, it made it very difficult for him, for his Cabinet officers and for others to impose Administration guidelines on labour and industry.

'In a way, we have reached a point of paradox in this country, in that if liberal measures are called for, it is best to elect a conservative President. Nixon has been very liberal in his State of the Union proposals and it is obvious that no Democrat could do this without having the roof raised by the conservatives. Conversely, perhaps if conservative measures are needed it is best to elect a liberal President. For instance, John Kennedy has a continuing reputation for liberalism because of his "style", but actually his programme was quite conservative—it increased our military involvement in Southeast Asia, it expanded our military forces and in many ways domestically, also, it was a very conservative programme. In this conservative President, Nixon, you may have the beginning of a new liberal era.

'The problems we face have a sort of intractability to them. Whoever thought that Nixon, for instance, would ever be a Keynesian? He was always going to have a balanced budget. Now he talks about a deficit budget, pump-priming and the rest to beef up the economy.

'There are only certain options open to any President. If Nixon fails to persist in his withdrawal from Vietnam, if we are still caught with 200,000 men in the field and American helicopters all over the place, he will lose in '72 and he should. But if his policy has proved effective, if we are well on our way out of Vietnam, if the economy is healthy again and inflation is under control, he will win and he should.

'There is, however, one interesting caveat about that—the possibility that Nixon won't win a new term, no matter what. This is because he isn't liked—he just isn't liked as a man. There is no warm feeling towards Nixon in the country. It's an odd phenomenon. There's no real warmth or enthusiasm for the man. He is no longer viscerally hated and he is not viscerally loved. There is a sort of negative reaction. Maybe if the Democrats put up a man who is likeable, attractive, appealing in a human sense, there will be a change, no matter what. A President is measured not so much by what he does, but by what he does not do—and by his personality.

'Nixon cannot afford to fail. But it is not necessarily true that his success will guarantee that he will be re-elected.'

NIXON PREPARES A CUT OF BILLIONS IN BUSINESS TAXES
... NIXON CONSIDERS AGENCY SHAKE-UP. OVERHAUL WOULD
CREATE FOUR DEPARTMENTS AND DISSOLVE OR ALTER
SOME OTHERS ... JEWISH DEFENCE LEAGUE PLANS TO
HARASS RUSSIANS.

Attorney General John Mitchell is full of pipe smoke and chuckles, much discretion—which sometimes raises the question whether he really knows all that much about the subject he is being discreet about—and an occasional shrewd comment.

He is faintly reminiscent of Alfred Hitchcock about to launch into a description of his latest thriller and loving all the intrigue of it. I forebore from asking about his wife.

'I have no real idea yet about the shape and emphasis of the 1972 campaign, although it is true, as reported in the press, that I will head it up. The economic picture is, of course, the prime issue, and the Democrats would insist on keeping it that way even if it weren't. If the Vietnamization programme succeeds the war may well be behind us by the time the campaign begins. The Middle East could also be a problem, and so could crime and riots, although they are under much better control than they have been in a long time.

'The President hasn't changed a hell of a lot since the first day he came into office. I really don't believe that he has changed one iota. I've been amazed at the ability he has to make decisions and then go on without worrying about them or bitching about them when things go wrong. He allocates his time very effectively and appropriately and I think he handles the job very well. There probably has never been anyone who became President who had studied the office so long. He knew which doors to open and which to close. As for temper, he'll let fly with a couple of cuss words or expletives now and then, let off steam, and go on from there. He doesn't hold grudges or stay mad for long. It isn't his nature.

'I think Agnew is set. I don't think the President is going to lock himself in on it at this time, although he may—it's not his nature to do so, but he may. Most people fail to realize that Ted Agnew has been absolutely loyal to the President and 1000 per cent co-operative. The President is not unmindful or unappreciative of that.

'The Democrats in these remaining two years are going to use every trick in the book. The Republican Administration is going to have to be a lot smarter than we have been. We were mouse-trapped too many times in the first two years.

'If George Wallace runs in the South in '72 you will have one set of problems for the President to meet. If the labour and big-city boys get control of the Democratic Convention and nominate a Democrat like Scoop Jackson, you will have another set. McGovern in that case would probably break away and split the party. Muskie is going to have his troubles because obviously his competitors in the party are going to cut up the front-runner if they can.

'I think that as far as we're concerned, the Republican National Committee is going to be what it was intended to be —an aid to getting the President re-elected. As far as I'm concerned, I'm opting to get the Presidential politician out of the White House—I want him to be President and forget politics.

'In my particular area of crime and justice, I'm never satisfied with what we're doing, and I know he isn't either, because we both want to move faster than circumstances will permit. Our system of justice is so damned slow. And there is so much to be done.'

Cabinet comment (not John Mitchell): 'I have only seen once in two years an occasion in which he indicated any signs of emotion or stress. That was after some issue had failed on the Hill, I think the Haynsworth nomination. Next day I had a meeting with him and some people from the private sector in my particular area. As soon as we were seated he began to talk about the defeat in a way that showed he was resentful and under strain, and he talked about it steadily for a whole hour, until the meeting ended. I had never seen him do this before, and it was obvious that he was very upset. But that is the only time I have seen him in such a state.

'As a general rule, he seems to be able to adjust himself mentally, to take the good and bad, to deal calmly and pleasantly with his problems. When he is tackling a problem there is no indication he has any other problems. I have never heard him cuss out any subordinate, or cuss out any problem or individual, which is more than I can say for Eisenhower, Kennedy and Johnson. I have never seen him pound the table.

'He has a good sense of humour but not a frequent one. Occasionally he will make a clever remark, but mostly, for him, it is serious business.

'Nixon has intelligence, modesty and shyness. This causes people to say he is not a warm person. He can be very warm when in a setting where he is totally comfortable. His mind is so organized and so brilliant that not many things escape him. Not very often does he get on the track without knowing the details and knowing where he is going.

'He probably has fewer cronies than any recent President. He doesn't drive people the way Johnson did, or ask the impossible of them, or call them in the middle of the night. He is much more thoughtful than that.'

He holds a high and powerful position in the Republican hierarchy. He is tough, he is shrewd, he is intelligent. Sometimes he goes along with the President, sometimes he does not. Better than most, he understands the personality at 1600 Pennsylvania Avenue.

'I think I can agree with Pat Moynihan, who said that the President was the most civil man he had ever dealt with, courteous, deferential, listening carefully to other people's opinions and having great respect and consideration for them.

'Having said that I would add:

'Like every President before him, the desire to be a good President and be remembered in history as a good President is a stronger motivating force than any other crosscurrents with which he deals. Being a politician, he cannot help but be aware of political effects of what he does and political consequences. But in the way of leaders, often when you are desirous of acquiring good things and are proposing them, you sometimes cloak them in a political appeal.

'You sometimes fly in on your objective at a lower level than is necessary or than you need to, to achieve the objective.

'I don't think he has yet reached the point of feeling that the public is willing to accept him on the basis of the high idealism that he generally feels. He seems to be conditioned by the feeling that the public thinks of Nixon as a politician and therefore when he proposes something, it must be on a political basis—he does not feel that a more direct and honest appeal based on his own emotions and idealism would succeed.

'His attitude towards welfare is an example. I think he genuinely favours welfare reform and is sincerely for reorganization of the government. But while he genuinely wants people to get a better start in life and to have their government run better, what does he propose in the way of welfare—what appeal does he make to them? He presents it as a political issue: he appeals to the lower elements. It is a mistake to present welfare reform as just a matter of "getting the loafers off the payroll".

That is Chamber of Commerce and service-club talk, which goes over big in the churches and the poolrooms. But it lowers the dignity of the objective and I think it demeans his own approach to it.

'I think he still has the feeling that "People think I'm a politician and they'll let me have certain things if I present them as the politician they think I am." He seems to think that it is impossible for the public to accept him as being sincere, and therefore he will act and appeal in an insincere manner.

'I think this is a sad and unnecessary mistake.

'I think in a sense he feels he would be embarrassed in front of his old colleagues of Congress if he took the position that he generally believed in his own rhetoric. Now, if he took "the lift of a driving dream" and let his publicity people go to town on it, and conditioned his statements and appeal on that idealistic basis, I think he would be accepted by the public. They would like this idealism. They would follow it. But he does not do that.

'I think his finest hour came when he went to the Lincoln Memorial at the time of Cambodia. This was instinctive. This was human. This was the reaction of a concerned man and an honest man filled with a real desire to find out where his country was going. Also his speech to the Children's Conference and his speech in Nebraska to youth showed real evidence of a man who cares about his country.

'But this idealism he often derogates by dropping into such middle-class rhetóric as he has presented to Congress. The same thing seems to apply to the whole attitude of the White House in its relation to Congress. There is a political appeal rather than an idealistic appeal—this business of wearing buttons bearing the label "I care for Congress!" We are not button-minded here, we are not button-manipulated, we are not button-pushed. They don't seem to see the difference down there between caring for Congress and really understanding Congress.

'It is really as though the President is almost too embarrassed to look these guys in the eye, these tough politicians up here, and say, "I believe—I have a dream". He seems to feel "I can't sell them on that level", so he seeks the political level. I think he is trying to overcome this right now, but whether he can, I don't know.

'By the same token, revenue sharing and government re-organization will have to be sold, *I* think, on the basis of giving people a better government and a fair shake. It's going to be a long, hard road and he may not get what he wants, but he's going to have to keep at it and he's going to have to keep it on a basis, *I* think, of simple good government. I think if he does that, he will have a much better chance to succeed then if he puts it on a low political appeal.

'I think he worries too much about balancing his statements between liberals and conservatives. I think he sees a greater dichotomy between the two than is actually there. He moves too fast to give labels to people. He does not realize that most people, when they are asked to label themselves, say either "I'm a moderate" or "I'm a little left of moderate."

'He would be better off if he composed his appeals in terms of centrist or moderate policies and stopped worrying about whether liberals or conservatives are going to be upset or can be appealed to.

'As for '72, I don't think the American people vote too much on issues or on even the man himself. I think they want to know what is being done for them. Then they have sort of an instinctive feeling as to whether it would be better to change the guard or let the incumbent go ahead and continue the job. I think they regard all politicians with suspicion and so from time to time they think it's wise to make changes, because they just figure it's time to let the other guys do it. I don't really think the American people trust either crowd, but they feel that if you shift them around from time to time, you're apt to get a better shake. I think '72 will be decided by their fundamental feeling, "Does this guy care for me, is he giving me a fair shake, or is it time for a change?"

'As far as the White House staff is concerned, the Congressional liaison men who come up here are sincere and hardworking. The leadership has no complaint at all with them. There are some fellows around here who want their hands held, who want the President to pay attention to them, or want these staff members up here to pay attention to them, all the time. But most people, at least in the higher-ranking leadership, find it a very satisfactory relationship.

'However, at the Ehrlichman-Haldeman level there is failure

to understand the extreme complexity of assuring Congressional approval. It doesn't come about simply because you believe that something is a good thing. There is a tendency down there to just wish that Congress would go away and stop bothering them, to say, "Why do they bother us—can't they see that what we propose is good?—they just want to get headlines—they're just being ornery—we've explained it and it makes sense, so why aren't they with us?"

'Ehrlichman, Shultz and Haldeman never ran for public office, and while Finch has had some experience with the legislature in California, they really don't believe Finch when he says that they are heading for trouble if they don't really understand the personalities and the problems up here in Congress. They much prefer the soft life of San Clemente or Key Biscayne or Camp David: they like their little cakes and ale, they like their cushy prerogatives, they just don't want to do the job of getting along with Congress, because they really don't understand how important that job is.

'They are very zealous in the President's interest, but they are often very stupid in what Congress is all about. They believe they can cure their faults by working harder, but that is not the answer.

'Now, if the President continues working with Congress as he is beginning to do much more actively this year, then the results will show. It will get to the point where Congress will call Ehrlichman "John" and bicker pleasantly with him, and things will get on a nice personal basis.

'It is a search for rapport between people who basically consider themselves naturally superior to Congress and people in Congress who resent and criticize the palace guard.

'I never have understood why the President and the people around him fail to understand our problems up here on the Hill. When I took my oath of office, I took it because millions of voters in my state had pulled a little green cloth across the booth and marked my name. My first obligation is to them. My second is to my colleagues here in this body, and *then* my obligation is to the President. If there is a conflict between these prior obligations and my obligation to the President, then I simply have to tell the President that I cannot go along. But they don't seem to understand that down there.

'Possibly the reason for this difficulty in the staff, and the fact that it has continued, is that the President delegates power and then he has strong loyalties to those to whom he delegates it and strong reliance upon them. I think in the last couple of years he has been so involved with his first love, foreign policy —and so commanded by it— that he has let other things slip away. I think that now he is realizing that he must pay more attention to domestic matters, and also I think the staff is beginning to get an inkling that they must pay more attention to the real feelings and the real desires and sensibilities of the Congress.

'Whether this will prove out in actual fact and operation, however, is another matter, and one that remains to be seen.'

PRESIDENT WARNS ON STEEL RISE, HINTS IMPORTS MAY BE SOUGHT TO HALT BOOST ... SOVIETS DELAY ALLIED TRAFFIC ON AUTOBAHN ... U.S. CUTS MORTGAGE RATE CEILING TO $7\frac{1}{2}$ PER CENT AS AID TO HOUSING MARKET ... BERRIGAN INDICTED IN KIDNAP PLOT.

In the grey old Treasury Building across the street from the White House, outgoing Secretary David Kennedy, quiet, white-haired, soft-spoken, had a fire in the grate against the winter chill. Persian rugs were on the floor, light blue wallpaper on the walls. He had just been appointed special roving ambassador by the President to make way for John Connally's appointment as Secretary of the Treasury. The change did not appear to disturb him overmuch. He was amiable, dignified and pleasant.

'It has been my custom in this office not to worry a lot about how often I see the President. I meet with him on a basis of his interest, which is the way it should be. Sometimes we have met frequently and at other times when he has been engaged in other areas such as military policy, it may have been once a month. We have found that it is hard to separate the economic issue from the international. It becomes a question of how to fit into the departmental hodgepodge with our own problems over here.

'I feel that I have seen him whenever necessary. A Cabinet officer can't run to the President all the time. Actually'—with a little smile—'I probably didn't go running over often enough.

246

Perhaps I should have made a bigger thing out it.

'But I remember one episode that seemed to sum up his own attitude. We had a major decision on finance to reach. I called the White House to say I'd like to come over and see the President sometime in the next few hours. I said I needed his full co-operation and support. Within twenty minutes he called back himself and said he would come on over here. He did so, we had a meeting with all the top people involved and in about two hours we had our programme worked out. That direct approach I have found to be typical of him.

'I have no feeling that he is isolated from us. I could very well *feel* isolated if I wanted to see him every five minutes, but he has an impossible task in the sense of just finding time to do the things he has to do. So I don't feel that I should bother him unless I have something really important to say.

'We have had this problem: lots of people outside the government want to see the President. I have friends who are very anxious to get in and see the President, principally, I think, just so they can say they have seen the President. In those cases, I send the information on them along to the staff and let the staff make the decision. Most of the time my friends don't get the appointment.

'Now, I know they could if I went over and made a big case out of it, hit the table and shouted—and I know some in the Cabinet who tend to do that, because they want to show their friends how important they are and what influence they have. I'm not trying to impress anybody. The only thing I worry about is when someone down the line in the staff is in a position to isolate the President without really having any necessity to do so. That, it seems to me, *is* a problem and a danger, and I don't know quite how you handle it. But it is there.

'The question is how far to go in putting on the pressure to get to see him. The staff in some instances has to decide, because they could not possibly take everything to the President himself to decide. The same thing happens to me here—my staff turns down many things that I don't even hear about. The real danger does come down the staff line in the White House, and sometimes there is an isolation of the President at that point. There is also the danger that sometimes when the President tells them what to do, possibly in a hasty moment or a moment of annoyance, they take it as a cast-in-stone order. The word comes back, "The President wants this done." Well, does he or doesn't he? It becomes a real question. I have had the word many times from the staff that "The President wants it done." I've said, "You go back and tell the President he doesn't want it done." And often that's been the end of it.

'I had a long talk with the President before I joined up, and he said at that time that he was going to operate with a very small staff. I raised the question whether he could, but he thought then he could do so. As it turned out, he wasn't able to.

'I'm convinced, however, that the White House staff can't run the government. The confidence of the country and the bureaucracy is in the departments. We have to formulate things and be on the firing line. While we have all those telephones and all those buzzers, it's still a problem of decision by the people who really have the confidence. And that is something the White House staff in some areas does not have.

'The President has been deeply involved in economic problems. I think from my own point of view that handling the economy has been more difficult than I foresaw. The correction of inflation and recession have posed major problems. I think we went about as far as we could go in solving the inflation without adding to the economic problem.

'I am very optimistic that things are going to continue to pick up—more optimistic now than I have been in some time. The problem now is to get the economy back on a growth basis and at the same time reduce unemployment. Things have to be slowed down a bit—we can't let them run wild. It's a lot of fun to let it grow, put on the gas rather than the brakes, but sometimes government has to put on the brakes.

'The problem now is that we have had thirty-four years of running at full capacity, putting pressure on the economic boiler, and somebody had to slow things down: it was up to us to do it. We've got great strength in our whole business setup and also in the fundamental structure of our economy. In the old days when something like the Penn Central failed, the whole system might collapse. Nowadays we have a much more stable situation.

'In my new job as a roving ambassador I'll have special assignments from the President—in fact, he's already lined up a couple for me even before I leave this office. I'll have a principal interest in international economic matters, but in a way it will be more than that. Whatever comes up is where I'll be active, and I know from experience that the special places occur where the President needs help, and he will call on me then. I won't have a staff, and in some ways it won't be easy, but I am looking forward to it. I really wanted to go back to private life. But the President said he wouldn't give me my chair in the Cabinet Room, I had to stay and be a member of the Cabinet. So I agreed to do so.

'I am not a politician. I have said this many times to my disadvantage, but I love to say it. I think it's going to be a very difficult time in the Treasury in these two years. I hope John Connally can get bipartisan support. If he can, then revenue sharing and the family assistance plan may get through, even though both rouse some very strong feelings. His work is really cut out for him: it is not going to be easy. On the whole, however, the economy will get stronger, the schools are settling down, we're getting a better balance in the country. If we get the era of peace that the President wants, it will be the greatest thing that ever happened.'

He is in his first term in the Senate, from an area traditionally Republican. He looks sour and he is.

'It's an odd thing to assess, why they act the way they do down there. It's like dealing with a different institution at different times. Of course, I opposed them on the ABM and on Haynsworth, and have been critical of Vietnam on occasion. The whole attitude towards me has changed completely.

'The President talks a good game on co-operation, but they don't know what it means down there. Most of us have found that if you disagree with the President once, you don't see him again. I disagreed on ABM and Vietnam, and that's the end of it. Now, I'm very much interested in his State of the Union programme, I think it's very ambitious and laudable, but it is extremely hard to help the President on things like this, because they don't let you. You're either with them all the way or you aren't with them at all.

'The problem seems to be with the people around him. But

it is also with the President himself.

'They don't have any understanding or any concern for people in Congress who don't go along with them 100 per cent. Ehrlichman and Haldeman deal with you in a way that is colder than a mother-in-law's kiss. In an effort to protect the President they have smothered him.

'When you talk to him he listens but there is no follow-through. You get the feeling that it's simply a programmed deal and that once you've said your piece, that's it.

'They have things so out of focus down there that your vote on ABM or Haynsworth or Carswell is more important than everything else. You may vote for everything else they want, but if you vote against some key measure, then you're on the list. They're more worried about what they get beat on, than on their successes. They bruise easy and they don't heal much.

'I will say it has changed the attitude of a lot of Senators around here about running for re-election or even staying any longer at all. Because it's just God-damned unpleasant to take what you have to take from the White House when you oppose them. Many Republican Senators have told me that they had more contact with Kennedy and Johnson than they do with Nixon. They just don't understand it and they just don't like it.'

(And yet, of course, three months later when a group of Republican Senators mounted a staunch defence of the President's policies in Vietnam, he was in the forefront. Somebody in the White House apparently found the key.)

About ten days before I was scheduled to leave town I began asking the staff to find out what had become of the President's answers to my questions. Margita White reported that she was telephoning various people about it. Days passed without an answer. Two days before my departure she said she thought she was making progress: Alex Butterfield was going to be seeing the President, and had agreed to ask.

Next day she called back: the President said he was very sorry, he had been too busy to answer as fully as he would like, he was working on it, he hoped I would understand, it would be along by mail in due course. I said fine, no hurry.

Apparently the lengthy delay in finding this out was caused

*by the fact that everybody assumed that he had already given
the answers to someone. The universal questions then became:
Who's to blame? And if I am, how can I find a suitable excuse?
When someone finally got to a direct man with a direct question
he got a direct answer and the mystery was solved in half a
minute.*

*In this, as in all administrations, a straight line, in the White
House, is sometimes not the shortest distance between two
points. Staffs become very timid about treating a President as
though he were a reasonable man.*

*Which is not a good thing: for them, for him, or for the
country.*

Secretary of Commerce Maurice Stans is a quiet, grey-haired,
pleasant-faced, soft-spoken, thoughtful gentleman in his sixties
who served Eisenhower as Director of the Budget in his last
term and is thoroughly familiar with government and with
Nixon. He has a mammoth office with panelled walls, an
enormous desk, a large picture of Herbert Hoover and a staff
member sitting in on the interview.

'We have had very little problem over here with the White
House staff. The initiative is up to us to contact the staff most
of the time—90 per cent of the time, I would say. About 10
per cent of the time they contact us over some question of
policy or ask us about a business-related or department-related
programme. Our contact mainly is with Peter Flanigan. He
raises questions with me two or three times a week and occasionally we have breakfast together to discuss our problems.

'I think the staff as a group is extremely able, although in the
beginning there was an inevitable uneasiness among them. But
this has settled down to a very high level of confidence and
general intelligence. As of now, I would say the staff is working
extremely efficiently.

'I am glad to see the President initiate his new policy of
Cabinet meetings every two weeks because contact with the
President is without doubt important to the individual Cabinet
officer when he needs it. I have had no difficulty on that score.
My presumption is that the President wants me to run my
department and come to him only when I have something of
sufficient importance. Therefore I try to reduce the times when

I do come to him. I tell his appointment people whether or not what I want to see him about is a matter of urgency or a matter of time, and then they work it out in his schedule.

'I probably haven't seen the President for private meetings more than once every six weeks. I usually have some eight or ten subjects that I have saved up for that period. The Commerce Department generally, of course, is a lot less emotional and political than something like State or HEW or Defence. We can work in a calm atmosphere and generally we do so.

'I think in the beginning there was covert opposition and foot dragging from some holdovers in the department, but I think that disappeared rather promptly and I am not aware of any now. Here I think the Administration can claim some credit, because the Commerce Department was sinking in prestige under my predecessors in recent years, partly because there were so many of them who came in and went out so fast. We have now rebuilt some of the prestige that the department needs to do the job with the business community which needs to be done.

'I only knew Ike in his last years. I would say that he had a great warmth, that he was a bit more temperamental than Nixon on some subjects—less pliable. He was less dynamic and less determined to effect change. He had several reorganization plans which were nowhere near as bold as Nixon's. Nixon's plans are very bold. Eisenhower would never have proposed such a plan because that was the sort of issue that would provoke problems and potential unrest and he did not want to do this. So he would have refrained from putting in anything as extensive as this. I would say the staffs of the two Presidents have been much the same in what they do, as it has finally turned out. Nixon originally was going to use a lot of generalists but he has found himself in a situation where he has finally settled down to using specific channels and experts on specific things.

'The principal problem of my department is to keep the general public from forgetting the importance of the American business system and how much it has contributed to developing our society. Any enthusiasm over environment and consumerism has to have a sense of balance. Some things require a trade-off between the best interests of the public and the consumer, the environment and the market place. There is a price the public has to pay for getting these things done. For instance, on the question of power plants you have to balance off how much damage they might do to the environment against the fact that we are coming into a power-shortage period and have to have the power. Our most difficult problem is to help bring a sense of balance to issues such as this.

'The government has to approach corporate entities with some attempt to understand their problems, instead of simply making them the whipping boy for everything.

'Business is making quite clear that they are willing to undertake voluntary efforts both in consumerism and in cleaning up the environment. Our job is to give them credit for this and to work with them so as to encourage that voluntary impulse.'

PRESIDENT WEIGHS TOUGH WAGE CURB FOR CONSTRUCTION
... EGYPT OFFERS PEACE PLAN TO MEDIATOR ... CAMBODIA
VIABILITY TESTED IN OFFENSIVE ... COPTER-BORNE ISRAELIS
HIT IN LEBANON ... ENVIRONMENT AGENCY ACTS AGAINST
DDT.

'It's difficult to judge a man with whom you have no communication. It simply does not exist.'

He is young, able, a relative newcomer to Republican ranks in the Senate; tagged by the press as 'liberal', probably somewhere in between; originally disposed to be friendly to the White House, but cooling fast.

'I'm very hard put to say whether the President is at fault or the staff—except that the President sets the tone. The President always sets the tone.

'Many of my constituents are directly involved with government and are very much interested in their personal security. When a new administration comes in, they pause and wait for the wind. Then they turn their faces toward it.

'This time there is no wind....

'There is an attitude: there are perfectly good Republican lawyers who would be excellent federal judges. But because they were not pre-Miami supporters of the President, they are ignored. That represents the attitude.

'When I was a poor little back-country back-bencher in the

253

House, Jack Kennedy had my wife and me down to dinner. I have been mildly critical of some Nixon policies. I have never been invited to dinner by President Nixon. That too is an attitude....

'How do you communicate when there is no communication?'

MUSKIE, KOSYGIN CONFER FOUR HOURS. EXCHANGE VIEWS ON MIDEAST AND INDOCHINA AT KREMLIN—NEED FOR AMITY CITED ... ISRAEL RAIDS VILLAGE ON LEBANESE COAST ... FULL FUNDS FOR ARTS SOUGHT BY NIXON.

The top men in the Defence Department are alike in several major and—given their task of riding herd on the military establishment—vitally necessary respects. Both Secretary Melvin Laird and Undersecretary David Packard are shrewd, intelligent, pragmatic—and tough. This does not make them too popular with such bodies as the Senate Foreign Relations Committee, which prefers Cabinet officers it can bully. But it makes them very good from the President's standpoint.

Mel Laird, who served in Congress from Wisconsin for sixteen years before his appointment as Secretary of Defence, is bald, bullet-headed, pleasant-faced, with small, deep-set eyes that look up at one from under lowered eyebrows. He gives his boss the highest marks—'Oh yes, he's always cool under pressure. He's been very cool always. Never flustered. Very calm about everything'—but aside from what he seems to regard as that necessary duty, he speaks with a reasonable candour and some pride in the legislative record of the DOD.

'We're the only department that hasn't lost a vote on Capitol Hill in two years. We haven't lost a single vote. I've had over sixty-five breakfasts with members of Congress since I've been in office, to explain our position. We haven't lost any votes and we don't expect to lose any votes.

'Morale is pretty good over here, though I do find some difficulty with the military, who continue to press their points of view regardless of budget considerations or policy considerations, and never give me a direct or unqualified recommendation on anything. I'm not criticizing them, that's their job, just as it's mine to keep them in line and mediate between their various claims and wishes. They have been quite alarmed by the withdrawal of troops from Vietnam and South Korea, but they go along when the decision is made.

'I find the President very well prepared on military matters. He certainly listens well. It is up to all of us over here, of course, to point out the pitfalls along the way in the major decisions he has to make. But he listens very carefully and we feel that he takes our advice under very serious consideration, and that it enters into his final decisions.

'I had a little problem at one time with Henry Kissinger and his staff, who attempted a bit at first to interfere with DOD budget and policy. But we worked it out. I have not really had any major problems in the budget sector—certainly none of the problems that existed between the National Security Council and the DOD before I came into office. That kind of problem has not existed, as far as I'm concerned. I think we've got a very good working relationship. The NSC staff has always given me good support, and the President I would say has given me 100 per cent support. I only recall one major disagreement over policy, and on that one both NSC and State were opposed to me. That was the case where I felt that 20,000 troops should be withdrawn from the NATO forces in Europe. I lost that one. But most of the time I have been successful in winning my point of view.

'The threat in the Middle East has to be met by keeping a proper balance of forces and a proper-strength Israeli force. We're doing that. I personally approve all the Israeli requests and watch it very carefully. I am confident we are going to maintain the proper balance that the President wants.

'It is true that the Soviet Union is apparently engaged on a progressive and aggressive programme of expansion, and apparently intends to try this for the next ten years or so, but within that time period we are confident we can maintain our forces and overcome that particular threat. If it continues beyond that point'—confident Mel Laird looks thoughtful and then shrugs—'we will just have to see what we will do then. . . .'

Dave Packard, tall, bluff and no-nonsense, has had his run-ins with the White House staff too. But he too has managed to survive them nicely.

'I have found from time to time'—a dry little smile—'that some of the boys at the White House do try to get into the defence area. But fortunately Mel Laird is a very good and very close friend of the President, and so we don't really have too much trouble, because he can always go straight to headquarters and get what he wants. Also, I guess I'm pretty tough myself. We have our little run-ins now and then, but on the whole the Defence Department manages to do pretty well. Henry is disposed to get into our area sometimes, but we have not had any real quarrels, and on the whole we manage to work together.

'There is, admittedly, a tendency on the part of some of the White House staff to be a little high-handed, and perhaps even arrogant, in their treatment of the departments, and this does sometimes cause problems—for others perhaps more than for us.

'We are engaged over here essentially on a constant series of decisions on how to balance factors against one another as regards growing Soviet strength and our own military position. We have to decide between many things and many pressing demands on our strength, and this is not so easy. It seems to me that on the Hill we get along fairly well with most people, although some of the committees like to give us a hard time and some of the members seem to be looking for headlines by attacking us. Of course'—a cheerful grin—'one of my strong points in this job is that I don't have to stay. If I get mad enough I can just pack up and go home. This gives me a certain independence which comes in handy both with the Hill and the White House.'

SOME PRICES RAISED 6.8 PER CENT BY U.S. STEEL. STEP
FOLLOWS INCREASE OF 12 PER CENT BY BETHLEHEM THAT
NIXON DECRIED ... NIXON SENDS AID TO MIDDLE EAST TO
BAR OIL CRISIS ... SECURITY GROWS TIGHTER IN NATION'S
COURTROOMS ... 6.6 PER CENT ARE UNEMPLOYED, CANADA
REPORTS ... MUSKIE HEARTENED BY SOVIETS.

He's a swinging kid, this perennially youthful Republican: in the last year or so the hair has grown longer and longer, the shirts have grown modder and modder and the highly intelligent and supersensitive political instinct has moved in channels far from the placid ways of his older and more sedate colleagues. But there is no doubt the intelligence is there, and along with it a very astute and perceptive understanding of the personalities and problems at the other end of the Avenue.

'The Presidency is a matter of style—personality—manner. In my opinion, Mr. Nixon has moved towards the traditional concept of the Presidency in both manner and style. The manner in which he has handled it has, in a sense, restored the symbolic importance of the Presidency to the nation. He has rebuilt the respect that most people, whether they agree or disagree, generally tend to feel toward the institution of the Presidency.

'In reference to his family, people tend to look to the White House for the family that represents them, and I think this family has a very high standard in Mrs. Nixon, Tricia, Julie, David and Grandmother Mamie. It is the typical American family, and there is a great dignity and warmth about it. There is a sort of non-flamboyancy, of non-pretence, a sense of well-being, of peace, about the family. The activities around the White House are also relatively quiet and not flamboyant. Those activities also reflect the President's desire to restore the dignity of the office—the emphasis on the white tie, the welcoming speeches to visiting dignitaries, the toasts at the dinners. These represent to America and to the world something which should be symbolized in that office. I give him high marks for that.

'As for his political leadership, his personality is against him in some ways. Personally, I haven't known him well over the years—I don't know *anybody* who has known him well over the years. There is a shyness, almost an uncertainty—not an uncertainty of intention, but of personality. I think he strives to be warm and strives to be friendly, but these things become wooden and automatic: the gesture'—he waved his arms upward—'the smile'—and he gave a very good imitation of the quick, embarrassed smile. 'It is all too mechanical. He is trying to respond. I think the guy has difficulty in simply letting himself go. Now, you take his visit to the Lincoln Memorial at the time of Cambodia. He talked to those kids about football, and of course that was entirely away from what they were interested in at that moment.

'I don't think the staff is as big as he is. It has become very petty, vindictive and revengeful. Their attitude is that if you are not with us 100 per cent, you are just not with us at all. They're as bad as the labour unions in this respect. They tend to do things that hurt Nixon. The staff can damage him, particularly in its personal relationships with Congress, and I think it has.

'If I, as a liberal Republican, have felt this, then think what Democrats have felt. Think what conservative Republicans have felt, for that matter. It is common talk in the cloakroom. I have heard conservatives such as X, Y, and Z complain bitterly about it. Z took a job with the leadership up here. He said it didn't mean much, "but at least now I'll have a chance to tell him what I think face to face when we have those Congressional breakfasts."

'A good part of the problem is really the problem of the staff and its pettiness. For instance, I came out before the convention for Nixon, worked hard in his campaign and right up to Cambodia I was thoroughly for him. I was totally shocked by Cambodia, because I thought it would complicate the political situation at home and a political solution of the war.

'Well, I said so, and in consequence I could tell immediately that I was on the White House staff list of those they don't like. This example is petty but there's been a special project pending in my state for some time. I've taken it up with the appropriate Cabinet officer, he's all set to announce it this afternoon at 2 p.m. As of now [twelve-thirty] I have had no word from the White House staff that this has been approved. But last night they called my colleagues in House and Senate and told them about it. They immediately issued statements for distribution back home. I was able to recover because friends called me and said I was being scooped and had better get on it. But it was a deliberate thing, done by the staff in revenge. I have a feeling that Richard Nixon would never condone that sort of thing. But his staff is like that.

'Where the national image abroad is concerned, I think he has a great capacity to communicate, to give the right image to foreigners who come here and to those he visits on his travels. I think he makes an excellent impression.

'I think he has failed miserably in reaching certain major areas in this country and certain segments of the population such as the blacks, the poor and the young. He has just not come across. He has failed both substantively and personality-wise. These groups have been given the press stereotypes of Nixon over the years; they stick to those and he seems unable to break them down. They are also unaware of the steps he has taken in the environment, in integration and so on to help them. They are ignorant of his leadership. He complicated it for himself by buying the wrong campaign strategy in 1970. All the hatred towards Agnew piled on to Nixon. He got sold a bad bill of goods in that campaign strategy. We had lots of money, good candidates, a lot of campaign chances—and he and the whole party took a beating.

'I think there were two times when he really had the ear of the American people. The first was his inaugural, to which people really listened, which they really liked and which really impressed them. But he really fumbled the ball in not following through on the spirit he aroused at that time. I think that in this last State of the Union message, those who did listen and read were caught up again in something of the same spirit —he had almost the same, if a somewhat lesser, chance to get to the groups that he failed to reach and communicate with before.

'I don't think he has utilized a lot of people who could be helpful to him. I know many of us liberal Republicans have initiated requests that we be allowed to help on many things, but we simply have not got through to him. He needs us and we need him. One time he did send over about a dozen of his people, including Ehrlichman, Haldeman and Klein, but that was it. There was no further attempt to communicate with us.

'Now, I have the ability to keep up certain contacts with students, with black groups—responsible black groups—and with some of the poor, and I am willing to go down the line for the Nixon programme. I'm saying, "Look, man, send me into battle. I'm ready to go." But instead'—making a gesture with his hands as though holding off something—'they keep me at arm's length and don't make use of me.'

U.S. AID GROWS IN CAMBODIA. ARMY COPTERS REPORTED
EN ROUTE FOR FIGHTING ... TWO GUERRILLA GROUPS SPLIT
OVER HUSSEIN ... NIXON AT MID-POINT: TWO YEARS OF
CONTRACTION BRING FEW TRIUMPHS OR TRAGEDIES.

Secretary of Labour James Hedgson is roundfaced, youthful-looking, amiable, easy-spoken; a former vice-president of Lockheed and obviously a very confident and intelligent individual. He too had a fire burning cheerfully in his panelled, high-ceilinged office. He was not accompanied by a protective aide.

'I'm fascinated by Washington—awed and excited, but not intimidated by it. I am not sophisticated politically, I really did not know too much about this aspect of it, since all my work has been in California. I am carried along by the challenges of the day—by the crises that emerge and the things that have to be met and handled each day.

'Here in the Labour Department we reflect the condition in the country. This is a time of people-ferment. There is people-ferment in the world and in this country. There is a high ferment base in everything, with a kind of lateral unrest that extends through everything, an uneasiness, a loosening of traditional bonds. We are trying to establish new bases of manners and morals. Our business in this department is essentially people business, our job is people as groups, labour and industry and minority groups in their relations to each other and to the nation as a whole.

'The President's objective in his first two years has been basically to cool it. My role is to assist the Administration in that cooling process. I think we are helping to solve it by persuasion, and mainly by providing a climate of quietness and discussion and co-operation. It's a problem of the proper climate, of tone, of style.

'We consider ourselves accessible here in this department, we believe in listening. We think we can work in the most effective manner if we do not identify ourselves too closely with one segment or another of the population which might alienate other groups in the population. We are essentially peacemakers and that is the way we try to operate here.

'As for the minorities, with whom we deal a good deal in this department, they have been so subjected to overpromise and to the exaggerated rhetoric of the previous ten years that they have been easily disappointed in government. I got in Art Fletcher to head the Federal Contract Compliance Division, which had only twelve people, and we now have expanded it greatly. Art is a real dynamo and is making considerable headway—but in a very strange climate, because there is a great deal of hostility and suspicion towards what we are trying to do.

'I feel that in the end we are going to get what we want, and then with the economic things taken care of for the minorities, we are going to be able to move forward to the full development of their social roles, the roles which they have a right to expect.

'The unions are in a very critical stage in which they are now being described by some as being "establishment". It is a transitional phase from a kind of mass, almost messianic movement to more of a standard special-interest concept. The top leaders, when the chips are down, come to the aid of the country, as they did when we reached near-chaos in the postal system. On international issues, their reaction to Cambodia and so forth, they have stood up and been counted as they have on such issues as ABM.

'They have been in a very difficult public position in the past four years when their people did not gain a cent in real earnings, even though they did gain on paper, because inflation wiped it out. These have been years when they didn't make any major gains and this adds up to "It's time to get ours." They're now in a catch-up phase, with many demands for big increases. This, of course, is being felt, and will be felt, by the economy, because they are contributing to the inflation that has made them ask for increases.

'This Administration has tried to follow a hands-off policy but sometimes the unions have gone too far, particularly in the construction area in trying to recover a measure of the increase in the cost of living. They are harassed, and we have got to try to be understanding about it. At the same time, we have got to see that their thrust is not carried so far as to add decisively to the very thing they are complaining about.

'I would say our main jobs are to help the disadvantaged groups, to restore the health of our economy and to stress and increase the safety of our workers. We have a worsening record each year in worker safety and the only way to turn it around is for the federal presence to make itself known in the workplace. We got the Safety Act passed and it's going to cause a considerable change in this area. In the long run I think it will be as significant as the Labour Relations Act.

'I think one of our major needs is legislation to deal with

national emergency situations such as railroads. We must get something like this. The Administration is now trying to get hearings on the Emergency Public Interest Protection Act and I think that we are going to make some progress. Labour is against it, but something must be done in this area. I think the logic of that is going to work its own changes in the government and in the way we do things.

'As for labour-management co-operation, when it's in their self-interest to work together, they do so. Where the public interest is concerned, they are not so co-operative and in fact are more sceptical. However, I think the top union level is gradually acquiring a lot more responsibility and co-operation than is present at the second and third levels.

'As for the President, I really have no trouble in working with him. That son of a gun has a marvellous understanding for this business. He played a significant part in settling the 1969 steel strike. He instantly recognizes the basis of the interests involved. He is a man who is much more interested in getting at fundamental matters than at the temporary peripheral systems. It is a joy for me to have such a man for my boss.

'I've heard it said, and I think it's true, that for President Nixon, happiness is having a country to run. I think he is probably as enthralled by his job as I am by my job as Secretary of Labour. The job is twenty-four hours long. But as long as the job is fascinating, who cares?

'As for Washington itself, there's no place where there is a higher calibre of people or more interesting people, but in a sense they are very inbred, and there is sometimes a terrible feeling that unless something emerges from this area, it isn't worth discussing. This I think is a real handicap for a lot of people in Washington.

'There is some resistance from holdovers in the department but I don't think that it is political. I think it is more bureaucratic in nature—I think they are committed to old programmes and when they are faced with the necessity to change, then this creates a resistance in them. In a few instances I have run into some political resistance and there have been some leaks to the press designed to embarrass us, but I think we have taken care of most of them and I think that things are in good shape.

I don't think there is really significant resistance just for the sake of resisting.

'I think "jawboning" will do some good in labour disputes in that it lets the country know that this is a subject about which the President and Labour Department are concerned enough to speak out. There is some evidence that this helps in settling things, or at least in setting a climate in which things can be worked out. Setting a climate seems to be the element of the battle that will do general good and in some cases will create specific solutions.

'It is a good technique if the President does not misuse it or overuse it. And I don't think he will.'

U.S. PLANS TO USE ALL AIR WEAPONS IN CAMBODIAN WAR. SAYS IT WILL FERRY SAIGON'S TROOPS—AIM IS PROTECTION OF AMERICANS IN VIETNAM ... BETHLEHEM CUTS STEEL PRICE RISE TO 6.8 PER CENT. U.S. 'GRATIFIED' BY ROLLBACK ... NIXON ATTACKS 'SPIRAL' IN CONSTRUCTION WAGES ... MCGOVERN ENTERS '72 RACE, PLEDGING TROOP WITHDRAWAL.

He is seventy-two, kindly, paternal, veteran of three terms in the Senate: one Republican who can always be counted on to go along dutifully with whatever a Republican President desires. To him, both as manager of the White House and as manager of the nation, Richard Nixon appears in a friendly light.

'I think the President is not only in firm command of the White House but I think he is operating it more in terms of a planned programme than a day-to-day relation to events. This is a definite contrast to the way it operated the last time.

'As near as I can see, he is personally quite unflappable. I have not seen him upset, and I have seen him courageous. This new programme enunciated in the State of the Union message certainly shows that he is willing to lay his own political career on the line to accomplish the basic reforms he believes necessary for America. Every major thing he suggests indicates that he is thinking of a basic change looking towards the future, rather than current manoeuvring to get him by in 1972.

'"Isolated?" I have never asked for an audience so I have

263

never been offended. But I have been in a number of meetings where my position justified my being present, and I would say the atmosphere when he was there was an atmosphere of interchange, rather than of someone talking down. The President has always listened, and he has, as much as possible, tried to put himself on the same footing with the rest of us. When one is with him, it seems to me, he brings himself down to almost an equal basis—as near to creating an atmosphere of equality as a President of the United States can.

'My own relations with his staff have been very cordial. I consider them to be completely successful. I haven't been snubbed or ignored. I feel as free with them as I do with members of my own staff. I have had no experience of arrogance.

'As for '72, the President has a great many stresses and strains and pressures upon him, but I don't think you can write him off. I don't think the things he has done or the things that have been done to him thus far have destroyed him. I think the country is getting a little tired of basic policies that were developed thirty or forty years ago. I think it is tired of people who simply feel these policies can be maintained if they are adapted to modern problems. The President said he is going to face these problems and try to do something different—to wrench the government into shape in a number of areas.

'I think there is a general attitude in the country of disillusionment and lack of faith in the system because it has not produced all the things that have been promised by past administrations. If the President can really present us with ideas that match the future instead of the past, he will have something to build upon for 1972.'

DEMOCRATS NAME ALBERT AND BOGGS TO TOP HOUSE JOBS. LIBERALS DEFEATED 140-88 IN ATTEMPT TO ELECT UDALL AS MAJORITY LEADER ... U.S. IS NOW FLYING COMBAT MISSIONS FOR LAOS TROOPS. NEW STEP-UP IN AIR WAR. WHITE HOUSE SAYS ITS POLICY BARRING USE OF GROUND FORCES IS UNCHANGED.

Dr. Arthur Burns is the resident pixie at the 'Fed'—the Federal Reserve Board—of which he is now chairman after having served both President Eisenhower and President Nixon as chairman of the President's Council of Economic Advisers. He is sixty-seven and looks younger, roundfaced, dark-skinned, white-haired; extremely intelligent and shrewd and aware of it; speaks like a wry and ironic W. C. Fields. 'Pixie' is the word, at least to those who are in a position to enjoy his pungent and perceptive witticisms. For the President, who must deal with him as the very independent head of the very independent Fed, it must sometimes be another matter, although personally their relationship seems to be cordial and close.

'My relations with the President are very good. He talks to me with complete confidence. He says things and asks things that he wouldn't ask unless he had a great deal of confidence in me. I'm pretty sure that he really does have this confidence, partly, I suppose, because my point of view is that of a pretty objective economist, no matter where I am.

'I do have a little more freedom here at the Fed than I had before. I'm happier here than I would have been if I had continued on the White House staff. In fact, when I joined the White House staff initially for President Nixon I had an agreement that I would come over here when the opening occurred in the chairmanship.

'I can't say honestly that I was drafted for the White House staff—although yes, I suppose I came pretty close to being drafted—although no man is really drafted for a job like that.

'What happened was that I came down here on January 20, 1969, after having worked on the transition report for the President. I arrived with it on the twentieth and was asked to come to the White House and present it to him on the morning of the twenty-first. When I saw him he was very much the President: he didn't give me a chance to speak. I tried to speak up and say that I didn't really want to come to the staff, but he took me into the Cabinet Room and showed me my chair and told me that was where I was going to sit. Then he asked me to come in the following morning and report on the document I had been working on, about the transition period. In the course of this first conversation he gave me a dozen different assignments and before I knew it, I had agreed that I would join the staff. Damn it all, an independent cuss like myself could have said no—but his Presidential style was most impressive. He was in command and acted as though he had lived in that White House ten years. He is not always euphoric, but I think he loves that job and all its aspects.

'As for the White House staff, now that I am over here at the Fed I get along pretty well with them—although that perhaps is not entirely true—but I recognize my own independence even though it is sometimes very difficult for the White House staff to recognize my independence, or indeed anybody's independence. Of course, we always have tensions between the Fed and the Treasury, between the Fed and the White House, between the Fed and the Commerce Department. In a way this is a good sign, because if you didn't have tensions it would mean that people were not really working.

'I like to think of it'—a sunny little twinkle—'as a zeal for excellence on the part of the White House staff ... but sometimes I can't escape the feeling that it's a zeal for power.

'The economy I feel generally optimistic about. Some reorientation of economic policy is desirable and I think the President is moving in that direction—not as fast as I would like, but I can't be too critical of him.

'I don't know when the economy will make the real upturn, but I think it is coming soon. I can't exactly say why I can't give evidence that I myself consider cogent, but I really think this is going to happen.

'What is important politically is recovery—not necessarily a rapid recovery, but a recovery of basic confidence. The slow accumulation of confidence will bring about the upturn. There are some eager beavers who want to stimulate the economy, but you could so easily get a reversal in 1972 if you move too fast.

'By far the most important factor in the economic situation is confidence. There has been some significant erosion of confidence. The task now is for the Administration to rebuild it.

'People are distressed by inflation in the midst of recession. It is a new problem. For the moment, the President and his advisers are dealing with this with classical remedies. But classical remedies are no longer sufficient.

'He may not be moving fast enough, in my judgment, but he is moving. If things continue as they are with this expansionary budget he has submitted, you might find employment down to 4 per cent but inflation up to 8 per cent, which would not be a very happy situation, politically or otherwise. It is hard for the President, ideologically, to interfere with the classic wage-price policy. To step on toes economically is not good for a politician.

'However, I keep urging, and I think events will drive him further in my direction. I wish he'd move that way for his own sake and the country's sake.'

BYRD DEFEATS KENNEDY AS SENATE WHIP. KENNEDY'S SPANKING DIMS '72 OUTLOOK ... NIXON TO SEEK RECONSTRUCTED GOVERNMENT ... REDS RAID AIRPORT IN CAMBODIA. SENATORS CALL AIR ACTIONS [BY U.S.] BREACH OF FAITH AND LAW.

'I have known Richard Nixon for twenty years,' he says thoughtfully, from his vantage point as one of the most independent, and most likeable, men on the Hill, 'and I like him very much. I think he has done a good job in foreign affairs.

'In domestic policy I am damned if I know where he is driving.

'A year ago he said the federal government had to balance the budget. Now he submits a budget which will be very badly out of balance. LBJ's unbalanced budgets became a major cause of the inflation we have now. I don't see how Nixon thinks he can unbalance the budget and control the inflation.

'It appears the President has changed direction radically.

'I still think the most important thing is to put the government's financial house in order. I don't think the government in the long run can continue to operate at a deficit. Sooner or later somebody has got to pay. I am afraid this new budget is strictly politics. It is such a sudden change from just a year ago. It just doesn't make sense to me, what he is attempting to do now. I think he has reversed his field completely, and I am afraid it is for political reasons.

'I don't think the President is going to have much success with revenue sharing, and there are great problems involved in the reorganization of the Cabinet. There again, he has offered us only a broad outline with no details, and it is difficult to understand what he is driving at.

'I have to confess this whole change baffles me.'

Elliot Richardson, Secretary of Health, Education, and Welfare, has his offices in an older government building, plain, utilitarian but pleasant. The reception hallway is a dark-panelled corridor with a blue rug. He is fifty, square-faced, dark-haired, wears glasses, speaks slowly and thoughtfully with a dry little twinkle of humour and impresses one as being extremely intelligent and extremely competent. He is a former Undersecretary of State who was moved over to HEW when Bob Finch resigned to go to the White House staff. Since Richardson has been in HEW things have been much quieter there, at least on the surface. He has apparently managed to defuse a lot of the upsets and hysteria that seemed to revolve around, and be inspired by, the department's black staff members. Whether it is a real defusing or simply a smooth sweeping-under-the-rug remains to be seen.

'I have found the White House staff easy to get along with when you make your position clear and state it effectively and determinedly. I had a year and a half in the State Department dealing with Henry Kissinger and the National Security Council. I found right away that there was a need to get a clear understanding and respect for people whose role in the State Department gives them importance. There was some inclination on Kissinger's part to try and dominate the thing, but I think we worked out an agreement early in the situation and got along very well.

'There are people in the NSC whose role transcends that of the State Department, and at the same time the head of the department, the undersecretary or other officers there also have a responsibility to their own people. This inevitably creates a certain tension between the interest of the President on the one side and the people in the department on the other.

'Here in HEW, the best way we can help the President is to do the best job we possibly can in solving the social problems which are the responsibility of this department.

'Creation of the Domestic Council several months ago has caused a good many things to be shaken down, and I think that has helped much over here. I like and respect Ehrlichman, I find him astute, quick, basically sympathetic with what we are trying to do and very fair in managing the relationships between the staff and this department. As for George Shultz, you couldn't ask for a better or more broad-gauge man. The budget was already a pretty good operation and he has made it much better.

'The Executive departments are much less capable than you might think they would be of good staff work from the standpoint of the President. I understand why the President has to have the capacity to see things he needs to make decisions. One of the things the President has to do is act as decision-maker between conflicting claims for limited resources. He must consider the needs of both domestic and foreign policies. He alone has the responsibility.

'The White House staff can assure you as a Cabinet officer of the opportunity to be heard as an advocate of your point of view and to explain why you think certain things should be done, before decisions are reached. This is very helpful to us and helps make the government run much more efficiently. It improves relations by getting the people in the department involved early in the decisions. I have attempted to do something of that nature here in the department and think I have succeeded pretty well. I think this has helped to calm down the situation over here which existed when I came in.

'The President seems to be in tremendous spirits these days. He is buoyant, humorous, on top of things, impressive in the range of his grasp and his understanding. I think this is more true than ever as he goes along. He really likes the job and this helps. Cambodia, I think, was a real trial by fire for him, a very lonely ordeal by fire, and having emerged wholehearted from it, he feels better. In many respects he is quite definitely, if not a shy man, then very sensitive, but with an inner core of great toughness and confidence in his own judgment, derived from the six crises he wrote about in his book and various crises that have occurred since—particularly including having been President for two years and found that he can do it, and do it very well. He is buoyed up by what the opportunities are for the country, and he knows how he does it as President now, and this makes a real difference.

'The family assistance plan, health insurance and the like are the outcome of heightened forces brought to bear on the government. They are having difficulty in Congress because on the negative side there are purely political aspects involving individual aspirants for the Presidential nomination or the Vice-Presidential nomination on the Democratic side, jockeying for power and credit. This tends to heighten criticism of the President. Some proposals are going to be more difficult for them to support if support indicates approval for the President's ultimate aims.

'However, some of the same factors can be exerted for affirmative results. It's possible there will be a conclusion with more or less divided credit going to both the Administration and the Congress. In the Congress they do have a choice between an affirmative record, for which no one can claim entire credit, or a mutually destructive record, which will bring public lack of faith in both the Administration's and Congress' capacity to govern. I don't really think Congress wants that, and I so think there will probably be a positive record. Whether it emerges to the extent that each side would like to see is another matter. It will depend to the extent on which each side is prepared to share the credit. I think we in the Executive Branch are reasonably willing to share the credit.

'In the area of welfare reform, the options are not as wide as you might think. There are not many major alternatives to the President's programme, when you come right down to it. The atmosphere is pretty good for getting it through. There's been a lot of participation in the process of decision and determination to reach an agreement on the problems that exist. Making decisions is a small part of any government job. A great deal of the job is getting to the point where you are ready to make a decision—getting everybody involved so that when it is made they will support it wholeheartedly and be able to move forward.

'Looking back at my former home in the State Department, its principal problem is that it doesn't have any jump on events. It does not anticipate enough. It doesn't plan how to use U.S. resources or influence in the best way around the world. That was my constant cry over there, that State did not look forward enough and did not make use of the things it had, to plan for the crises which might occur. Again, this goes back to involving many more people in the decision-making process.'

He has served in the Cabinet, been eighteen years on the Hill, wandered from dove to hawk and back again on several occasions; has now done so again and ended up a dove. He is tall, dignified, pleasant, a very likeable gentleman whose scalp the Nixon-Agnew campaign of 1970 almost succeeded in getting. He doesn't like the President, but manages to be relatively objective in his comments.

'Some of these fellows up here are very bitter because of the way in which the President and the Vice-President went out against them. Of course, they did that to me and I survived, and I hopefully am not as bitter as some of them. But some are really feeling quite upset about it. That campaign is going to make it extremely difficult for the remainder of his term for him to get Congressional support for the things he wants on critical issues. Chotiner and Colson were his hatchet men, they spread the dirt around for him, as did Agnew, and he's going to have to pay for that, up here on the Hill.

'I think the President, in effect, has stripped the Cabinet of power. This is a process that began really under Truman, although he delegated a great deal to the Cabinet. Ike began to put more and more stress on the White House staff, Kennedy did even more, Johnson even more than that, and I think Nixon has increased it even further. The White House staff and its operations increasingly control the government. Henry Kissinger is recognized as the second man in government, with the power to override Laird, Rogers and everybody else. Cabinet members under Nixon are just figureheads now. I think Rogers looks sort of silly. I'd have got up and quit long ago if I had taken the things he has taken from Kissinger.

'As for the President'—a shrug and a smile. 'He is what he

271

is—he is what he is. We all know what he is, and—he is what he is.

'He's the same fellow he has always been. Ideologically he is a hard-line anti-Communist, a superb politician and one who is always looking at both sides to try and find his own advantage. He must be aware of what the war is going to do to his political future, and yet he has flubbed his chances. If when he first came in he had said to Hanoi, "This is going to stop or I'm going to take out the harbour of Haiphong and if necessary knock out Hanoi itself"—or if he had said, "We're going to get out right away—period," he would have been a lot better off. Either one would have been better than to try to drag along and try to work this both-sides-of-the-street policy that he is doing now.

'He is caught in about the same spot that Johnson was in.

'We have a real problem with the economy, because these fellows around him are hard-money men. As a result of the election and increasing unemployment, he has now abandoned the concept of balancing the federal budget, and has abandoned it for political reasons. His policy had better work or he could wreck the economy of this country. It could get worse very quickly, and I don't think he has any real plan to prevent it from doing do.

'Nixon's trying to pull everything in under his wing—he wants to know everything about everything. He ought to delegate more. I think he is in very deep trouble—politically, militarily, economically. The people are getting fed up. Now his credibility is beginning to crumble as Cambodia and Laos come back into the picture.

'I think he's in deep trouble.'

HILL TO GO SLOW ON CABINET, BUT NIXON PLAN IS
PROMISED EARLY HEARING . . . CAMBODIA: END OF ILLUSION.
HILL OUTCRIES BARE EXTENT OF U.S. INVOLVEMENT . . .
MUSKIE, MCGOVERN ASSAIL STATE OF THE UNION MESSAGE.

He is extremely intelligent, extremely articulate, extremely sarcastic, one of those typical younger-than-they-are young men who come into administrations and then quit in angry bitterness because the President has not done exactly what they thought he should do when they dedicated their idealism and their hearts to him in the days of his campaign. 'I suppose,' he concedes after two hours of bully-ragging, 'that maybe it's because so many of us came in expecting so much that we are taking it harder now. Maybe that does make us a little bit unbalanced on the subject. But I still think there's a lot more that could be done ...' Mostly he remains stern and righteous:

'They're just wallowing, over there in the White House. Nixon is surrounded by cronies and they aren't even smart cronies. They are people like Ehrlichman, who managed an insurance firm, and Ron Ziegler, who used to be a guide at Disneyland and was charged with the great responsibility of using his pole on the Jungle Ride to fend off the hippopotamus. They're suburban cronies: the Hot Shoppes vote.

'They're a bunch of second-raters. Everybody is very adept at pushing papers, but there isn't any sense of policy to be found among them. They're great at programming papers, but no real planning or intelligent, constructive programming in the policy sense comes out of them, because they just aren't capable of it.

'If Nixon has an over-all policy, I wasn't able to find it when I was working over there. It isn't so much that liberal forces have "taken him over", it's just that there isn't any incentive or capability to get a good, constructive conservative programme going.

'He is trying to do things that will please the New York *Times*, and when they give him a little pat on the shoulder he is pleased to get it. It is quite contemptuous on their part. They just toss off a little crumb now and then for his ego to lap up, and that way they inhibit him from doing things that he might do to remain true to his campaign promises.

'The same applies to the Washington *Post*, that gang of kooks, who really are quite insufferable. They cut him up right and left and yet he is very concerned about what they say, and perhaps naturally so, because they have a lot of influence in this town. However, I don't think he is doing what he ought to do, or what he could do as President. I think he ought to tell them to go to hell and do what he ought to do.

'If he would run a campaign against the press—a real campaign, not just a few little stabs here and there, but a real campaign against the press, and against Congress as Harry Truman did in 1948, then I think Main Street America would be with him 100 per cent and he would be re-elected in good style.

'But as long as he tries to appease all sides he is not going to do it.'

CAMBODIA AIRPORT HIT AGAIN ... SHAH THREATENS OIL CUTOFF BUT PLEDGES TO SEEK PACT ... NIXON TO INCREASE BUDGET FOR SCIENCE ... McGOVERN URGES U.S.-PEKING TIES ... MUSKIE STRONG IN CALIFORNIA.

He is a very liberal Democrat, a Nixon-Agnew target in 1970 who survived handsomely; very pleasant, very intense; one of the few people on the Hill, and the only one I interviewed, who has a real, genuine, visceral hatred of Dick Nixon, to the point where it keeps him in an almost constant state of tension and really blurs his approach to legislation.

'I just don't like him. This has nothing to do with his capabilities or talents, it's just a feeling that he isn't likeable and I don't like him. I don't think his policies are wise, I don't think his approach to them is sound. I think we can fiddle along and take our time on inflation and things like that and go down the drain while we are doing so, simply because he doesn't have the guts to come to grips with the problems.

'The war in Vietnam is one thing I am convinced has come close to destroying us, and could still destroy us if it is not straightened out quickly. I don't think the President has any real understanding of the attitudes of the young people towards this, nor does he have any real relationship to the young people, to the poor, to the blacks.

'What I don't like about him is that by calling for lowered voices he attempts to sweep everything under the rug. He just has no inspiration in him. If an individual lives in a constant attitude of despair because of race or because of economic condition, the President offers him nothing. This man offers no inspiration to people like that. This man may be appealing to people who he thinks have got problems, but he doesn't know how to appeal to them, really, because he has no real relation to them. He may reassure small-income people, he may reassure small business men, he may reasssure that particular type of citizen. But they don't really have problems. The people who really have problems are at a dead end, and they just don't get anything from the President in that area, no real understanding —nothing.

'The chemistry of Richard Nixon just doesn't permit him to relate genuinely to these people in trouble. Richard Nixon symbolizes nothing of the things that people in a serious dead-end condition are looking for—nothing.

'Now, it may be that a man might come along who would have no simple solution for things of this nature, but if he simply showed that he genuinely cared, at least that would give something to these people. It would let them know that somebody is aware of them and is working for them, is trying to find a place in the sun for them. That would give us time to work out these problems. Our desperate need is time, but Nixon does not offer even the comfort of an inspiration that would buy us time.

'I think he is one of the least likely public figures ever to give hope to anyone. It's a lack of style, a lack of spirit, a lack of heart. I don't know what his motives are—you don't know your own motives, so how the hell can you tell what his are?— but he should be more sensitive, he should have more relationship to these people, he should show that he sincerely wants to do something.

'He can understand the Penn Central's going bankrupt and the government's responsibility in that area, but he can't seem to understand his responsibility all down the line to all the citizens.

'His own memory of being poor and of having to eat cheap foods as a child relates to a world that was different then. Now the difficulties are much greater, the tensions are much more important. It takes much more skill and luck to climb out of these situations than it did when he was coming along. And he just doesn't realize this. He just doesn't know it.

'When the poor people, the blacks and the young look at this guy, he simply confirms them in their belief that there is no opportunity left in the system.

'Of course, I don't know what the Democrats will come up with—maybe I'm letting myself get too swept away by what appears to be Ed Muskie's appeal—maybe he doesn't really have it, either. But I do know this:

'Nixon is a bum choice for this period.'

PRESIDENT PRESSES '71 GOALS. LOCAL OFFICIALS, MILLS OPPOSE REVENUE PLAN ... U.S. EXPORTS CLIMB TO THREE-YEAR PEAK ... ARMY SEIZES CONTROL IN UGANDA COUP.

Thoughtfully, as the winter twilight darkened rapidly over Washington, an old friend of the President had the last word on these many musings on the subject of Richard Nixon and the people who serve him:

'He dreamed of that job for years, prepared himself for it, must have seen himself as President so many times that it really was natural to him when the moment came. I remember at the inaugural I turned to look back up at him as he came down the stairs to the platform to be sworn in, and I saw a glint in his eye. If I read his mind correctly, I got the feeling he was not going to take an oath before God—he was going to take an oath that he was going to be a good President. He looked pleased to be "Mr. President", he looked like a high school boy who had won the prize. I thought the President should commune with God at that moment, but I think he was genuinely pleased with himself, as though he were saying, "I've made good, Mama, now why don't you cheer for me?"

'I am not sure I know him; I am not sure I understand him. I sometimes feel he lacks assurance—that he is hungry for love and applause. Most of the time I feel that he is master of the house and wanted to be master of the house; that he is entirely at peace in the job and believes he is doing it well. This doesn't mean that he is blind to his failures. He knows when he has done well, when he has not done so well and when he has failed ...

'You ask if he has humour. There is more humour in the man than I saw during the long Eisenhower years. It is humour in the sense of quick repartee, humour in turning a phrase. He is quite good at it, quite spontaneous—but it is not the humour of a relaxed man. It is not humour such as Eisenhower had, which was a release and relaxation. Eisenhower would fume about some man who had just left the office, he'd just relax and let himself explode for a bit, and then he would crack a joke and start laughing about it and get it off his mind. Dick Nixon is rarely like that. Eisenhower had a terrific sense of humour—he'd rage and he'd laugh. I'd say on balance that Dick Nixon's humour is limited, but he does have a good sense of it.

'That staff makes me so tired! Particularly when they say that he never shows any sign of emotion and is always calm and quiet. Of course I've seen him upset and tense. I wish the general public could see him like that, because he is really a very decent man and he reacts in very human ways to things.

'There is an effort on the part of the staff to deify the President. I think the staff has done him considerable harm because of this. They are over-protective. They are very loyal, very devoted, but they are over-protective. They have the feeling that *they* know—*they* know what is right for the President and no one else does.

'I don't think the President sees enough people. I remember that Tom Stephens, for Eisenhower, had enough good sense to let Cabinet members in. This is not the case nowadays. Haldeman is not a politician and his understanding of human nature is quite limited. He keeps people out when it would serve the President for the people to see him.

'There is a certain pathetic air around here on the part of some people who claim that they see the President all the time. I know that one Cabinet member who told me he had seen the President frequently hadn't seen the President for four months. I don't blame the President for that. I blame the staff. As far as I'm concerned, I take advantage of my years and tell him what I think. He'll say, "Yes, you're right, that will be corrected." Then for two or three weeks we proceed with a new plan of access. Then the old one comes back again and the staff once more is surrounding him.

'They respect his every whim, and that's a mistake. They would serve the President better if they told him what people think. Most people around the President—any President, over the years—do that. They become protective—over-protective. Presidents can be frightfully isolated and frightfully ignorant ...

'There are too many fellows around that White House. They get in each other's way. And a lot of them are men who have not had political experience. Instead of building good will for the President they have created a great deal of resentment, because they are so devoted to the President that they simply isolate him. They are at this job ten to twelve hours a day. There can be an excess of virtue, or a misdirection of virtue, in such practices.

'Eisenhower was loved by every member of his Cabinet. This is not true of President Nixon. His personality is a factor, but the chemistry of that office is so powerful that you may come in with a sense of rancour, but just because you're in that room with the President, you feel so warm and wonderful that it seems to dissipate. In other words, it is so easy to get the love of these men that I blame the President too, because he says, "Keep these fellows out!" But he doesn't mean it, and the staff makes a great error in thinking he does.

'For instance, there was Hickel. He asked for it, true enough, but he had some fine assistants who were discharged in the most immoral manner, and this I attribute to the overzeal of the staff. The President probably said, "Get those men out of here!" Hell, he didn't mean that literally or immediately. But the staff immediately acted on his whim, they take him at instantaneous face value, and therefore they sent a minor aide over and he fired six men in an hour's time, and there was a great deal of criticism from the press and rightly so.

'You don't carry out the President's orders when you know that they're given in a mood of anger and you know that once he calms down he wouldn't mean that, or do that.

'There is a question of humanizing the White House. As far as the outside world is concerned, the White House lacks a soul. This comes not from the President's part of it. It's a feeling that the staff gets in the way so people don't have a chance when they want to humanize him. Actually, of course, the President had no administrative experience when he came into office. His first mistake was in not bringing in a top staff man who really knew administration and really knew Congress. He should bring in someone like Mel Laird, a seasoned politician who can become political without becoming belligerent about it.

'The President is a kindly, very shy man at heart, who has been driven by ambition to reach this point.

'People feel strongly about Dick Nixon—they love him, or

they don't like him, a great deal. There is a great deal of good and a great deal of decency in the man that many Americans have never recognized. At the same time, he has all the faults of human nature. If they would stop deifying him over there, and if he would only let himself go a little and relax sufficiently, that would do it—people would understand.

'But can he?

'The answer is probably no, because if he could do it, he probably would have done it by this time.'

U.S. WILL OVERSEE CAMBODIAN USE OF ARMS SUPPLIES. DELIVERY TEAMS WILL TOUR COUNTRYSIDE TO ASSURE PROPER DEPLOYMENT. ADVISORY ROLE BARRED, BUT PENTAGON SAYS AIDES MIGHT SHOW ALLIES HOW EQUIPMENT WORKS ... JORDANIAN STAND ON TALKS IS TOUGH. NOTE TO JARRING REITERATES DEMAND ISRAEL LEAVE ALL ARAB TERRITORY ... MANSON, THREE WOMEN GUILTY. PROSECUTOR TO ASK DEATH ... SENATE PANEL CALLS ROGERS ON CAMBODIA.

II

'THE MOST DANGEROUS CRISIS'

He is a friend of the President, a veteran observer of foreign affairs; in a position, relatively detached and thus relatively objective, to know pretty well what happened in what he describes as 'really the most dangerous crisis this Administration has faced'—the civil war in Jordan, when the United States and the Soviet Union came to the brink of final confrontation in the Middle East.

As he sees it, the episode contained all the key ingredients of the Nixon approach to foreign affairs, as well as demonstrating conclusively what it takes for this country to live in the same world with the Communists: cool heads, iron nerves, steel will. There was here, as he relates it, particularly on the part of the President and his principal adviser, Henry Kissinger, much courage and few hesitations.

'The situation in Jordan in the spring of 1970 involved a combination of several explosive factors—the relationship of the Israelis to the Arabs, of the Arabs to one another, of the great powers to the principal participants, of the great powers to one another. When these blew up into crisis, they were further complicated by intense bureaucratic argument in Washington.

'The State Department regarded the Middle East as its own particular bailiwick, for which it claimed responsibility and regarding which it felt a considerable jealousy. All during the summer, as the Middle East simmered, and as the situation between King Hussein of Jordan and the Palestinian guerrillas became increasingly tense, the bureaucracy found it almost psychologically impossible to acknowledge that things were getting worse. Its Middle East experts maintained that stability was being achieved, that the situation was easing instead of aggravating.

'The Palestinian hijacking of four international aircraft ended that illusion with a bang.

'The immediate issue grew out of the fact that, while the fedayeen released most of the foreign nationals aboard the planes, they held the foreign Jews, including American citizens, and proposed to barter their lives for release of Palestinian guerrilla leaders held by Israel, Britain, West Germany and Switzerland.

'This posed three grave problems: Israel could not assume the responsibility of bartering the lives of foreign Jews for those of guerrillas she held—the United States could not accept the proposition that her nationals could be used as pawns in other peoples' quarrels—and an overwhelming challenge was posed to King Hussein as to whether he could preserve order, or even his throne, in his own country. If the fedayeen won their demands involving the hostages, and if they succeeded in toppling Hussein, there would be a very serious question as to whether general peace negotiations in the Middle East could go forward at all.

'As I got the story, the government received on Tuesday night, September 15, an intelligence report from the British that Hussein had decided to make an all-out effort to crush the fedayeen. The official bureaucratic attitude was to be somewhat sceptical of the report, and to wait and decide what to do if the event occurred.

'Henry Kissinger, who had come over the years to have a considerable respect for British intelligence, was attending a black tie dinner at Airlie House in Warrenton, Virginia, together with several members of what is known as the NSC "Washington Special Actions Group"—which includes himself as chairman, the Undersecretary of State, the Deputy Secretary of Defence, the chairman of the Joint Chiefs of Staff and the Director of Central Intelligence. During the dinner a hot-line call was received at the White House from No. 10 Downing Street, asking what the U.S. was going to do, since it was clear to the British that a major battle was about to break out the next morning in Amman, the Jordanian capital.

'Dr. Kissinger was immediately notified of the call, understood its significance and called the senior officials out of the dinner. He commandeered a White House helicopter and by 9.30 p.m.—the report had reached him at 8.30—they were in the West Wing reading intelligence reports and discussing contingency plans. They met until past midnight, still dressed in their tuxedos.

'It was clear to this group that if major fighting erupted and the American hostages, and American citizens in Jordan, were in danger, they might have to be rescued and evacuated. At the same time, if it looked as though Hussein—who was regarded by this government as the principal stabilizing factor in the Arab world—was in danger of being overthrown, the Israelis would feel compelled to intervene. And that could mean confrontation with the Soviet forces backing the Arabs.

'There was also the delicate question for both the U.S. and Israel—of how to use the possibility of intervention as a means of cooling down Arab hotheads without at the same time accelerating and snowballing the crisis.

'It was a lively set of problems.

'For the moment it was being tackled by the Special Actions Group, which explored the range of possible U.S. responses to the possible contingencies. Henry then called the President and told him of the group's meeting, stating that the group would have a memorandum for him first thing in the morning, setting out the issues and possible actions this government might take. On Wednesday night the President met with him prior to going to Kansas City for a scheduled address.

'The President's first reaction was that the group was too pessimistic, though he was, of course, deeply concerned about the dangers of outside intervention and wanted to look carefully at the situation before it escalated. Later in the day Kissinger and Assistant Secretary of State Joseph Sisco flew to Chicago to join the President in a foreign policy briefing for Midwestern editors and publishers. They met with the President for an hour and a half after the briefing, discussing the latest developments. Kissinger and Sisco then returned to Washington, the President remaining in the Midwest. That night at 2 a.m. Kissinger was awakened and told that the fighting in Amman was spilling over into civil war. He notified the President, who immediately took charge and asked for full contingency plans.

'Acting with the advice and support of most of his principal advisers (over some continuing reluctance on the part of the bureaucracy), the President next day ordered several moves by

American forces to discourage any irresponsible action, including outside intervention. A parachute brigade in Germany was put on well-publicized alert. A carrier which had been scheduled to join the Mediterranean fleet in six weeks' time to replace another was ordered to sail at once. Another carrier which had been scheduled to join NATO forces for exercises in the Mediterranean a month later was also dispatched at once. That night, a Friday, the Soviet chargé d'affaires in Washington solemnly assured Sisco that Russia knew of no country that had any intention of intervening in Jordan.

'On this basis, Kissinger at first told the President that while the crisis was by no means over, he thought it could be handled on the local level. This time the President told him this was too optimistic. The next morning—Sunday—Syria invaded Jordan, after having massed three hundred tanks on the border, an operation of such magnitude and time-consumption that the Soviet Union could not possibly have been in ignorance of it when the chargé gave his assurance the night before.

'At that point the bureaucracy, reacting according to its customary way of doing things, recommended that this government get in touch with London, Cairo and the UN and start a discussion of the situation. This, in the view that finally prevailed at the White House, could have meant the end of Jordan and, in effect, a bloodless Russian conquest of the Middle East, since the United States would have been unable to move until the talks ended—and the Russians and Arabs would not let them end until a Soviet-supported Syrian victory was complete.

'The President forbade any communication with anyone but the Soviets, and to them his message was terse: "Call your boys [the Syrians] back." Just that, in about that length and about those words.

'There still, however, was no Presidential decision as to whether American troops would intervene or whether we would support Israeli action if the war continued and the situation deteriorated. Again the Special Action Group gathered in a night meeting, this time with the President. It was decided that if the war were permitted to continue and Syria knocked over Jordan, a general war in the Middle East was inevitable. The President reached the decision that if worst came to worst, U.S. forces would be in reserve to back up the Israelis by deterring Soviet action. The meeting was just breaking up when word came that the Syrians had broken through and the King of Jordan was in dire straits and asking for any help he could get.

'The group re-formed, reviewed the new situation, decided on psychological warfare steps the President immediately put into action. A courier plane was flown to Tel Aviv to pick up information on the situation, and was duly noted on Egyptian and Syrian radar. The 82nd Airborne at Fort Bragg was put on alert. And the parachute brigade in Germany was sent to the airport with great fanfare. At that point, the bureaucracy had a heart attack.

'Monday evening the Soviets delivered a mild note saying that they were doing what they could to contain the crisis, even though this government knew their officers had advised the invading Syrian tank brigades. The battle in Jordan continued unabated.

'The President, in the face of intense and even agonized bureaucratic opposition, stood firm. It was understood that if Jordan really started collapsing, the Israelis would have no choice but to move. That would mean that the Egyptians would probably feel that they had to move. If this seriously threatened the Israelis, the United States would have to move. In order to prevent the final play in the game—the Russian move—the Russians had to be made to understand that under these conditions the United States *would* move, which meant that a confrontation would be inevitable if the Russians moved. The Israelis had to be made to understand that they were not to go too far if they did move, only enough to turn back the Syrians. And the Arabs generally, as well as the Russians, had to be made to understand that the United States had no desire to make any fundamental changes in the Middle East, only to stop the fighting.

'Partly by intimation and partly by incident, these points were put across. One chance to do so came quite by accident to Henry Kissinger, who went that night to a party.

'He says that he "practically never" goes to embassy parties but the Egyptians were holding a reception and he decided to attend—"to show the flag", as he puts it. Soon after he arrived he had an unexpected opportunity to make the U.S. position once more emphatically clear to the Russians. He did so, reiterating the stand already emphasized by the President.

'At two-thirty the next afternoon, while Kissinger and Bill Rogers were having a vigorous discussion of the situation in the President's presence in the Oval Office, word came that the Syrians were withdrawing.

'In a few more hours Hussein had vanquished the fedayeen and re-established his control of Jordan. In a matter of days the President was calmly departing on his previously scheduled visit to the Mediterranean fleet. And the crisis was over.

'But it might not have been. If the President had wavered and waffled, as some proposed, Hussein would have gone and Jordan would have fallen to a Soviet client state. Russia would have been implanted squarely astride the Middle East, very swiftly Israel would have been in danger, complete chaos would have ensued and war between the United States and the Soviet Union would have been almost impossible to avoid.

'This was the crisis the President referred to in his foreign policy report to Congress on February 25, 1971, as "The gravest threat to world peace since this Administration came into office". It is difficult to disagree.'

III

TALK AT THE BEACH

I saw him for the second time in San Clemente, on March 30, 1971. The SST had been defeated in the Senate, in Laos the unhappy invasion had surged in and limped back. It was a typical overcast Southern California day, the sun trying vainly to break through the persistent light clouds. Off in the distance the cold Pacific curled in upon the shore; occasionally a train passed along the track that separates the Coast Guard station, site of his 'Western White House' offices, and the house, hidden next door in its clump of trees, from the open beach. In the corridors and offices there was an air of quiet, the pace obviously slower, more relaxed, more comfortable than it is in Washington. King Timahoe wandered in and out looking sleek and beautiful, submitting graciously to the pats and greetings of staff and visitors.

The President looked tanned and rested. He apologized for not having taped answers to my questions as he had promised, but explained that he had been rather busy: it was obvious from his comments throughout that he had studied them very closely before deciding on what the staff likes to call his 'one-on-one' method. I showed him my newspaper horoscope for the day: *'Consulting with bigwigs opens the door to greater opportunity now but don't try to criticize them in any way.'* He laughed and said, 'Oh no! Oh no! Don't worry about that!' He played with a single silver cuff link the entire hour and a half that we talked, but otherwise seemed as calm as ever, and as convinced that the course he had chosen was right.

We began, as my written questions had begun, with the Presidency itself. It had held for him, he supposed, 'fewer surprises than it does for most. I had been Vice-President for eight years, I knew what a President could do and couldn't do. The main thing I had learned was that Presidents come and go, but the bureaucracy goes on forever. I knew that no President who is not in tune with the mood and the ideological bent of the bureaucracy can bend it to his programme without a great deal of difficulty and hard work. I also knew how difficult it is to deal with Congress, particularly with both houses in control of the other party, and no such bipartisanship as Eisenhower was fortunate enough to have when Lyndon Johnson was Majority Leader of the Senate.

'That bipartisanship is so fragmented now that it practically no longer exists. We don't have many supporters on the Democratic side, and sometimes not so many on the Republican side. Mike Mansfield is a very responsible Majority Leader now, very responsible in his disagreement about Southeast Asia—but he does disagree, and in fact disagreed with Johnson and with Kennedy too on that subject.

'So now it has crumbled away and now we have partisanship —or perhaps not so much partisanship as what you might call a new isolationism, in which the old internationalists and interventionists, who supported World War II, the Korean War, the Alliance for Progress and the rest of the war and postwar programmes, are now turning away and trying to turn America inward again.

'They are concentrating now on America's internal problems, the alienation of groups and generations, the economy and all those things which our so-called "intellectual elite"—self-appointed and self-described—have made their top priorities.

'We now have what could be termed basically a new "America First" doctrine, not in the sense of "look to America's defences and forget the rest of the world", but in the sense of "forget the rest of the world and concentrate on our own domestic problems and social commitments".

'But I don't feel frustrated or disillusioned—I really don't. I went in with my eyes wide open. I knew Congress was against us, I knew we were in a period of great domestic torment, I knew we had Vietnam to face and many social problems. Essentially, of course, those problems would be here whatever happened internationally, and they will continue to be with us long after Vietnam ends. But I want to make sure Vietnam ends in such a way that it does not leave us with disenchantment, bitterness, even greater alienation of one group from another. If it ends that way, it will not end, in a sense—it will go on to plague us for many, many years to come.

'I think we are at one of the great watersheds of American history—where America, having acquired world leadership really without consciously seeking it or wanting it, having met that role as best she could since World War II, is now determining whether she will continue to play the part of a leader in world affairs or would prefer to abdicate her responsibility and let it go. If she does, freedom and democracy will go, we all will go.

'I am convinced that what has happened in Laos will prove in the long run to be as sound as Cambodia. After all, what really matters is what actually happens, not what instant analysts have to say about it. They over-reach, grab at straws, see it through their own prejudices and report it the same way. They jump to conclusions and then a few weeks or months later, they prove to be wrong. Cambodia was an enormous success, and yet you go back and look up what our friends in the press and television were saying about it at the time it ended, and you'll see they weren't about to concede it was any success. Now they've finally and grudgingly accepted it. I'm convinced it will be the same with Laos.

'You have to be quite fatalistic about these things. After all' —with a sudden sharp, direct look—'I know more than they do or you do about it. I know what has happened to the enemy. I know he has taken enormous losses. I know how the South Vietnamese as a whole really behaved, in spite of what three of four units may have done. They proved they could hack it. Everybody ought to wait awhile and see how Laos affects our continuing withdrawal. The enemy will not be able to launch another offensive this summer. He will not be able to interfere with the timetable for the ending of our involvement.

'I know when American involvement will end, though I can't state it, because to do so would be to give up certain tactical advantages, and also to remove whatever chance—little, not big—may remain to have meaningful negotiations in Paris.

'I think we're going to make it, in this situation—I think withdrawal is going to work, Vietnamization is going to work —not in the sense that "Vietnamization" would mean the withdrawal of all of the American presence, but in the basic sense of South Vietnam being able to handle its own affairs. In the sense of seventeen million people having a chance to decide their own destiny and their own future, which is what we will have achieved for them with our help and our sacrifice.

'If we can do this, it will be one of the major achievements of this nation in all its long history—to keep a Communist enemy from conquering our friends, to give a nation the right to live as it wants to live.

'If we fail in that, and if South Vietnam goes Communist in spite of all we've done, then communism will indeed be the wave of the future in Asia. But I don't think it is, and I don't think that is what will happen ...

'You ask about my comment to Cy Sulzberger that this would be "the last war". I meant, of course, the last general war, the last big conflict. Of course, there will be brush-fire explosions, things like Pakistan, Nigeria, things like that. But any Soviet leader who comes along—or any Chinese leader, for that matter —will know what I know: that if he begins a major war, he almost instantly kills seventy million of his own people. The same applies to me and my successors. I don't think that kind of national suicide is feasible any longer, for any sane man. Of course'—wryly—'there seems to be one or two around the globe right now who talk as though they could contemplate this with equanimity, but I don't really think they can when they come right down to it. At least, I hope they can't, and you have to live in that hope.

'If the United States maintains its sufficiency of nuclear deterrent, then there will be a balance in the world. The superpowers are going to be extremely careful about becoming involved in local conflicts that might bring them into confrontation with another superpower. In Southeast Asia, the Chinese are not going to come in because they know very well that would bring a very serious risk of confronting the United States. And they don't want that. In the Middle East, things are more ticklish with the Soviets, but the same thing applies: they don't want a confrontation. In Cuba and the Caribbean, the situation has been handled very well as regards the Soviet sub-base. With quiet and very firm diplomacy, we have avoided another Cuban missile crisis, and for the basic reason that the Soviet Union *does not want* to have a confrontation with us over Cuba.

'The United States as I see it must continue to play a world role, because if we retreat from that responsibility it will result either in another war or in a defeat without war. If we maintain adequate strength, keep our commitments to our friends and don't let ourselves get involved in brush-fire wars, I believe we have a good chance to have a generation of peace.

'Critical to all of this is the way the Vietnam War ends. If it ends in a way that can be interpreted as an American defeat—a retreat—a bug-out—inevitably those in the world who are inclined to use force to gain their aggressive or imperialistic ends will be encouraged to do so. And all our friends be in disarray. The world will say, "Look, at Vietnam. If the United States could not be counted on there, where can she be counted on?" The way to avoid more Vietnams is to be sure that this Vietnam ends in a way that will not dismay our friends and encourage future aggressors.

'A corollary of our strength is that we must build up the strength of others. We must vigorously implement the Nixon Doctrine with assistance to smaller countries that will enable them to build up their economies and their defences so that if they are threatened they will not need to call on us. They will be able to take care of themselves. They will be strong enough to withstand the threats, and very likely their strength will mean that the threats won't even be made, or not in a way that will lead to conflict ...

'The press?' His expression changed, became earnest, stubborn, close to contemptuous. 'I probably follow the press more closely and am less affected by it than any other President. I have a very cool detachment about it. I read it basically to find out what other people are reading, so that I'll know what is being given the country and what I have to deal with when I talk to the country and try to influence people for my programmes. And of course I read it also because sometimes there will be a very thoughtful article on some subject that is enlightening and of value to me. Presidents are like other people : they don't know everything, it's good to get another point of view on something. Providing, that is, that it's a matter of substance and not just something somebody has dreamed up because he doesn't like Nixon or wants to make points with his own boss or bureaucracy, who don't like Nixon.

'I'm not like Lyndon as regards the press—we're two different people. The press was like a magnet to him. He'd read every single thing that was critical, he'd watch the news on TV all the time, and then he'd get mad. I never get mad. I expect I have one of the most hostile and unfair presses that any President has ever had, but I've developed a philosophical attitude about it. I developed it early. I have won all my political battles with 80 to 90 per cent of the press against me. How have I done it? I ignored the press and went to the people.

'I have never called a publisher, never called an editor, never called a reporter, on the carpet. I don't care. And you know?'—a grim but rather pleased expression—'that's what makes 'em mad. That's what infuriates 'em. I just don't care. I just don't raise the roof with 'em. And that gets 'em.

'Anyway, that isn't my style. I don't stomp around. I don't believe in public displays of anger. I don't raise hell. I'm never rough on the staff about things just for the sake of being rough, or making an effect. But they know how I feel. The things we've faced in this Administration have taken a lot of hard decisions and I've had to be firm about things, but I've *been* firm—I haven't shouted about it. There are some people, you know, they think the way to be a big man is to shout and stomp and raise hell—and then nothing ever really happens. I'm not like that, with the staff or with the press.

'I never shoot blanks.

'I respect the individual members of the press—some of them, particularly the older ones—who have some standards of objectivity and fairness. And the individual competence of many of the younger ones, I respect that too, though nowadays they don't care about fairness, it's the in thing to forget objectivity and let your prejudices show. You can see it in my press conferences all the time. You read the Kennedy press conference and see how soft and gentle they were with him, and then you read mine. I never get any easy questions—and I don't want any. I am quite aware that ideologically the Washington press corps doesn't agree with me. I expect it. I think the people can judge for themselves when they watch one of my press conferences. It's all there.

'I can tell you this'—and his eyes narrowed, he swung his chair around and stared out across the distant grey Pacific—'as long as I am in this office, the press will never irritate me, never affect me, never push me to any move I don't think is wise ...'

How did he appraise the relative strength of the superpowers? When he spoke publicly of the United States as 'the world's greatest military power' in the face of steady Soviet advances on land, sea and in the air all over the globe, was he really convinced of this or was he simply engaging in diplomatic bluff? (One of the questions that had perhaps prompted him to lay aside his tape recorder: although he faced it squarely enough today.)

'At the present time, the Soviet Union has passed the United States in land-based missiles and it will be equal to us in nuclear submarines by 1974. We are much ahead on the sea and in conventional armaments such as long-range bombers, for whatever they're worth, aircraft carriers and other standard equipment. However, unless we get some kind of agreement in the SALT talks, some kind of limitation of offensive and defensive weapons, the United States is going to have to make what will very probably be the most important decision of its whole existence: are we going to keep up our strength or are we going to accept second place and sink to the status of a second-class power?

'Of course, there are other aspects of power than just the strictly military—the strength of the economy, for instance, and the fact that Russia is essentially a land-locked power, a land power, while we are a sea power. We must continue our modernization of the Navy. We cannot ever give up our leadership on the seas, it is essential to us to show the flag, to deter aggression, to protect ourselves and maintain stability in the world.

'I am constantly concerned because Congress keeps trying to bite too much out of the defence budget. If we are going to have peace in the world the United States *must* assume responsible world leadership, and it can't be done without strength. And I don't mean strength in the sense of the sort of awesome advantage, maybe 10-1, we had at the time of the Cuban missile crisis—but strength in the sense of superiority on the sea, nuclear capability, the general balance of armaments. We must have enough so that regardless of what our opponents may have, any foreign leader will know that an attack on the United States will be clear suicide.

'We must also maintain our support for friendly governments

around the world, because our aid and encouragement is vital to them. We must encourage them to strengthen themselves. Europe is not going to do more for itself if the United States does less.

'We have to recognize in this country, in Congress and in the country generally, that the world these days isn't made up of nations as devoted to peace as we are. The whole trend of our history in recent decades has been to become less aggressive— we are in effect engaged in a long historical process of giving up the ideas of conquest and expansion. But there are a couple of powers in the world that haven't given them up—that talk conquest and aggression and have the strength to move in that direction. The United States is the only barrier to protect the world from it. We have to be strong to uphold that responsibility ...'

What kind of a country would he like America to be when he leaves the Presidency? What would he like history to say Richard Nixon had done for America? His face sobered, he fell silent, stared again out the window at the restless ocean, turned back, spoke slowly and thoughtfully, repeating, refining, rephrasing.

'What kind of country?

'I would like first to get this war ended in a way that Americans can look back upon not ashamed, not frustrated, not angry, but with a pride that in spite of our difficulties we have been totally unselfish—that we have enabled seventeen million people to choose their own destiny, and in so doing have preserved and strengthened the chance for peace in the Pacific basin, and probably the world.

'I would like to leave with a new relationship between the U.S. and the U.S.S.R. It will be intensely competitive, of course, we are different peoples with a different history and we want different things—but I believe we are at the critical point where we can finally decide that we must have a live-and-let-live relationship. I think we are making some progress in that direction. I hope we may have achieved it when I leave. I would like to leave some structure on which at least the beginnings of genuine world peace can be built.

'Domestically, this nation is never going to be wholly at one. But I would hope that we can reduce the tensions, reduce the demonstrations, reduce the dissent—not the constructive dissent that is the yeast of a free society, but the destructive dissent that wants only to tear down the system.

'I want everybody in this country to recognize that our system provides for peaceful change—to get people to work within the system and find better methods to make the system work.

'You said something in your questions about how could I, a basically conservative President, propose such "liberal" things as revenue sharing and the family assistance plan. That isn't "liberal". It's common sense. I believe revenue sharing is one way to make the system work better, because it means decentralization of government—and I think decentralization of government is the key. The modern twentieth-century liberal is *for* big government. He likes concentration of power—*he likes power*. I don't go with him in that.

'I hope to give more people a chance to participate in the action—to believe that what they do counts. I want to restore as much as we can the concept that this country has grown great by adhering to the principle of shared responsibility and peaceful change.

'I would like to make some progress in restoring some sense of understanding and of pride in this country and in its greatness—get away from this idea that America's foreign policy is rotten, its domestic policies are rotten, the whole damned thing is rotten. I know that because of slavery, black Americans have not had an equal chance; I know that there are many injustices in other areas. But we are working, we are trying, we are making progress. I know these things *can be changed*, and in a peaceable and constructive way, through the system we have.

'When you look at the United States with all its pockmarks, you realize that, nonetheless, a person born in this country has more freedom and more genuine opportunity than a person born in any other country.

'I would like to leave a renewed conviction in America that the system *does* work, that democratic government *is* better than the alternatives, that reforms *can* be made through peaceful change. I would like to leave re-established the idea that in this system things can be achieved and made better. Not that we can say, "We've solved them, now we can forget them and live happily ever after": nobody ever lives happily ever after, that's not life. But the idea that while challenges will always exist, they are not insurmountable, in our free system. *They can be met*. It does work.

'In foreign policy, the greatest contribution a President could make would be to leave a world in which the United States is at peace with every nation—and has the strength and the will to guarantee that peace.

'In a sense'—hitting the desk firmly with his hand—'it's all right here in this room—right here in this chair. Whoever is President of the United States, and what he does, is going to determine the kind of world we have. His leadership must be strong—and firm—and, we hope, wise.

'But more than that. He must be supported by the belief and the conviction and the faith of the American people, in themselves and in their country. That's why I want to restore some sense of balance, of perspective, of understanding and pride in America's role in the world, and in her institutions.

'This is a noble country in many ways, and somehow we must restore the feeling that we should take pride in it—that we should believe in its system and its policies and its future.

'The important thing is not our capacity to do things—we have that. The important thing is our will. It is not going to be there unless we restore to Americans more faith in themselves and their country.

'The problem now is the American spirit. This is a crisis of the spirit that we face. The most important thing of all is to restore the American spirit.

'That is what I would like to do before I leave this office.'

On that day the headlines were full of post-Laostian backbiting, of Lieutenant Calley and My Lai, and of Leonid Brezhnev, calling with a fine, stern, moral righteousness for world peace, in the city whose leaders have done, are doing and will continue to do, more than any other members of the planet to destroy it.

The sky was still grey, the sea cold, the air chilly when I left. From the doorway Timahoe wagged amicably one last time, and at the gates the guards smiled, saluted and waved me through to the roaring freeway and the hastening world.

IV

THOUGHTS ON FIGURES IN A FAMILIAR LANDSCAPE

Trying, as much as one can, to penetrate The Enigma of Presidents, which with each occupant of the White House develops its own obscure peculiarities, one arrives presently at several puzzles about Richard M. Nixon.

One also arrives, if at all fair-minded, at a considerable admiration for the courage and integrity with which he is pursuing the policy he believes best to save his own country and the independent peoples of the world from the domination and control of communism, be it monolithic, fragmented, Muscovite or Asian.

The ultimate question becomes: are the courage and integrity of a President of the United States enough, in a world whose citizens—even in his own country—seem to be not at all sure that they want to make the necessary sacrifices to keep themselves from being dominated and controlled?

And how much do his personal characteristics, deliberately exaggerated and misrepresented by many in press and television who profess to disagree patriotically with his methods, handicap him in persuading his countrymen that yes, for the sake of themselves and their posterity, they do want to do whatever is necessary to keep themselves and their country free?

The problems of a contemporary American President, as exemplified in this mid-term tour of the Nixon Administration, seem to come down to common essentials, varying in degree from Executive to Executive but basically the same in continuing detail. There is the staff, there is the Hill, there is the press, there is the country—and finally there are his own aims, ambitions, personality and way of doing things, which perhaps are the most important of all, for they are the things against which the others react, to which they respond and towards which they take up positions of loyalty or opposition, approval or dismay.

There can be said of the Nixon staff the things they like to say of themselves: they are young (to middling), they are earnest, they are intelligent, they are honest, they are loyal, they are dedicated, they are devoted. They have among their number probably more bright young men and women and skilled technicians of government than have been present in any other administration. They are adept at programming, supreme at preparing memos, superb at offering options. Almost without exception, they give to their boss an absolute support which must make it easier for him to fall asleep at night. He can count on them to carry out his every directive, respond to his every whim. Some of them may occasionally, as one inside observer noted earlier in these pages, take their own sweet time about responding to Presidential requests, but sooner or later they do respond. By far the majority of them respond smoothly, efficiently and at once.

But there are also voices on the other side. Admittedly many of them are Congressional, and it is very little secret in Washington what some of the White House staff think of *them*. Nonetheless, they are experienced voices, they are older voices, they are, perhaps, sager and wiser voices; and they make points to which a White House staff, if truly intelligent and truly devoted to the best interest of its boss, might well pay heed.

'There is an effort on the part of the staff to deify the President. I think the staff has done him considerable harm because of this. They are over protective ... I don't think the President sees enough people ... Haldeman is not a politician and his understanding of human nature is quite limited. He keeps people out when it would serve the President for people to see him ... You don't carry out the President's orders when you know that they're given in a mood of anger, and you know that once he calms down he wouldn't mean that, or do that ... These wise-guy Presidents surround themselves with bright young men who feel they have to be cynical and smart and have to play a game with the American people; and finally the game becomes more important than anything else. Because a President very seldom gets into details, these bright young men around them feel great. They're able and they're dedicated and they believe they're serving a President well, but basically what they're really serving is their own egos ... I don't think the staff is as big as he is. It has become very petty, vindictive and vengeful.

Their attitude is that if you are not with us 100 per cent, you are just not with us at all. They're as bad as the labour unions in this respect. They tend to do things that hurt Nixon. The staff can damage him, particularly in its personal relationship with Congress, and I think it has ... Ehrlichman, Shultz and Haldeman never ran for public office, and while Finch has had some experience with the legislature in California, they really don't believe Finch when he says that they are heading for trouble if they don't really understand the personalities and the problems up here in Congress. They just don't want to do the job of getting along with Congress, because they really don't understand how important that job is. They are very zealous in the President's interest, but they are often very stupid in what Congress is all about. They believe they can cure their faults by working harder, but that is not the answer ...'

Now, some of this can be heard in any administration, and some of it can arise very naturally when you sit at 1600 Pennsylvania Avenue and look up at a Hill containing an ornery bunch of cantankerous obstructionists who show a devilish propensity for thwarting the dreams of the pure and the noble. But a lot of it is particular to the Nixon Administration, because there have been other administrations, particularly the Kennedy and the Johnson, which had a very lively basic contempt for Congress and yet somehow managed to smooth it over, conceal it and get along reasonably well (in a personal if not always political sense) in spite of it.

The staff can be most helpful and most kind to a project such as this volume—in those areas where it has decided (sometimes without consulting him) that the project will be helpful to the President. But this kind of project doesn't pass legislation; it doesn't require political expertise; it doesn't necessitate the subtlety and human skills of dealing with 535 touchy prima donnas, any one of whom has instant access to press, television and lecture platform if he or she perceives a real or fancied grievance. This kind of project, essentially, comes under Programming, Protectiveness and Paper-Pushing; and those are not the talents that enable an administration to make headway on Capitol Hill or allow a President to emerge before his countrymen as the basically idealistic, decent and kindly man that this one is.

And sometimes even here the protectiveness—or what the staff apparently genuinely considers protectiveness—is carried too far. Legitimate requests for information or for photographs, things which the President himself may have suggested, get buried in a shuffle of memos, phone calls, overlapping jurisdictions and excessive caution. Sometimes they are lost altogether, simply because there is no way to get through the staff barrier to remind the President that, yes, you did suggest so-and-so, and it's being all messed up down the line. Sometimes this arises from sheer timidity on the part of the staff—sheer unwillingness to go frankly to the President and check with him: did you agree to such-and-such, or didn't you? More often it is the quality that so infuriates many members of Congress—the bland assumption that the staff knows best, that it is not going to bother the President with it and so that's the way it's going to be, and to hell with anybody who doesn't like it.

So things need to be done with both Congressional relations and day-by-day relations, in terms of human maturity, human understanding, human astuteness. They are things that come with age and time. History may not grant this Administration the time in which to acquire the age, and with it the maturity. But it would be well if a conscious attempt were begun—and not just the conscious attempt of buttons and slogans and clever little press stories about how everybody is going to be nice to everybody and, above all, just love that old Congress to death. That old Congress just says, 'Yeah, boy? Is that right, now!' and goes its merry way. That old Congress is a very human institution and it recognizes very human people who deal with it on a very human, grubby basis of give-and-take and haggle-and barter. Some very nice white collars are going to have to get frayed, some very nice neckties are going to have to get yanked askew, some very nice neat hair is going to have to get mussed before, in the words of one of the ablest and most sympathetic veterans on the Hill, it will 'get to the point where Congress will call Ehrlichman [or any other staff member] "John" and bicker pleasantly with him, and things will get on a nice personal basis' upon which really major legislative accomplishment can be founded. And the same applies to general public relations as well.

Not, of course, that this will ever come fully about in this

Administration, even with the best of intentions, as long as it must deal with a Democratic majority in Congress and as long as the Democratic majority is swarming with would-be candidates for President and/or Vice-President. As Pat Moynihan truly says, there are some on the Democratic side of the aisle who are opposing the things they have believed in all their lives simply because they will be damned if they are going to give Dick Nixon credit for getting them done. Such deliberate obstructionism is sometimes hard for the average citizen to believe, but noble leaders of the nation can become very petty very rapidly when the bauble of the Presidency dances before their eyes; and it dances before many these days.

Still and all, there remains a substantial group of men of good will, many of them in senior position, their views represented in these pages, who have their criticisms of Dick Nixon —as of any President—but who nonetheless are fair-minded enough, and concerned enough with the welfare of America, so that they will come a reasonable way towards honouring and supporting his position if he will reciprocate and honour theirs. It is on such as they, in both parties, that he must rely if his legislative record is to be very much more than earnest rhetoric. And with them, as their spokesmen shrewdly note, it is not the phoney public relations approach that works, but the practical, the pragmatic—and, although the President still perhaps cannot quite bring himself to believe it a touch of the idealistic as well.

The relations of the Nixon Administration with Congress will never be easy, even should he be lucky enough someday to have a Republican majority. But they can be easier than they are, if there is a genuine—not a forced—respect. In spite of the bitter exceptions, there is an amazing amount of respect for Richard Nixon in Congress, as a politician, as an individual and as the President. If he—and above all, those around him—can relax and show a genuine respect in return, much can be accomplished, even under the difficult circumstances in which he finds himself. And if he can, as one clever elder states it, relax enough to express clearly and forcefully the basic idealism he feels about America and her role in the world.

'If he can relax'—and therein lies the problem. It is a tribute, of a sort, to the media (and those who are so natured can revel in it) that it is largely because of their tender ministrations

307

that he never has, and perhaps never can, fully relax in the office his dutiful choristers insist he was 'programmed to occupy'.

He loves the Presidency, true enough; but he loves it looking over his shoulder. He says they 'will never irritate me, never affect me, never push me to any move I don't think is wise'. But neither he nor his family nor his staff can ever forget they are there.

Day after day, hour after hour, month in, year out, hatred of Richard Nixon snarls from the news columns, sneers from the editorial pages, smirks and sniggers from screen and air-wave. 'Unfortunately,' murmurs someone when the President of the United States is announced: the word accurately reflects the personal feelings and the professional slant of three fourths of the Washington press corps, four fifths of the major news-papers and periodicals of the country, all of the television and radio networks. 'From the hacienda White House at San Clemente,' says someone, a sneer in his voice as he uses the pejorative adjective. 'In what the White House hopes will be called a major address,' says someone else, ever so smoothly emphasizing the snide description. The President holds a press conference at 6 p.m. and next morning as the lead item the radio carries North Vietnam's *condemnation* of what he said, without ever stating what he *did* say. The examples are endless, and the effect on the country unfortunately almost subliminal by now. America is so used to hearing Richard Nixon mocked and sneered at by those who convey the news (or their arbitrary decisions as to what the news is) from Washington that it takes a really conscious effort to halt the automatic agreement of the mind and say, 'Eh? What was that again?' It comes and goes so fast and so often that very nearly a majority of the country (and the world, for that matter) is now conditioned to regard the current President of the United States with disparagement. It is not a happy condition, for him or for the country; and it is not really a happy condition for those who do it, eaten and shrivelled inside as they are by their fanatic obsession with how awful Dick Nixon is. The two are linked in a sick and unhappy relationship from which both suffer, and from which neither can break free.

By the same token, and in the same sometimes obvious but

more often almost subliminal fashion, there is a fawning adulation upon those who oppose him. 'They are so anxious to find an alternative to Dick Nixon that there is a built-in tolerance of the Democrats.' It is apparent all the time everywhere. All any member of Congress, Democrat or Republican —or any publicity-seeking citizen, for that matter—needs do to get instantly on nationwide television and into the major journals of the land is attack the President: the attacker is an automatic hero. It does not matter whether his words be wise or wilful, sound or silly: if they contain the magic ingredient of opposition to Richard Nixon, he's got it made. And if he is a potential candidate for President, one who might possibly be able to dislodge the hated one, it is better yet: the worshipful promotion of his person and cause becomes wondrous to behold. He can, almost literally, do no wrong.

Things that bring the media howling down upon the incumbent's head are happily and deliberately smoothed over, forgotten or ignored altogether for anyone who has the potential to make him an ex-incumbent. Not only have the fashionable lightweights of the media abandoned objectivity as a standard of professional conduct, telling us all how impossible it is for people like them to achieve, but they have abandoned the self-respect that objectivity used to confer upon its practitioners in the press. They have no more self-respect. They grovel now in their adulation as they wallow in their hatred; and it is a sad and shabby sight to see.

And it does, unfortunately, influence, handicap, weaken and thwart the President as he tries against enormous odds to hold his country to a firm and consistent policy in the world. He says it does not affect him personally but it certainly affects the climate in which he operates, and it certainly destroys with termite determination the popular support he must have to exercise his powers and lead the nation. It may be that an easier manner and a friendlier approach would slow down the lions a little; but this Daniel will never be granted the slightest charity or the slightest shred of human kindness as he passes through the den.

It is pointless, for instance, and a little silly, for Pat Moynihan to write, and the President to circulate to the staff, frantic letters about how the Administration's work for the Negroes is not being understood by the country. Both Pat and the President know very well that the members of Murderers' Row in press and television are bound and determined that those achievements, and most others, *will not* be understood by the country. All their energies and talents—and some of them are very good —are devoted to that end.

The reasons for this are partly historic and partly personal and they go in final analysis, in all probability to the fundamental puzzles of Richard Nixon.

The attack began when he had the temerity to expose Alger Hiss, the darling of certain powerful elements in the media whose reputations and professional support were committed to that unhappy individual. They have never forgiven Richard Nixon for catching their hero, and their virulent and vindictive vengeance has pursued him down the years in a million direct and indirect ways. 'The press stereotypes of Richard Nixon,' as a friendly observer characterizes them in these pages, did not come about by accident, nor have they been hammered home to the country unceasingly for two decades just by casual happenstance. The cold, cruel, ruthless, inhuman, uncaring, *political* (God save the mark) man who goes by the name of Nixon in millions of minds is the deliberate creation of his enemies in the media, and it is no wonder that a whole new generation of journalists and a whole new generation of voters have been brought up to dutifully parrot the same old clichés. That has been the purpose and the intention, and it has come very close to total success. He beat it by winning the White House, but it may beat him in '72. And if it does not, he will almost certainly face another unsatisfactory four years because of it.

By now the reactions to him are so automatic that the younger journalists and voters who froth at the mouth when the bell rings never even stop to think; the instant disparagement, the easy slander and the vicious wisecrack are articles of faith. It is so because a previous generation said it was so; and unto the last, in many minds, it will still be so.

This does not, however, absolve Richard Nixon from everything; and there are things to be said on that score as well. He is human, he is ambitious (as what Democratic candidate for President, what candidate for local dog catcher, is not?), he has his weaknesses and he has his strengths; and no tour of his uneasy White House can be complete without a few comments on them too. He is the target of opportunity of many, but there are areas that justifiably invite fire. And there is some final judgment to be rendered that only history can render, but whose outlines may even now be apparent in his character and his Presidency.

Underneath the public mask and off in the actual area unrelated to the constant caricature of his enemies, he is, to begin with, exactly what all these intimate witnesses attest: 'a kindly, very shy man at heart, who has been driven by ambition to reach this point'—the decent, courteous, deferential, considerate, thoughtful, 'most civil' man who never shouts, rarely explodes, very seldom criticizes those around him who deserve it for their errors and is generally agreed to be 'very warm in a setting where he is totally comfortable'.

The ogre of the media and those they have conditioned, in short, is no ogre at all, but in all probability one of the most decent men who ever sat in the White House.

He is also, of course—and here even his enemies concede—one of the best-organized, most competent and most intelligent.

Why then, leaving aside the artificial and politically inspired obstacles thrown in his way, is he not recognized as such by more of his countrymen, and why does he not achieve more than he does? Why is there that lingering feeling, even on the part of many of the most loyal Republicans, that 'he isn't doing anything ... I wish he'd *do* something'? Why is it that he and his staff, sitting on top of an ever rising pile of good speeches, sound recommendations, excellent legislative proposals, erudite reports, studies, projections, plans, have somehow failed to connect (at least consistently) with the current of history that can carry even a President with an opposition Congress over the shallows to a reasonable record of achievement? Why has he failed, in some curious fashion, even aside from media hostility, *to get through?*

After considerable thought I arrived at the title *Courage and Hesitation* for this book, because that, it seemed to me, goes quite directly to the essential character of this Administration and the man who heads it.

'I never bother to read the psychological studies of myself,' he told me with some contempt in San Clemente; and yet the psychology of Presidents is a vital matter to our times—none more so. The psychology of this one (in the judgment of this reporter, at least) balances pretty well between courage and hesitation; and so it is that the graph, instead of a consistent pattern which by now would have set at rest the sincere concerns of both responsible critics and loyal supporters, shows instead a sometimes unsettling erratic pattern of challenge and avoidance, achievement and bombast, boast and withdrawal, advance and retreat.

It is true, as one of the senior Senators quoted herein expressed it, that there is an odd hesitation, an odd incompleteness, about the Nixon leadership. For example, offering one of the most revolutionary overhauls of the Executive Branch ever proposed by any President, he first elects to go to Congress for a straight up-and-down vote, rather than make the changes by Executive order, as he is empowered by law to do; and challenge Congress to veto them, as Congress is empowered by law to do. Then, having chosen the method of direct approval by Congress, which, considering all the interests involved, is probably the fairest (and in some ways the least embittering) way to do it, how does he go about it? He makes his State of the Union address, the phrases swing—the rafters ring—and then there follows, for many weeks: nothing.

Here, as in many of his domestic policies to date, there is a curious lack of follow-through, a curious inertia that could almost be called disinterest, a curious reluctance, almost, to come to grips with it—to get down to the guts of it—to get into the arena, tear off those nice neat ties, unbutton those nice neat shirts, muss up that nice neat hair and *fight*.

Consequently, by the time the actual proposals come along to Capitol Hill, weeks or months later, the impact is lost, the momentum is lost, the enthusiasm of staff and Congressional supporters has lost its essential freshness and vigour, and an attrition has set in which further rhetoric and further propaganda cannot do much to reverse, because that is exactly what they are understood to be—rhetoric and propaganda.

'We sometimes seem to have the feeling,' said one of the younger and more candid staff members, 'that if we just state it, it's enough.' But it isn't enough, and another of the curious things is that the man who is supposed to be the veteran of Congress, the connoisseur of the legislative process, the master politician, seems to fly so drastically in the face of what is claimed to be his own experience and knowledge.

'I never shoot blanks,' he says: and yet somehow there has arisen in Congress, and in many other places throughout the country, the unhappy impression that he does; and that sometimes he too thinks that wishing, providing the wish is stated with enough rhetorical flourish on the public record, will make it so.

These, of course, are essentially domestic problems of the Nixon Administration. They are part of the same package with keeping a sharper eye on the staff, not letting yourself be isolated, looking for really negative advice once in a while. All of these go to the heart of whether he really does want to be remembered as a great, or at least very good, President. If so, he is going to have to fight for it, and a lot more shrewdly, expertly and toughly than he has so far: because he is up against some shrewd, expert and tough people all along the way.

Shrewd, expert and tough as they are, however, they are nowhere near as shrewd, expert and tough—and malignant— as those who confront him, and all independent peoples everywhere, on the broad stages of the world.

Here there are no blanks; and if you shoot what appears to be one, you are apt to find, now or at some horribly embarrassing moment later, that it was loaded, after all.

Yet here too, on occasion (Jordan, the mustering of past administrations to oppose reduction of American Nato forces and his scheduled visit to China, as brilliant exceptions), there has appeared to be that odd, and possibly dangerous, dependence upon rhetoric; that tendency to boast about the greatest nation, the mightiest military force, the most super of superpowers. At San Clemente he worried about building up the Navy and Congress' desire to whittle; yet it would seem that the prudent man, confronted by such wearings-away, would, at least temporarily until they have been corrected, moderate the rhetoric somewhat. It does not fool the enemies of independence, who know exactly what the relative balances are, and how rapidly they are shifting to the Communist side.

He assumes, it is true, that no sane man, confronted by the knowledge that war means instant incineration of himself and seventy million of his countrymen, would attempt it. Yet he acknowledges also that some on the other side who have the power may not be, by their own public statements, quite so sane as all that. He says with some pride that one of his own purposes in foreign policy is to be 'a little bit unpredictable, so they will know they can't count on me'. Is he prepared to find out that they have the same idea? It is possible that he is counting too much on their believing, as we believe, that world war is no longer feasible, that it is the ultimate insanity as it would in all probability be the ultimate destruction. But maybe they don't: maybe they are still insane enough to make the gamble. Hitler would have. Stalin would have. What gives anyone assurance their military counterparts do not sit in the Kremlin and Peking today?

There is a certain amount of trying-to-make-points about the Nixon foreign policy, and it sometimes appears that he is trying to make them with the people he purports to deprecate most, those members of the media who have been most harshly critical. This will possibly help, in some small way, to ease the task of winning re-election. But does it fool the Communists? One wonders. (A very tentative 'agreement' to consider both defensive and offensive weapons in the SALT talks is hailed with ecstatic pomp in Washington. In Moscow it rates a terse two lines on the official news broadcast and another cartoon in *Pravda* attacking the United States as the home of capitalist imperialism. Who is kidding whom? And why?)

Behind the dynamic and forceful Chief Executive of the trip to China, the economic freeze, the Moscow visit, lies the President who must make good on these great, dramatic gestures after the first fine burst of publicity and world amazement has died away. We do not yet know the full capabilities of this second figure. It is one thing to make the gestures: it is another to do the tough, dirty, undramatic work of making them come true. Many a long hard mile lies between initial headline and final result. History, ever sceptical, will have to wait a bit to render judgment.

He cannot be faulted by any halfway decent and fair-minded person (which very many of his critics on the issue are blatantly not) for the fact that he has indeed, just as he said he would, halted the war in Vietnam, reversed it, brought home many thousands of troops, established in his own mind a terminal date for military involvement towards which he is steadily proceeding. He has not explained how a power which voluntarily reduces its strength in a vast area of the world can continue to act as though its strength were the same as ever, but obviously he is relying on sea and air power to maintain the balance that ground troops will soon no longer be part of. It will be a great trick if he can do it. So far, though his howling detractors will never give him credit, he has managed it amazingly well. Barring some new crisis, he may finally bring it off. It is the one great consistency of his administration, and perhaps it, with Jordan and the move towards better relations with China and the maintenance of the NATO shield, will be enough in the eyes of history to give him the accolades he, like all Presidents, would like to have: statesman, humanitarian, peacemaker.

Aside from these, however—and sometimes even in these, here and there along the way—the dominant themes of courage and hesitation remain: challenge and avoidance, achievement and bombast, boast and withdrawal, advance and retreat. And the puzzle of why so astute, intelligent and basically idealistic a man should have an almost unbreakable tendency, as one of his leading supporters on the Hill expressed it, to fly in at a low political level upon objectives that might better be achieved by an avowed idealism backed up by the toughness to make it stick.

And yet—and yet. 'I know more than they do and you do.' Very true: he does. And no outsider, pontificating in book, editorial, news story or television broadcast, can possibly bring to his comments the inside knowledge and immediate factual background that come minute by minute, from all over the globe, to the President of the United States.

Nor can any outsider truly know the human pressures and incalculable burdens of the office he holds.

Perhaps it is enough to say: this is a decent man who does his best—and his best is better than that of nine tenths of his critics. Perhaps it is enough to say: who are we to jab and jest and snarl and bellyache? What makes us so almighty certain, sitting at our typewriters, spouting into our microphones, smirking from our television screens?

True, he should give more attention to the staff, shake it up, raise a little hell, keep it from becoming complacent, find somebody with enough experience and maturity and general savvy to recognize the importance of a little black poster girl or a senior member of Congress—and give him the authority to make his recommendations stick. True, he should get himself a naysayer, something few Presidents can tolerate but all Presidents should have, someone old enough and wise enough and disinterested enough and fearless enough to say, when he needs it, 'Slow down, there! You don't mean that, do you? You don't really want to do that, do you?' True, he should free himself of his awkwardness about his own idealism; true, he should truly ignore the press; true, he should adopt more instant follow-through on legislative proposals; true, he should really understand and cultivate Congress; true, he should get in there and fight; true, he should drop the tendency to bombast in foreign affairs; true, he should—

True.

He should—he should—he should.

But these are easy things to say when you sit on the opposite side of the desk. He sits behind it and—'he is what he is'. Politically, philosophically and, above all, personally. And at fifty-eight, though a fast learner in one of the hardest schools any public official in America has ever had to go through, it may be that some of these things he cannot change.

Yet one would hope so, for the sake of his own achievement and above all, for the sake of America and those independent peoples whose continued independence depends upon the American shield. He is a decent and worthy man, leading an Administration composed, for the most part, of decent and worthy men. He is deeply devoted, with great courage, to the policies he sincerely believes best for his country and the world. We do indeed face, as he says, a crisis of the American spirit whose successful solution is imperative if America, and with her the independent world, are to survive in all their marvellous multiplicities of weakness and of strength.

How good for us all, therefore, if, on the fundamental realities that confront the world, he can somehow come to trust his own instincts, trust his own idealism, trust his own courage—stop worrying, stop calculating, stop zigzagging—stop hesitating.

That way, if history is any guide, lies the true greatness of Presidents.